SpringerBriefs in Economics

More information about this series at http://www.springer.com/series/8876

Ahmed Naciri

The Governance Structures of the Bretton Woods Financial Institutions

A Case of "Beggar-Thy-Neighbour"

Springer

Ahmed Naciri
University of Quebec at Montreal
Montreal, QC, Canada

ISSN 2191-5504 ISSN 2191-5512 (electronic)
SpringerBriefs in Economics
ISBN 978-3-319-97905-2 ISBN 978-3-319-97906-9 (eBook)
https://doi.org/10.1007/978-3-319-97906-9

Library of Congress Control Number: 2018953165

This Springer imprint is published by the registered company Springer Nature Switzerland AG
The registered company address is: Gewerbestrasse 11, 6330 Cham, Switzerland

Preface

In the aftermath of the Second World War, the world community came to the conclusion that a similar catastrophe should never occur again and made the pledge to uproot insecurity and unfairness. Toward this aim, it pledged a fundamental commitment to global development and to fighting poverty and considered major means of global security and prosperity. Accordingly, it created specialized multilateral organizations, particularly the Bretton Woods Financial Institutions (BWFIs); it also initiated the official development assistance (ODA) movement. For a layman, Bretton Woods Institutions and development assistance are one and the same. Indeed, many people would confuse them. John Maynard Keynes, for instance, considered to be founder of BWFIs, admitted to being confused by the names IMF and World Bank: "he thought the Fund should be called a Bank, and the Bank should be called a fund. Confusion has reigned ever since" (Driscoll 1996). There is obviously a fine line of distinctions between BWFIs, which is underlined in this book. The consecration of the world strategy for development and against poverty was the 1944 Bretton Woods Agreement (BWA). This agreement has, indeed, set milestones for a postwar new economic order, one that is based on the fundamental principles of consensual decision-making, cooperation, and the promotion of international economic development assistance (Bretton Woods Project 2005).

Although development assistance was first meant to be for the reconstruction of the war-devastated European countries, it was quickly switched to cover economic assistance of postcolonial regimes. The objective is "compensating" countries that do not adopt communism (Howard-Hassmann et al. 2011). For opponents, official development assistance has metamorphosed into what they call a semipermanent, "neocolonial" regime, which, by their logic, actually perpetuates the former colonies' dependence (Anderson 2011). For them, the Bretton Woods movement seems to have been derailed from its founding spirit, and it is fading, giving its detractors the unexpected opportunity to assign it detrimental blows. This is a sentiment that no better than President Eisenhower of the USA can express, when he proclaims:

Every gun that is made, every warship launched, every rocket fired signifies, in the final sense, a theft from those who hunger and are not fed, those who are cold and are not clothed. […].[1]

Unfortunately, Eisenhower's affirmation was not widely accepted and was not able to discourage the humanity from its mad race for armament, nor did it keep the planet military expenditure from soaring, as it continues to, to the point where it is estimated that today an amount of $1686 billion a year is burned in the hell of arm race. This is an equivalent to 2.2% of the global gross domestic product (GDP) (roughly, seven times the amount dedicated to development assistance). This is equivalent to $227 per human being on earth that is wasted in military expenditure (Tian et al. 2017). At the same time, indeed, world assistance to development is stagnating at under 0.03% of the GDP threshold, and only very few countries, five at most, seem to meet the long-standing UN target of 0.7%, which only equates to 7 cents for every $100 of national income, and is deemed enough to meet the Millennium Development Goals.[2] As human beings "we have the power to save humanity from this shameful scourge (of poverty)" (Kofi Anan[3]). Why don't we do it?

There are, however, people inside institutions and outside who believe this can be done, just as there are cases where development assistance has scored positive results. For opponents, however, development assistance should not be looked at in just monetary terms; its worth also should be considered in terms of its impact "fundamentally corrosive of democracy and self-determination" (Anderson 2011). According to them, no assistance program is known to have been determined by the people it is supposed to assist but rather in contradiction to the first article of the International Bill of Rights (IBR). Development assistance decisions gain, indeed, to be left to assisted country decision-making. The governance of international financial institutions may consequently be at stake. However, while relating some of the legitimate critics toward BWFIs and development assistance system governance, we must be careful not to unfairly put the whole blame on those, who are very numerous in international agencies, whose sole objective is to sincerely try to secure the human being more decent living conditions.

If, however, international institutions want really to contribute to the reduction in poverty, they must first consent to giving poor people and countries a more effective voice within their decision-making processes (UK government White Papers 2000a). Indeed the enhancement of developing countries voice and vote in BWFIs' governance would also upgrade their appropriation of the policies advocated by institutions, as well as the relevance and impact on development of these policies (Griffin 2002). It might be possible that the speed of change might also be challenging to the capacity of BWFIs to deliver and make those they serve more resilient and adaptable to change (World Bank_FY_2017_AR, p. 10).

---

[1] (*Dwight D. Eisenhower Quotes Military Industrial Complex*)

[2] http://www.un.org/millenniumgoals/

[3] #HumanRightsDay (Kofi Annan,10 décembre 2017)

It is obvious that the sought positive impact of both the action and development assistance of BWFIs may not stem from the published raw data, and, therefore, an empirical level may be necessary. This book tries to test both the conformity of the BWFIs to their founding spirit and the efficiency of official development assistance that they are supposed to administer. The results show impacting weaknesses the governance of Bretton Woods Institutions and inefficiencies in development assistance. Faced with the results, the book also explores other avenues of explanation, besides the international institutions' weak governance, only to find out that international development aid's efficiency greatly depends on the quality of the public governance in assistance receiver countries. There are two types of public governance, namely, social public governance and economic public governance, and both of them should exist in order for development to take root.

The problem of development assistance appears, therefore, to be neither solely with the governance of international institutions nor solely with the quality of development assistance programs; rather, the problem seems to be with the way these marvellous creations of the 1940s are managed. Consequently, as inefficient as international institutions might be, and as inoperative as international assistance might be, these systems should not be beyond appropriate reform, keeping in mind that there could be no possible development assistance without unconditional assistance, fair trade, and firm commitment from all interested parties. The only way to secure such "unconditionality" may be to channel international assistance through independent international means, without shareholding dominance and having in mind that the development gap is mainly a knowledge gap, which can be tackled only through availability of education and training.

Montreal, QC, Canada Ahmed Naciri

Contents

Abbreviations

ACCSF	Asian Currency Crisis Support Facility
ADF	Asian Development Fund
AfDB	African Development Bank
AfDBG	African Development Bank Group
AfDF	African Development Fund
AIIB	Asian Infrastructure Investment Bank
APIF	Awqaf Properties Investment Fund
AsDB	Asian Development Bank
AsDF	Asian Development Fund
b/f	Brought forward
BRICS	Brazil, Russia, India, China and South Africa, collectively called
BWA	Bretton Woods Agreement
CABEI	Central American Bank for Economic Integration
CAF	Corporación Andina de Fomento
CDB	Caribbean Development Bank
CEB	Council of Europe Development Bank
CEO	Chief executive officer
cGS	Government Size
CIM	Islamic Society for Private Sector Development
cOM	Open Market
cRE	Regulatory Efficiency
cRL	Rule of Law
DAC	Development Assistance Committee
DAM	Development Assistance Movement
DRC	Democratic Republic of Congo
EBRD	European Bank for Reconstruction and Development
EDB	Eurasian Development Bank
EEC	European Economic Community
EFW	*Economic Freedom of the World*
EIB	European Investment Bank
EU	European Union

FAO	Food and Agriculture Organization
FFP	Fund for Peace
FSI	Fragile States Index
FY	Fiscal year
G8	Group of Eight
GCI	General capital increase
GNI	Gross national income
GNP	Gross national product
IaDB	Inter-American Development Bank
IaDBG	Inter-American Development Bank Group
IaIC	Inter-American Investment Corporation
IBR	International Bill of Rights
IBRD	International Bank for Reconstruction and Development
ICIEC	Islamic Corporation for Insurance of Investment and Export Credit
ICT	Information and communication technology
ID	Islamic dinar
IDA	International Development Association
IDB	Inter-American Development Bank
IEF	Index of Economic Freedom
IFAD	International Fund for Agricultural Development
IFC	International Finance Corporation
IMF	International Monetary Fund
IRTI	Islamic Research and Training Institute
IsDB	Islamic Development Bank
ISFD	Islamic Solidarity Fund for Development
ITFC	International Islamic Finance Trade Corporation
JFICT	Japan Fund for Information and Communication Technology
JFPR	Japan Fund for Poverty Reduction
JSF	Japan Special Fund
MDB	Multilateral development bank
MDG	Millennium Development Goal
MIF	Multilateral Investment Fund
MIGA	Multilateral Investment Guarantee Agency
MoU	Memorandum of understanding
NDB	New Development Bank
NGO	Nongovernmental organization
NTF	Nigeria Trust Fund
OAS	Organization of American States
OCR	Ordinary capital resources
ODA	Official development assistance
OECD	Organisation for Economic Co-operation and Development
OFID	Organization of the Petroleum Exporting Countries Fund for International Development
OIC	Organization of the Islamic Conference
OPEC	Organization of the Petroleum Exporting Countries

pcGDP	Per capita gross national product
PEG	Public economic governance
PG	Public governance
PRC	People's Republic of China
PSG	Public social governance
SDR	Special drawing right
Shari'ah	Islamic law
SPDA	Special Program for Africa's Development
SSC	South-South Cooperation
TrC	Triangular cooperation
UK	United Kingdom
UN	United Nations
UNAIDS	Joint United Nations Programme on HIV/AIDS
UNDP	United Nations Development Programme
UNESCO	United Nations Educational, Scientific and Cultural Organization
UNIDO	United Nations Industrial Development Organization
US	United States
USAID	United States Agency for International Development
Waqf	Charitable endowment under Islamic law
WB	World Bank
WBG	World Bank Group

List of Figures

List of Tables

List of Appendixes

Chapter 1
Overview: Historical Development of International Financial Institutions, Development Assistance and Conceptual Issues

There is, among the general public, insufficient in-depth knowledge about Bretton Woods Financial Institutions (BWFIs) and the global fight against poverty movement. BWFIs were specifically established for the reinforcement of the Bretton Woods spirit, and they translate into global cooperation, poverty alleviation and development assistance. When we dwell on the Bretton Woods financial system, we realize how ingenious this extensive funding program is, as it is inclusive and covers the entire spectrum of development finance. Development assistance provided by BWFIs proves to be one of the main sources of world development assistance. There is, however, a growing concern about BWFIs and about development assistance, resulting in an increasing demand for improved governance and transparency regarding their activities. It is commonly believed that, as global public institutions and development assistance administrators, BWFIs ought to be accountable to the world public and should act in its common welfare. The governance track record of BWFIs may, however, seem far from perfect (Bank watch network[1]).

"Development assistance" and "Bretton Woods Financial Institutions" are terms that stir strong emotional reactions: some see them as keys to the improvement of well-being across the planet, while others see them as malign instruments of increasing dependency and disempowerment of poor and developing countries, while, at the same time, enhancers of inequality within nations.

Governance of institutions and development assistance, have not been examined in any depth since the institutions establishment decades ago, nor has their performance in fighting poverty and sustaining development been studied. This book tries to fill the gap and proceeds to evaluate the efficiency of Bretton Woods financial institutions and development assistance in scoring success against poverty, measured mainly by the economic progress that might be linked to their direct actions. Because of their status as intermediaries in global development financial assistance, it makes sense to use official development assistance as proxy to the institutions'

[1] https://bankwatch.org/

A. Naciri, *The Governance Structures of the Bretton Woods Financial Institutions*, SpringerBriefs in Economics, https://doi.org/10.1007/978-3-319-97906-9_1

action and the per capita gross domestic product as proxy to the economic advance that may result from their intervention. This book will address this mentioned lack of understanding and will try to clarify the relevant issues of the governance and development assistance of BWFIs by examining and analysing their present and planned governance structures: Section one discusses the historical establishment of the Bretton Woods Financial Institutions and development assistance; Section two discusses the conceptual issues; Section three discusses the main argumentative principle of the book; Section four lays down the structure of the book and presents chapter summaries; and section five concludes the chapter.

Historical Establishment of the Bretton Woods Financial Institutions and Development Assistance

In the aftermath of World War II, the world community made an important pledge to global development, cooperation and fight against poverty, as major means of universal security and prosperity. Major specialized Multilateral Financial Institutions (MFIs) were then established, including, for the financial chapter, the International Monetary Fund (IMF) and the ancestor of the World Bank Group (WBG), the International Bank for Reconstruction and Development (IBRD). The two are collectively known as the Bretton Woods Financial Institutions (BWFIs). These will also include the Regional Development Banks (RBDs), which subsequently emerged. MFIs were meant to be “influential funders, proponents and enforcers of economic and development policies, and global opinion formers” (Bretton Woods Project 2005a, b). The function of BWFIs becomes more prominent as globalization increasingly links the interests of developed and developing economies. Since their establishment, BWFIs have provided estimable services to the global financial system, but the period of the mid-1990s unearths profound weaknesses in their modus operandi, particularly a decisive democratic deficit (Nye Jr 2003), which mainly refers to the inequitable voting structures that favour rich country members and their use, for political purposes (Held 2006). Many other shortcomings in the management of BWFIs and of the development assistance have also been underlined. The purpose of this book is to study the Bretton Woods financial institutions in order to examine their governance structure and to assess the extent of their action in the fight against poverty and the enhancement of development.

Conceptual Issues

Crafters of the BWFIs were deeply convinced that global and fair economic development was necessary to international peace sustainability. Reducing poverty is not, however, just a moral issue, “[…] and if we don’t take action now to reduce global inequality, there’s a real danger that life for all of us—wherever we live—will become unsustainable" (UK White Paper 2000). Crafters of the BWFIs also strongly believed that global development and reducing poverty aims would justify major global involvement and strong universal commitment, on the part of the newly established international institutions. Consequently, the original aim of the International Monetary Fund (IMF) was the creation of "a stable climate for international trade by harmonizing the monetary policies of its members and maintaining currency stability" (Bretton Woods Project 2005a, b). Simultaneously, the original aim of the World Bank was the promotion of economic and social progress in developing countries, more specifically by inducing an increase in their productivity. The activities of BWFIs were quickly supplemented by the developing activities of four regional development banks (RDBs) that were assigned similar development objectives and were established on similar governance structures. Other regional development banks emerged later, apparently out of frustration with the first hours BWFIs.

BWFIs were built around roughly a common governance structure with a board of directors composed of representatives of both rich country members, who were generally funders, and poor country members, who were generally borrowers. As might be expected, voting rights on boards were determined on the basis of the percentage of equity held by each country member, and ultimately, it was, as it still is, the contributor to the equity capital who decides. Indeed, Contributor countries have always held full control over decision-making within BWFIs, and even in some rare instances where borrower member countries might be able to hold a majority of voting rights, there was always there a specific rule, intended to keep them from realizing their will: the so-called "rule of 15% of votes", which has effectively constantly allowed contributor countries to block any non-desired decision at the institutions' board meetings. It can be argued, indeed, that after all, in a for-profit environment, this situation should come of no surprise, except that BWFIs are far from being business-oriented institutions, and neither having a business objective or equity interest. These are rather institutions of human and development orientation. As a result, decision-making at BWFIs was historically and persistently left to the hegemony of a few dominant rich economies, and the situation has not changed since the 1940s.

BWFIs were inevitably subject to much criticism, although most of it was directed at the World Bank Group (WBG) and the IMF, but RDBs have not been spared and have been also blamed for similar governance deficiencies. In fact, some dominant developed countries have been at the helm of institutions since the start: The United States, for instance, is the largest shareholder at the IMF and the WBG, but also the largest shareholder at Inter-American Development Bank (IaDB) and the European Bank for Reconstruction and Development (EBRD). Together the US and its ally Japan are the largest shareholders of the Asian Development Bank (AsDB). The African Development Bank (AfDB) would appear to be the only RDB in which the US is the number two shareholder, after Nigeria (Ottenhof 2011). To protect their control positions, the US has always shown reticence to agree to any change at the capital structure of institutions, nor to concede more weight to new global economic players at institution capital. Major shareholders have also worked out a kind of gentleman's agreement, reserving the chairmanship of the IMF to a

European member, namely France and the chairmanship of the World Bank to an American. The marginalization, and even the systematic exclusion, of economically weak countries and their entire populations, from the decision-making process of international cooperation and development unfortunately appears to be the rule (Diallo et Vogel 1996).

The governance of BWFIs has barely been examined in its entirety, and appears to overlook the consequences of institutions' decisions on the real economy. In the opinion of developing countries, this situation obviously violates the very spirit of Bretton Woods, and fears are expressed that the system of absolute control of development funding, exercised by BWFIs, may have been used as a global political lever (Katasonov 2014) and may have had as an immediate consequence the subjecting of institutions to a *modus operandi* whose objective is submitting them to decisions imposed by the major western economic powers. The policies of BWFIs would in fact reflect prejudices emanating from domestic policies of major Western powers (Ottenhof 2011). The IMF, for instance, is constantly struggling to free itself from the US, to secure sufficient funding sources out of fear of diluting US share ownership. The U.S. has, indeed, constantly engineered the rejection of every proposal to expand share ownership in the IMF while refusing to increase its own interest (Held 2006). Unfortunately, in scenarios in which the decision-making process at the BWFIs is politicized, poor countries will pay the price. They will usually find themselves exposed to the risk of being unable to meet their own development agenda, or even facing the risk of seeing their development projects wrecked for political considerations, which can lead to financial waste and needless funding. Not to mention that very often developing country borrowers, once under pressure, will usually sign disruptive agreements, without even being aware of the reasons for their signing (Cissokho 2009). This, of course, is done with an obvious lack of respect for the International Bill of Rights (IBR), which recognises the right of poor countries to of their own economic decisions (UN 1948).

The limitations of the governance of BWFIs should not, however, darken their successful action in some development sectors, particularly in infrastructure and energy. Critics suggest that it is only to channel raw materials to developed countries, without consideration to the developing countries' needs. As a proof, they argue that the development model promoted by the World Bank is detrimental to developing countries and "partly explains the serious food crisis that Third World populations are suffering today." (Vivien 2009). Other opponents to the Bretton Woods financial institutions governance model, advance that in cases of inefficiency in decision making, rich countries (making the decisions) only insignificantly suffer from the negative consequences of their decisions (Held 2006). If wrongly made, BWFIs' decisions cannot be consequence free for developing countries, and can be detrimental to the quality of international relations and peace in the world, a situation that is roundly and emotionally condemned by Diallo et Vogel (1996), who proclaim that:

> *"there is something intolerable about the way international organizations have taken over our lives, together with the hypocritical stance of Western governments that pretend to be subject to the IMF and the World Bank when they are the ones making the decisions within those organizations!"*

Partial solutions to the dilemma of decision-making at BWFIs have occasionally been suggested, but few seem to have focused, even slightly, on the eminently political aspect of the BWFIs as a whole, despite their tremendous effect on the state of international relations. The governance of BWFIs was neglected for some time, and it was only in 2010, under strong protests, that major Western economic powers finally agreed to a review of the structure of the institutions' governance. On this occasion, quotas were in fact transferred from some developed country members to some developing countries. This has been particularly the case of China, whose economic weight was constantly increasing. Contributions were, however, correspondingly and simultaneously doubled, leading to the perpetuation of the absolute control over the decision-making of BWFIs, exercised by major economic powers. Finally, the recent reform of the governance of BWFIs does not seem to have alleviated dissatisfaction with the institutions, among developing countries.

The 2010 reform, shy and hesitant reform though it may be, was delayed for 6 years, by the US Congress, and could not really be implemented until the year 2016. Regardless, however, of what any reform may include, developing countries, for lack of choice, will still accept it and adapt to it. Unless the reform of the governance of BWFIs is driven by human considerations and fairness, nothing can be expected to change and the fate of communities around the world will still be at stake. Consequently, this book suggests a governance model for BWFIs and development assistance based on fairness, accountability, and a common destiny sentiment: a governance reform that is reflective of inevitable constraints, such as developing countries' public governance, institutions' inability to meet the financing needs of all developing countries and the difficulty facing poor countries in accessing financial markets (Hind 2002). It also suggests a development assistance that is mainly oriented toward the improving of public governance of developing countries through knowledge transfer and knowledge appropriation.

Main Argumentative Principle of the Book

The main contemporary challenge facing the world today is how to improve the lives and prospects for the nearly half of its population, which still lives in poverty with over a billion of these people living in abject poverty, while knowing that if only the economies in which they live grew faster, this challenge could be met (Masood 2000). The Bretton Woods Financial Institutions and official development assistance were established for this purpose. The performance and efficiency in the fight against poverty and the race for development can be measured by looking at the impact on the per capita gross national product (pcGNP), and this book has uncovered some inefficiencies of the Bretton Woods action and development assistance movement in the fight against poverty and development, and it may vindicate some of the critiques expressed. "Despite strong economic growth over the past two decades, income inequality has risen in many countries, [...]" (IMF_FY_2017_AR). For some critics, development assistance should not be looked at in just monetary terms. For them, benefit should be specifically considered in terms of its role in "fundamentally corrosive of democracy and self-determination" (Anderson 2011). The performance of BWFIs can also be assessed by other means, as suggested by institutions, by considering, for instance, the number of people that have benefited from schooling, sanitation, running water, and the like. Progress in all these elements is, however, supposed to result in progress in the gross national product.

Figure 1.1 underlines the fact that like in any bi-partite relationship, development assistance requires the two parties' involvement, and a strong performance, in order for the relationship to succeed. The possibility that development assistance can fail via either party's fault, the donor or the receiver or the two jointly, is significant.

Many people were quick to point out to the institutions' governance (as development assistance administrators), as the main cause of failure of the development assistance movement (DAM). Although institutions may be blamed for their possibly weak governance, notably their democratic deficit, in order to make the gears of development assistance effectively turn, both donors and receivers have to adopt the right tone, and also move in the same and the right direction. This will not happen, however, if donor or receiver does not move efficiently, moving in the wrong direction or moving too fast or too slowly. Consequently, putting the blame for the failure of development assistance on Bretton Woods institutions only can be just be one possibility among three, a possibility that can, quite naturally, be questioned by institutions. BWFIs can only be blamed for having allowed development assistance movement to locate outside the framework drawn by spirit of Bretton Woods. Development assistance seems, indeed, often to be granted for non-development objectives. The ineffective use of development aid is just the flip side of the coin, with subsidies and ineffective donations being the other. A willing receiver cannot get the funds without the consent of a willing donor, and blaming only one of them for failure may seem unfair.

Receivers of development assistance, mainly developing country governments, are quick to admit their part of responsibility, but would attribute it to the historical legacy of colonization that has left them destitute of material and human resources.

Fig. 1.1 Development assistance model

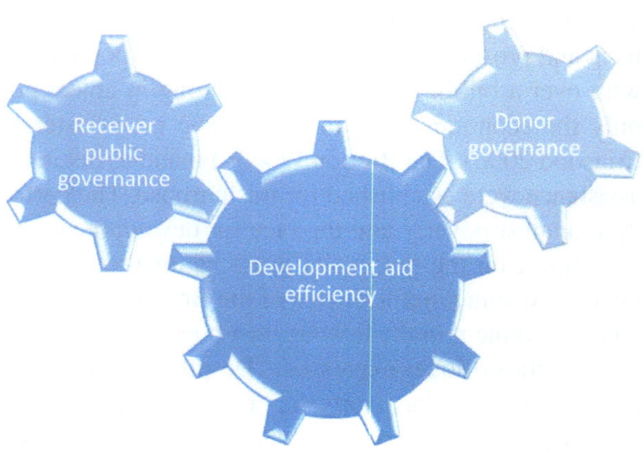

Such a legacy, they believe, has mortgaged their future and sustained their current development inertia and failure to take more advantage of the development assistance. History has certainly its own part in the unfairness, but there is, however, no point trying to correct these injustices by virtually revisiting the past; it pays more to try to interrupt their continuous negative spill-over. This is a moral obligation for all, developing and developed countries alike. Poor countries' governments in particular should not be distracted or feel exempted today from their responsibility, because others may have failed their own, in the past.

Empirical studies performed in the book uncover a significant deficit in developing countries' public governance that may have kept them from benefiting efficiently from the development assistance. Only countries that have engaged forcefully in their own development, by implementing governance rules conducive to achieving development have succeeded. In parallel, those that have relied solely on development assistance have generally failed in their development initiatives. Besides, although time has changed, all wealthy countries and recent economic success stories heavily relied on a state-interventionist model that had government playing a strong role in economic development (Global Exchange 2018).

The book concludes that for DAM to succeed in the fight against poverty and the sustaining of development, the governance of Bretton Woods financial institutions as well as the public governance of poor countries need to be reformed and enhanced, and for this to happen and to succeed, the approval of rich countries is needed.

Structure of the Book and Chapter Summaries

The book consists of 11 chapters, as detailed in Fig. 1.2. Each chapter provides the context for governance action and development assistance on the basis of the material covered in the subsequent chapters. The book aims to outline an international financial model, in which global development and cooperation would be central to every reform initiative, a model that would rehabilitate the founding principles of Bretton Woods, and allow the poor to take their destiny into their own hands, instead of a model that looks like one in which poor populations of the world appear to finance the rich (Pilger 1991).

The book is divided into two parts: the first devoted to theoretical issues and the second to an empirical investigation and a conclusion.

The theoretical part of the book aims to build a significant level of understanding of the international financial system and development assistance movement (MAD). The second part is devoted to an extensive empirical investigation into international assistance to development, to measure its impact on economic progress, as approximated by the advance of country per capita gross national product. The sought positive impact of international financial agencies and their role in development assistance does not stem from the published raw data, and so an extension of the analysis to an empirical investigation becomes necessary. The objective is to determine the impact of BWFIs and MAD governance in the fight against poverty and

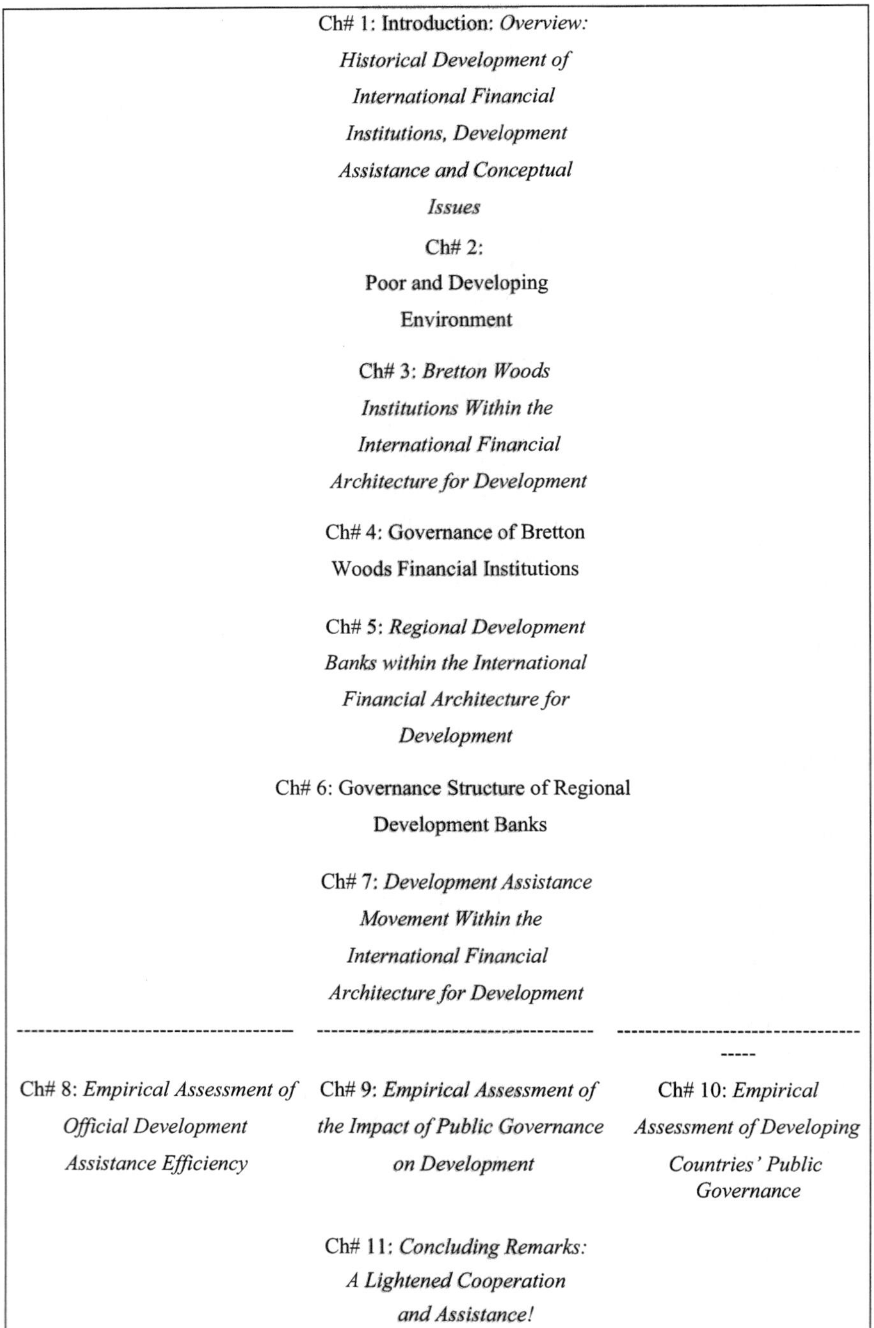

Fig. 1.2 Book structure

global development. The empirical analysis is further widened to explore other causes of failure, besides BWFIs and MAD, that could explain the lack of success in development assistance. The finding seems to indicate that the fight against poverty and development might be rather highly linked to the quality of public governance of developing countries. Public governance is of two kinds: social public governance and economic public governance, and the book analyses their respective effect on the fight against poverty and global development, both individually and jointly, only to find out that poor countries score a huge deficit on both levels that keeps them from advancing economically. It is even suspected that the impact of BWFIs and DAM, on top of being dependent on the level of public governance, may also be tributary to the level of development scored by the aid-receiving country; indeed, the positive effect of development assistance can only be felt at certain level of development, mainly among the lower-middle income group of developing countries. The book concludes by calling for a renewed international cooperation against poverty and under-development, which would put the poor of the world in charge of their development. "We have the power to save humanity from this shameful scourge. Let us summon the will to do it", declared, Kofi Anan. The following gives short summaries of the chapters:

Chapter 1 "Overview: Historical Development of International Financial Institutions, Development Assistance and Conceptual Issues" introduces the reader to the practical and pragmatic economic philosophy behind the Bretton Woods Agreement of 1944, which set milestones for a post-war new economic order, one that is based on the fundamental principles of consensual decision-making, cooperation, and the promotion of international economic development (Bretton Woods Project 2005a, b). The chapter raises the possibility that the development assistance movement may have failed not solely because of the fault of international financial institutions, which are themselves the product of the Bretton Woods agreement, and which are supposed to be entirely devoted to global development assistance and financial stability. Instead, DAM may have also failed in fighting poverty, because of weaknesses in developing countries' public governance. The chapter also gives sample, methodology and an overview of the book.

Chapter 2 "Poor and Developing Environment" aims to provide a clear picture of the environment of global poverty and underdevelopment. It underscores the regrettable fact that more than 10% of the world population is still living in 2018 with less $1.90 in purchasing power parity a day, making them easy prey to malnutrition, diseases and many other avoidable evils, and reducing their life expectancy. The chapter also suggests probable explanations for the real causes of poverty and underdevelopment and discusses their modern promoting factors.

Chapter 3 "Bretton Woods Institutions Within the International Financial Architecture for Development" discusses in detail the spirit of Bretton Woods and locates its financial institutions within the overall international financial architecture of development. It underlines how the IMF aims to create a stable climate for harmonised international trade and to provide temporary financial assistance to countries encountering balance-of-payment difficulties, and the World Bank aims to enhance the development capacities of poor countries by lending them funds for reconstruction and development projects. The IMF is funded by quota subscriptions from member countries, while the World Bank finances its activities by borrowing on the international bond market.

Chapter 4 "Governance of Bretton Woods Financial Institutions" aims to reinforce the understanding of the governance structure and policies of Bretton Woods Financial Institutions, considered essential to the understanding of their role and to the assessment of their effectiveness. It emphasizes their voting process and the "15% of vote rule" allowing a single member country to block any decisions at institutions.

Chapter 5 "Regional Development Banks Within the International Financial Architecture for Development" discusses the historical development of regional development banks, RDBs and highlights their respective roles within the development movement, DAM. The chapter distinguishes two groups of regional development banks: those of World Bank obedience, and those with weaker affiliation to the WBG. The chapter also emphasizes how the scope of RDBs can be uniquely suited to provide a more pertinent assessment of region-specific challenges and the development of country-specific expertise and strategic plans.

Chapter 6 "Governance Structure of Regional Development Banks" provides an overview of the current state of governance of Group 1 and 2 regional development banks and explains their structures and policies. It also shows how most development banks share the same characteristics of governance with the World Bank Group, and therefore also face similar criticisms issued against Bretton Woods financial institutions, in particular their decried governance models, which lead to "unfair" voting, ineffectiveness, opacity, and lack of democracy (Carrasco et al. 2009).

Chapter 7 "Development Assistance Movement Within the International Financial Architecture for Development" indicates that it was only at the end of the Second World War that the urgency of fighting poverty and stabilizing the international financial system prevailed, and with it the sudden consciousness of past mistakes and the strong desire to avoid them. This has ultimately paved the way for the inception of a new international financial architecture and the birth of the development assistance movement. Although such a movement was originally aimed at rebuilding European economies destroyed by war, it quickly took the form of the fight against poverty and underdevelopment in countries newly escaping the colonial yoke.

Chapter 8 "Empirical Assessment of Official Development Assistance Efficiency" indicates that although trillions of dollars have been used as development assistance over the last half a century, the world seems to be no closer to achieving the professed aim of eliminating poverty, famine, disease and war. The macro-economic success of the development assistance movement is therefore empirically assessed, leading to the conclusion that development assistance has been inefficient in diminishing poverty and sustaining development. Such apparent failure cannot, however, be attributed to the Bretton Woods institutions only.

Chapter 9 "Empirical Assessment of the Impact of Public Governance on Development, explores other answers to development assistance failure and suspects weaknesses in public social and economic governance as possible impediments to development and the fight against poverty. It explains the theoretical foundation of both social public and economic public governance, and concludes that they have a strong impact on development.

Chapter 10 "Empirical Assessment of Developing Countries' Public Governance" studies the overall effect of public governance on developing countries and also compares such effect on low income and high income countries. It tries to identify the relationship that may exist between public governance and development to find out that low-income economies are negatively affected by weak public governance and high-income countries are positively affected by good public governance.

Chapter 11 "Concluding Remarks: A Lightened Cooperation and Assistance!" underscores how the Bretton Woods Financial Institutions and the Regional Development Banks have the global objective of enhancing the development assistance movement. Given, however, the sacrosanct law of "whoever holds the shares rules," borrowing member countries have little voice in these institutions of development, and even in cases where they may hold a majority of the votes, voting veto keeps them from affecting important institutional decisions. Quite normally, Bretton Woods financial institutions were first to be blamed for the inefficiencies of international development assistance. The chapter argues, however, that even if the institutions' critics prove to be justified, this does not mean that the fate of development assistance may have been different. The failure of such assistance may be out of control of institutions, but rather to a greater extent, in the hand of developing countries. The chapter, therefore, suggests a new path for development assistance and the fight against poverty, embodied by improving both the institutions' governance and developing countries' public governance.

Conclusion

The role of BWFIs in development assistance administration is seriously shaken and challenged; however, it is firmly linked to the good will of rich countries, and unless they agreed to engage International institutions in more constructive power-sharing that may help dissipate clouds of the past and make developing countries engaged in more sound public governance, nothing can really change. The discouraging element of the BWFI governance reform is that any tentative reform was rejected by the rich countries. Bretton Woods financial institutions deserve to be allowed to free themselves from the hegemony of the few. There is still time for them to play a crucial role in global development. "The world's well-being depends on building an effective, open and accountable international system in which poor people and countries have an effective voice" (UK White Paper 2000). It depends on an enduring willingness to work together to face global challenges and build the foundation for economic growth that benefits all (Lagarde 2017a, b). Institutions have recently been attempting to build bridges by redefining their governance structures. Although it may be too soon to tell, available information suggests that the undertaken reform has done little to help the world's poorest take their destiny in hand, nor to renew commitments to cooperation and development. To our view, BWFIs and MAD governance should be built on closer collaboration with the United Nations Educational, Scientific and Cultural Organization (UNESCO).

Chapter 2
Poor and Developing Environment

Poverty and underdevelopment in the world today manifest themselves as a multidimensional phenomenon that strikes victims of malnutrition, privation, exclusion, diseases, and other avoidable evils. Poverty and underdevelopment also considerably reduce poor people's life expectancy and harden their quality of living. Although the percentage of poor people is steadily declining, as of the year 2016 it was estimated that as much as 10% of the world's population was living in serious poverty. Concerned with the misery and underdevelopment of the world, the crafters of Bretton Woods established in 1944 multilateral financial institutions and later initiated the development assistance movement (DAM) with the sole objective of fighting poverty and exclusion and promoting economic development. They were aiming for global shared well-being, particularly with countries and territories considered in unbearable insufficiencies. This original solidarity momentum was recently confirmed by the United Nations (UN) in their 2015 report on the Millennium Development Goals (MDG), which set itself the objective of ending all forms of poverty by the dawn of 2030, but which was also seriously questioned by opponents. "The most pressing economic problem of our time is that so many of what we usually call 'developing economies' are, in fact, not developing" (Friedman 2002).

This chapter aims to provide a clear picture of the environment of global poverty and underdevelopment, as well as to suggest probable explanations for their real underlining causes. Section one deals with the characteristics of poor and developing economies; Section two presents the poor and underdeveloped populations; Section three analyses colonial legacies as historical development impediment; Section four draws a portrait of a typical developing country; Section five discusses obstacles to modern development; and Section seven concludes the chapter.

A. Naciri, *The Governance Structures of the Bretton Woods Financial Institutions*, SpringerBriefs in Economics, https://doi.org/10.1007/978-3-319-97906-9_2

Characteristics of Developing Countries

Poverty and underdevelopment occupy important spaces in today's world. There are, in a world of expending wealth and material plenty, over a billion people "whose lives are blighted by poverty and robbed of their dignity" by exclusion (U.K. White Paper 2000). As of today, poor populations are forced to leave with less \$1.90 a day of gross national income (GNI). \$1.90 a day is the international poverty line, in purchasing power parity, set by World Bank in 2015. Most poor people belong to so-called developing environments, designated by the international community as "low-and middle-income countries". When they live with around \$3 a day, they are no longer considered to live in poverty. The \$1.90 GNI per day threshold of income corresponds to approximately \$700 per year, while the \$3.10 per day corresponds to \$1131 per year. This is barely the equivalent of the cost of a single usual luxury car repair, billed to a wealthy owner, belonging to a developed or developing country, alike.

The gross domestic product (GDP) and the gross national income (GNI) are alternatively used in this book to express economic advance, depending on their availability and opportunity. The GDP per capita is commonly expressed as the sum of the value added by all resident producers plus any product taxes (minus subsidies) not included in the valuation of output (World Bank 2015b). The GNI per capita, for its part, is expressed as the total income generated by domestic production, including income from trade. Unfortunately, as in the case of most measures based on private monetary data, GDP and GNI have their own inherent weaknesses: they do not, for instance, necessarily take into account a number of key impacting elements, such as insecurity, the risk of disease and the like (World Bank n.d.-e, Metadata). They are, however, the only measures available to analysts. The World Bank, for instances, uses the GNI to measure countries' levels of economic progress, while it uses the GDP to assess countries' economic advances. The two measures diverge, however, only slightly, as underlined by expression 2.1:

$$\text{GNI} = \text{GDP} + \text{BPI} \tag{2.1}$$

where:

BPI is the balance of primary income flows with the rest of the world. BPI is usually defined as households' income from economic activity, both directly and indirectly, excluding, however, social benefits.

Expression 2.1 underlines the fact that GDP can be computed by just subtracting net primary income from foreign sources from gross national income. GNI and GDP, once expressed in national currency, are generally converted to US dollars at the official exchange rate, using the World Bank Atlas method, to smooth fluctuations in prices and exchange rates. The Atlas method actually averages the exchange rate for a given year and the two preceding years, while adjusting for differences in rates of inflation between the country and the Euro area, Japan, the United Kingdom, and the United States (World Bank n.d.-h, Atlas method). Although income classification may not necessarily reflect the level of development of a given country, it nevertheless makes it possible to distinguish different levels of economic

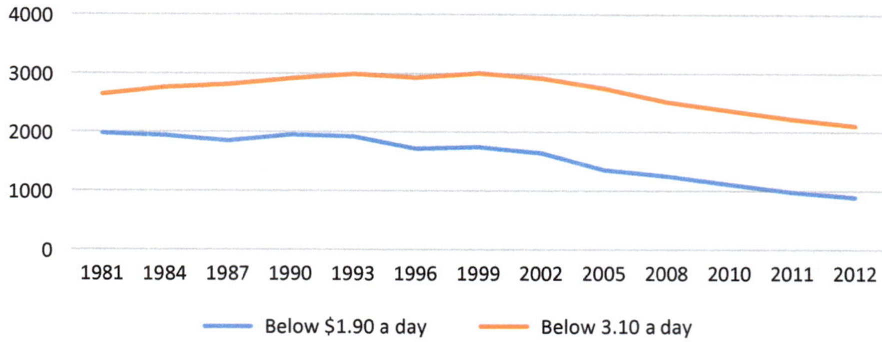

Fig. 2.1 Population living below $1.90 and $3.10 a day (millions, of 2011). Source: Computed based on data from PovCalNet, World Development Indicators, and World Bank Poverty and Equity databases

progress, achieved by different economic environments. For the year 2012, the World Bank country classification was as followed:

1. low-income economy (G1), composed of economies with a per capita GNI of $1,035 or lower;
2. lower-middle-income economy (G2), composed of economies with a per capita GNI of more than $1,035 but less than $4,085;
3. higher-than-average income economy (G3), composed of economies with a per capita GNI of $4,085, but less than $12,616; and
4. high-income economy (G4), composed of economies with a GNI per capita of $12,616 or greater.

The GNI per capita and the GDP may still be unable to give the true picture of a country's poverty or actual wealth. They stand to be complemented with an additional measure, namely their dispersion within the considered economic environment. Unfortunately, such measure of dispersion seems generally to be missing from the published international data. Figure 2.1 represents populations living daily above the GNI thresholds of $1.90 and $3.10, respectively, for each 3-year period for the entire period between 1981 and 2012.

Let's be honest: what can an individual achieve living on $3.10 a day, much less on $1.90 a day. How can he/she be said to be living at all? Still, data indicate that convincing and significant achievements have been made against poverty and a sizable improvement is emerging from Fig. 2.1, and this surely deserves to be highlighted with great satisfaction. Indeed, the population living below the $1.90 daily threshold has retreated, from its level in the year 1981 of around two billion people, to 897 million people by the year 2012, which corresponds to 14.9% of low and middle-income economies. This is a tremendous achievement, especially when we recall that the total world population has almost doubled in the meantime.[1] The level

[1] In 1982, the world population amounted to 3,531 billion individuals; it scored 7,81 billion in 2012.

Table 2.1 Developing economies within the world economy

	World FY 2012	Low income FY 2012		Low and middle income FY 2012	
	Value	Value	% of the world	Value	% of the world
Population (billions)	7043.90	846.50	12.02	5744.10	81.55
Population growth	1.10	2.30	209.09	1.30	118.18
GNI, atlas ($ billions)	71,692.40	499.40	0.70	21,916.10	30.57
GNI, atlas per capita	10,178.00	590.00	5.80	3815.00	37.48
GNI, PPP ($ billions)	85,986.80	1171.10	1.36	36,250.50	42.16
GNI, PPP per capita	12,207.00	1.38	0.01	6311.00	51.70

Source: Computed based on the little data book of WBG

of the population living with less than $3.10 a day has, however, improved only slightly, from 2,65 billion people living with less than $3.10, in 1981, and representing 71.5% of low and middle-income economies, to a total of 2,106 billion in the year 2012, corresponding to 34.9% of low and middle-income economies. This achievement is particularly impressive, given that these gains have been made while the global population has been on the rise (Oxfam 2015).

Despite the hesitation in qualifying the progress scored in the fight against poverty, an important fact remains: all regions of the world seem to have benefited from much improvement during the latest decades. Even if South Asia and Sub-Saharan Africa seem to have benefited the least (with these two environments in 2012 still reporting a high percentage of the population living on less than $1.90 a day), this represents 18.8 and 42.7% of their respective populations that year. Unfortunately, when the poverty line is raised to $3.10 a day, South Asia and sub-Saharan Africa show a near-zero improvement. Overall, 22.2% of East Asia and the Pacific's population still had, as of the year 2012, less than $3.10 a day to live on, and 67.0% in Sub-Saharan Africa, compared to 6.2% of the population in Europe and the Central Asia group, 12.0% in Latin America and the Caribbean group, 16.0% in the Middle East and theNorth Africa group, and 4.5% in the South Asian group.[2]

Table 2.1 gives an overview of some macroeconomic measures of the world economies, stratified by level of GNI. It places developing economies (low and medium-income economies) within the global economy.

Several characteristics distinguish developing economies from developed economies. For the 2012 financial year (the most recent year of recorded financial numbers appearing in the 2014 World Bank's little data book), developing economies accounted for 81.55% of the world's population (5.74 billion out of a total population of 7.04 billion) and were responsible for 118.18% of the growth rate of the world population. They accounted, however, for only 30.57% of the world gross income, and their GNI per capita represented only 51.70% of GNI per capita worldwide. The situation of low-income economies appears even more alarming when expressed in terms of wealth. These economies benefited from only 0.7% of

[2] World Development Indicators and Bases for poverty data and the World Bank.

world wealth, 0.01% once it is expressed in terms of GNI per capita in purchasing power parity (PPP). In 2012, the population growth, as a percentage of low-income economies, represented 209.09% of the average growth of the world's total population, thus reversing all progress made in the fight against poverty, and even increasing the risk of relapse for economies that have recently registered some progress in their fight against poverty.

Historical Evolution of Poverty and Underdevelopment

Poverty phenomena lead to the same consequence, embodied in preventing developing countries from laying down the solid foundations for productivity that required for development start up meaning these countries end up mortgaging their current and future outcomes. The World Bank, as underlined previously, assesses country economic progress through the behaviour of the gross domestic product (GDP), the overall market value of all services and goods within a nation's borders. The GDP growth, on the other hand, as defined by both World Bank and OECD, is the positive rate of change over 1 year of GDP. Recall that the World Bank uses the GNI for country classification. Table 2.2 provides an overview of the behaviour of GDP of world's economies, at three points in time (1990, 2000, 2012) and assesses the temporal progress made in the race for development and the fight against poverty.

Table 2.2 shows that world wealth, expressed in terms of GDP, increased by 326% during the period 1990–2012, from $22,246 trillion in 1990, and it totalled $72,496 trillion by the year 2012, scoring an average annual growth rate of 14.17%. Such improvement in material well-being seems to have been shared by all countries of the world, regardless of the level of their economic development. However, low-income countries seem to have benefited the least from this gradual and general movement in recent world wealth creation: they had recorded an increase of only 354% of GDP during the period 1990–2012, an annual average of 13.4%. "Lower Middle Income" and "Low and Middle Income" economies recorded higher increases of 562% and 719%, respectively. It seems that "extreme poverty rates have been cut by more than half since 1990" (Oxfam 2015), and the highest improvement occurred during the period 2000–2012. The GDP increased during this period by 310%, 390% and 401% for "Low income", "Lower middle income" and "Low & Middle Income", respectively, compared to 114%, 144% and 179%, respectively for the period 1990–2000.

Table 2.3 assesses for its part, the performance of developing economies at three points in time: 1990, 2000 and 2012. The variables used for the comparison are those suggested by international organizations, and they include: (1) the annual percentage GDP growth, as defined previously; (2) the value added in agriculture in millions of dollars; (3) the value added in the industry in millions of dollars; (4) the value added generated by service activities, defined as the net output of services, after totalling outputs and subtracting intermediate inputs; (5) exports of goods and services, defined as the value of all goods and other market services supplied to the

Table 2.2 Gross domestic product of FY 1990, 2000 and 2012, the world, low income, lower middle income and low and middle income ($ billions)

	The world			Low income			Lower middle income			Low and middle income		
	1990	2000	2012	1990	2000	2012	1990	2000	2012	1990	2000	2012
GDP ($ billions)	22,246	32,875	72,496	143	163	5,06	861	1,239	4,838	3,167	5,674	22,779
GDP growth (annual%) 1990–2000		148%			114%			144%			179%	
GDP growth (annual %) 2000–2012			221%			310%			390%			401%
GDP growth (annual %) 1990–2012			326%			354%			562%			719%

Table 2.3 Low income, Lower middle income and Low and middle income economies, in percentages

	Low income			Lower middle income			Low and middle income		
	1990	2000	2012	1990	2000	2012	1990	2000	2012
GDP growth (annual %)	93.10	74.42	262.50	117.24	97.67	195.83	82.76	120.93	204.17
Value added in agriculture (% of GDP)	633.33	850.00	933.33	333.33	325.00	366.67	333.33	325.00	366.67
Value added in industry (% of GDP)	57.58	72.41	88.89	93.94	110.34	118.52	109.09	127.59	133.33
Value added in services (% of GDP)	70.49	67.16	68.57	70.49	70.15	72.86	72.13	74.63	77.14
Exports of goods and services (% of GDP)	65.00	69.23	83.33	90.00	103.85	93.33	95.00	103.85	100.00
Imports of goods and services (% of GDP)	110.00	100.00	140.00	95.00	100.00	103.33	95.00	100.00	103.33
Gross capital formation (% of GDP)	72.00	82.61	127.27	96.00	95.65	131.82	108.00	108.70	145.45

Source: computed based on the little data book WBG

rest of the world, including the value of goods, freight, insurance, transport, travel, royalties, license fees and other services; (6) imports of goods and services, defined as the value of all goods and other market services received from the rest of the world, including the value of goods, freight, insurance, transport, travel expenses, royalties, license fees and other services; and (7) the percentage of capital formation, defined as total stock of capital that has been formed, expressed in % of GDP.

Numbers in Table 2.3 represent economic variables are expressed as percentages of GDP. The number 93.10, (column 1990 and line annual GDP growth in %), for instance, indicates that for the year 1990, low-income economies had registered a GDP growth rate of 93.10%, and they achieved in the year 2012 a GDP growth rate of 262.50%. The magnitude of the performance of developing economies, represented here by low- and middle-income countries, is best captured by comparing data for the year 1990 to those for the year 2000. We learn, for instance, that in the case of low- and middle-income economies (the three columns to the right of Table 2.3), annual GDP growth has improved by 121.41%, growing from 82.76% at its 1990 level, to 204.17%, the new level for the year 2012. Value added in agriculture, in % of the GDP, has improved by 33.34%, value added in industry by 24.24%, value added in services by only 5%, imports and exports have remained almost unchanged, and gross capital has improved by 37.45%. Such improvements have been observable since 2000, and they are shared by both medium- and low-income economies. Value added in agriculture continues to contribute the largest portion of the strength of developing economies, and it is much more important in low-income environments. Despite such remarkable achievement, however, one in five individuals in developing regions still live in poverty. Poverty doesn't only affect developing environments; several million people also live poorly within the boundaries of the richest countries of the world.

The encouraging performance of developing economies during the period 1990–2012, positive in itself, should not lead us to overestimate its real impact. It is clear that departing from a very low base, the least relative performance registered, can only be seen as significantly high. Further, in developing environments, more than elsewhere, a very small number of individuals often monopolize most of the existing or newly added collective wealth. Expressions like "enriching further the riches, without impoverishing the poor",[3] "a rising tide lifts all boats", usually heard, may only be attractive in theory.

The Colonial Legacy, a Major Historical Impediment to Development

A common denominator to most poor countries' misfortune, besides the fact that most of them are located in the southern hemisphere of the planet, is their sharing of the colonization misadventure. This is "the practice by which powerful country directly controls less powerful and uses their resources to increase its own power and wealth" (Collins dictionary n.d.). Colonialism was mainly fuelled by the industrial revolution, because the massive growth of colonial empires was pushing them to seek exclusive and huge access to raw materials, free man-power, and ever more captive markets for their industrial output. The most recent colonialist movement was, however, founded on more than just economic objective; it aimed for the systematic subjugation of nations, countries and cultures, through military and psychological means, and seemed to have played an important role and had a hugely devastating impact on nations and their capacity to develop. It stands as a system that draws its roots from racism, inequality, discrimination and the spoiling of other resources. Colonialism has irreversibly changed the cultural and economic destinies of most colonized peoples, and has caused their demise. Some nations never recover, as evident by the current life conditions of some aboriginal communities across the world, who are left to begging and homelessness in metropolises of extreme wealth. The colonizers had introduced and imposed new forms of inequality and new systems of oppression and discrimination, for the sake of facilitating the process of exploiting the free and abundant wealth existing in the conquered territories. A

[3] "Kuznets hypothesis" postulates that economic growth will first lead to an increase in inequality, and later to a decrease in inequality. (https://www.thoughtco.com/kuznets-curve-in-economics-1146122).

number of serious impediments to the development of the colonized nations have resulted from the colonialist system, particularly:

1. An outrageous spoiling of natural resources of colonized nations;
2. The bleeding of some colonially active manpower through slavery;
3. The denial of basic rights, notably the right to develop;
4. The denial of an international identity and sovereign currency, severely limiting international exchanges;
5. Investment in infrastructures orientated to export and that often become development impediments, in the aftermath of decolonization;
6. Imposition of arbitrary national boundaries, without cultural, linguistic or racial realities, and which subsequently resulted in problems that generated perpetual conflict and discouraged development initiatives; and
7. Abusive expropriation of most fertile lands, tapping countryside in archaic methods of agriculture production.

Most of these artificial obstacles to development have survived the colonialist era and have even been restructured to better suit decolonization and quickly transformed in collaborative exploitation systems between new elites in decolonized countries and old colonial powers. The inability of new independent nations to negotiate brand new and equitable relations with former metropolitan powers had often prevent them from taking advantage of the privileged and eventually positive relationship they might have had with the former colonial powers, and the common history they shared.[4] Such a relationship, despite some violent liberation wars that have preceded national independence, could indeed have been transformed, and still can be, into performing collaborative development systems.

Imperial powers have also brought with them innovative management practices that have resulted in wiping out local management paradigms, or at least confining them to secular marginalization. However, where colonial powers were able to amass optimal acceptance for their models, in terms of population size, the knowledge transfer seems to have succeeded. This is particularly obvious in colonized areas that have a small indigenous presence that was easy to neutralize (if not, to quasi-eliminate), such as Australia, New Zealand, Canada, South America and even the United States. Whenever a competing indigenous system existed—and in a significant form—the colonizer's system seems to have been rejected and eventually "ghettoed" and considered an instrument of assimilation. Such "ghettoization" was often the result of discriminatory orchestrations. Paradoxically, it is only after the departure of the colonizers that former colonies began to accept and adopt more seriously colonizing models.

The most devastating effect of the colonial era, however, is the generalization of the deep inferiority complex instilled in indigenous populations, which results for them in a loss of self-confidence, particularly in the area of entrepreneurship and economic development. This controversial era had sown the seeds of inequality and the false belief of

[4] In some developing countries, collaboration with former colonizer seems fruitful, but unfortunately to the benefit to an elite only.

incompetency among natives, which is still visible and even sometimes encouraged today, even sometimes within international organizations. In some environments, local people were not even permitted to learn a simple skill such as carpentry, or plumbing. When you are not permitted to learn how to do something, obviously you would not know how to do it. The colonizers have let themselves become convinced that they are the only repositories of human knowledge and that other cultures do not have the required intellectual predisposition for learning and so why bother to teach them? Nazism's subscription to theories of racial hierarchy, considering inferior literally every other race, showed in the 1930s how far such ideology can be extended.

Advanced economic concepts imported by the colonizer, combined with the arrival to colonized lands of larger and much better-organized metropolitan enterprises, led to the withdrawal of the traditional local managerial systems, which were unable to compete. The managerial contribution of the colonizer could have been beneficial, if only instead of exclusionary policies, appropriate measures of improving local management practices were taken. Fortunately, "the blessed time of the colonies" seems to have gone forever, and it seems today impossible to reproduce the misdeeds. It is also virtually impossible today for the great-grandson of an Antwerp trader to accumulate as much wealth as his great-grandfather, who had unconstrained access to the economic playground of Congo. Each era, of course, obeys its own logic, and the things we find repugnant today, were once considered acceptable, or even right. For colonisers, colonialism used to be viewed, as it may still be by some, as a manifestation of the "natural" rule of "the strong dominat[ing] the weak". For them, "every colony does or ought to exist for the benefit of its mother country" (Encyclopaedia). Since the end of the Second World War, however, the possession of colonies, for so long time a matter of pride and prestige, "has become a sin to be expiated by the granting of immediate independence" (Encyclopaedia). It is hard to deny that what we are witnessing today, at the level of economic underdevelopment and poverty, may, at least in part, be the consequence of this sad chapter of human history, one that ought to be corrected, not only in terms of aid, but also in terms of attitudes and historical imbalances correction. Those who still benefit from the outcomes of the colonial system of the past are not to blame on the basis of historical conditions, but the fact remains that they should today question the persistence of the damage and the inequalities that have been made and that are still at work. The strong commitment of the Bretton Woods spirit to development must, therefore, be defended and reinforced.

Closing this section without mentioning few of the positive aspects of colonialism, particularly in certain environments, would be unfair. In parallel with the colonial atrocities, certain benefits can be encountered. Colonial policies, for instance, seem to have led in some areas, to lasting stability and to the ending of conflicts, thus creating new states with well-defined and accepted boundaries, although these have sometimes been strongly decried. The colonial era, in some regions, was also an opportunity for the building up of basic infrastructure, albeit for metropolitan powers benefit. It has also linked the colonized countries to the international market, albeit for export to metropoles. Finally, it allowed a local elite to emerge through a modern educational system, originally established for colonial children, or for missionary objectives.

Modern Impediments to Development

Although expressed in terms of inadequacy of national income, poverty and underdevelopment turn out to be much more than just that. Gross national income per capita and gross domestic product seem to be only the consequences and not the causes of poverty. The precarious economic situation of developing countries appears to be structural and often based on damaging conditions of the past, but even more so based on inappropriate development policies and insufficient investment in basic services, such as education and health since those policies are often based, at best, on random or discriminatory government decisions. The situation is sometimes attributed to colonial legacies, but this can be only partially the cause. This section discusses some of the modern impediments to development that may be blamed for the low levels of development registered by poor countries. These are:

1. Inability of developing countries to build a stable income base system, allowing the collection of sufficient sustainable financial resources, such as taxes. Stable tax collection requires the government to insure citizens of the quality of its governance (World Bank 2017b).
2. Inability of developing countries to escape colonial formatting, leading to failure to reform old colonial systems, in order to make them more suited to local conditions, or just updating them to meet modern requirements (Globalization for All 2002, p. 72). Indeed, some poor economies find themselves trapped within underdevelopment, just by not having been able to escape out-dated organizational structures inherited from old colonial regimes and entirely geared towards export of raw materials.
3. Inability of developing countries to establish institutional contexts conducive to safeguarding income from natural resources, of which they are often very well endowed. This could help reduce the fiscal volatility they suffer from and promote a macroeconomic environment conducive to long-term investment (World Bank 2017b).
4. Inability of developing countries to recover the human education deficit and to take advantage of whatever educated public they may already have. Family and clan "relations" often keep them from entrusting able individuals with high national responsibilities, whenever they are not part of webs of relations. In such situations, developing countries find themselves trapped an infernal mediocrity circle, where incompetent people are hired for high ranking positions and surround themselves with incompetent relationships, themselves surrounded by collaborators of the same calibre and so on, perpetuating incompetence, down to the bottom of the ladder. In such environments, competency has no value; instead, it is only the relationship that counts.
5. The other impediment to development seems to come from the unfairness characterizing the international economic system itself, keeping developing countries from securing a fair share, mainly because of the enormous and outrageous asymmetries of power. The more obvious unfairness at this level includes the absence of clear international agreements on trade, forcing many poor countries into difficult and destructive compromises in order to survive.

The importance of the quality of institutions for development has been recognized for some time now, and real life experiences tend to point to institutional quality as the main guarantor of prosperity. Further, some types of institutions seem to determine higher levels of development, and this has led many policymakers and development agencies "to promote institutional reforms aimed at achieving institutional quality standards" (World Bank 2017b).

Portrait of a Typical Developing Country

Apart from the question of "whom to blame" for underdevelopment, it is possible to sketch a rough portrait of an economy struggling with underdevelopment and poverty. This is often a former colony with the following limitations (World Bank 2017b):

1. This is a country unable to set clear and well-defined development objective susceptible to mobilizing its citizens' energies in the fight against poverty and for the sake of development;
2. This is a country unable to prevent a small number of powerful groups of its citizens, often backed up by former colonial powers, from maintaining for their sole benefit, an exclusive control over national economic activities and resources.[5] Limited in number, such groups have self family professionals, lawyers, accountants, notaries, and even medical doctors, and they enjoy monopolistic activities whose rent is competition free. They are related to each other through subtle and informal connections, allowing them to maintain their iron grip on all sectors of the economy, in a way that no development project has a chance to get through, without their consent, often offered for royalty disbursements.
3. This is a country unable to promote or enforce good laws and regulations and where a law or any formal rule is unlikely to be promulgated,[6] when privileged groups do not want it.
4. This is a country where the government can increase national income only through informal and transaction-oriented way and finds it easier to reward supporters by violating its laws, or by allowing influential groups to violate them (World Bank 2017b).
5. This is a country unable to use its education system and its educated citizens as resources to better train senior officials and leaders, and where the academic community is kept from playing the key role it is supposed to play in

[5] The only external intrusion into family circles is by marriage, consequently any marriage request can then take the form of a family plebiscite.

[6] In some countries laws and regulations do not seem to be promulgated to be respected, but rather as punitive discriminatory means, applicable on the head of the client.

training competent managers, which are badly needed for economic development;

6. This is a country unable to take advantage of major technological breakthroughs. More than ever before, scientific methods and technologies can be used today to lay down the foundations for development that are more oriented towards progress and sustainability.
7. This is a country unable to value skills and knowledge for their real worth. In many developing countries individual and family relationships overshadow skills and competencies.
8. This is a country unable to provide its citizens with the necessary conditions for entrepreneurship freedom. Indeed, no amount of money can lead to development if citizens are not involved and a process of equitable interaction does not exist. This process involves first, an institutional context safeguarding revenue and reducing fiscal unfairness and volatility, and second, the establishment of macroeconomic environments conducive to long-term investment (World Bank 2017b).
9. This is a country neglecting to invest in information and statistical tools for political reasons, and the fear of seeing them used for criticism of its performance (World Bank 2017b).
10. This is a country failing to understand that the effectiveness of development policies depends not only on the policies chosen, but also on the way they are chosen and implemented, and that policy-making and implementation also imply their negotiation between different actors in the nation, to insure their broad acceptance.

Many aspects of development may therefore relate to public governance, particularly the notion of citizens' freedom. In economic terms, freedom can be seen as the opening and facilitating of access to opportunities and the eliminating of different types of barriers and irritants that keep citizens from opportunities, susceptible to reducing their ability to innovate and exercise their entrepreneurial ability (World Bank 2017b). The ability of an economy of putting citizens to work depends on its ability to invest in key sectors of development. No developed country has been able to make progress in terms of economic and social advance without getting around two main constraints: First, establishing a fair and sufficient income collection system, as well as a fair public expenditure system, geared towards the protection of individuals against the vagaries of life, and second, having appropriate policies that reduce social disparities between individuals (World Bank 2017b).

Unfortunately, social investment has never been quick to produce its expected outcome; it becomes economically profitable only once adequately trained and healthy generations have in adulthood accessed employment. Similarly, for a country to be able to collect enough revenue to finance its investments in public goods, its citizens must be cooperative in terms of compliance with tax laws. Such cooperation is usually only possible when the government behaves appropriately and demonstrates credible, consistent and fair application of its laws (World Bank 2017b). This, in turn, is, only possible when governmental institutions are of a good level of fairness and efficiency. The quality of institutions appears to be a main prerequisite for development, as the more prosperous and equitable countries also have the best institutional systems. It is therefore reasonable to think that certain types of institutions can determine the highest levels of development (World Bank 2017b). The impact of public governance on poverty and development will be empirically tested.

Conclusion

A large percentage of the world's population is still living in extreme poverty. Although, the number of misfortunates seems steadily in decline, it is still disturbing to most people to realize that in many developing countries people cannot expect to live to age 45 and in others, because of malnourishment and diseases a high percentage of children die before reaching their fifth birthday. In many other countries just half of the adult men, and less than one fourth of adult women, can read and write (Data from the 1999/2000 World Development Report, Table 2.2). This situation is as incomprehensible as it is unacceptable and "it is shameful that we could not eradicate poverty and privation despite in this age of unprecedented wealth and technical prowess" (Kofi Anan 2017) (#HumanRightsDay). Prosperity is not a closed space, where when one benefits when the other loses; it is rather, if intelligently managed, an open space that can benefit everyone. In contrast, extreme inequality can only be detrimental to everyone (Deputy Secretary General of the United Nations). In the face of the poverty and underdevelopment scourge, the international community has not remained idle since 1940; it has devised two far-reaching instruments: the Bretton Woods Financial Institutions and the Official Development Assistance.

Chapter 3
Bretton Woods Institutions Within the International Financial Architecture for Development

The Bretton Woods Financial Institutions (BWFI), established by the 1944 Bretton Woods Agreement (BWA), form a complementary web of international financial organizations composed of the International Monetary Fund (IMF), the World Bank Group (WBG) and regional development banks (RDB). They have the collective aim of the carrying of Bretton Woods spirit, by actualizing the promotion of economic development of their respective membership and the fight against poverty in suffering environments. They play a strategic global financial intermediation role within the international financial architecture. Despite their close links with the United Nations (UN) system, BWFIs are independent from the UN in terms of decision-making processes, sources of funding, and administration and budget. All Bretton Woods institutions are, however, submitted to the United Nations Security Council's agreed-upon guidelines, but they are not subjected to the United Nations General Assembly nor to one of its agencies' decisions.

This chapter discusses the spirit of Bretton Woods and locates its financial institutions within the overall international financial architecture for development and the fight against poverty; the first section introduces to the Bretton Woods institutions; section two deals with the International Monetary Fund; section three presents the World Bank Group and its constituencies; section four discusses the Bretton Woods institutions' financial models and the multiplicative factor; section five deals with the International Development Agency; and section six concludes the chapter.

Bretton Woods Financial Institutions (BWFI)

The spirit of the Bretton Woods Conference was strongly calling for the establishment of a new world order, free from belligerency, and able to prevent falling back into the global chaos that characterized the world in the aftermath of the first big wars and that presumably led to the second. In order to set up the theme of the

A. Naciri, *The Governance Structures of the Bretton Woods Financial Institutions*, SpringerBriefs in Economics, https://doi.org/10.1007/978-3-319-97906-9_3

Bretton Woods conference, president Roosevelt and PM Churchill, first agreed in 1941 on a determining document, known as the Atlantic Charter (AC),[1] laying down essentially the prerequisites for the United States' participation in the British war effort and mainly specifying what was really meant by the so-called new world order, by defining its founding principles, namely the abolishment of colonialism, the development of a fair global trade system and the improvement of labor standards and security around the world. At the end of the second war, the Atlantic Charter also became an operational vehicle for the Bretton Woods agreement (Consumer International 2005), that created the World Bank and the IMF, as part of a global initiative to provide the world with an appropriate international financial structure for development and the fight against poverty. In framework of the Bretton Woods' main objective was the strong will to avoid the repetition of the world war atrocities and the discouragement of their recurrence. The Bretton Woods crafters were indeed convinced that this was possible simply by establishing a fair and open global financial and trading system, coupled with an honest development assistance program, for those left behind due mainly to historical unfairness. Bretton Woods' liberalism was, however, hardly free from ideology. Indeed, in the face of the rampant communism, The Americans and British were deeply concerned and equally determined to ensure that the post-war order would stand in the way of the communist wave that threatened the then European countries ravaged by war. It was also meant to be attractive to the many countries newly promoted to decolonization, and to whom development assistance was offered as a reward for their rejection of the communist alternative.

Most BWFIs fund their loans and grants through borrowing from international capital markets, or through donor contributions and income from operations. They were established with the specific aim of transferring investment capital from rich to needy countries (Griffith-Jones 2002). History has shown that despite original geopolitical orientation, Bretton Woods' spirit still stands for much of its human aims, but surely needs some repair.

The Operating and Business Model of the International Monetary Fund (IMF)[2]

The International Monetary Fund (IMF), as a major creation of the United Nations Bretton Woods Conference, is entrusted with the mandate of preventing global economic depressions. The 44 signatory countries to the IMF's establishment act of 1944 sought to establish a framework for economic cooperation that would prevent the world from undergoing disastrous competing devaluations comparable to those of 1920s, which eventually led to the Great Depression of the 1930s, and subsequently

[1] This is the joint declaration of President Roosevelt and Prime Minister Churchill (August 14, 1941) resulting from a conference at sea that set forth the peace aims of their governments for the period following World War II. (Dictionary.com).

[2] http://www.imf.org/en/About

to World War II. Such an objective remains unchanged, to be expanded only in 2012, to encompass macroeconomic and financial policies and avoidance of global financial instability. To fulfill its mandate, the IMF provides loans to member countries suffering from real or potential imbalances in their balance of payments, thus enabling them to rebuild their international reserves, or to stabilize their currencies and continue to honor their international financial obligations. Unlike development banks, the IMF does not lend funds for specific investment projects; instead, it offers three concessional loan facilities for low-income and developing countries: Extended Credit Facilities (ECFs), Standby Credit Facilities (SCF) and Rapid Credit Facilities (RCF).

Extended Credit Facilities (ECFs) provide financial assistance to countries facing persistent disequilibrium in their balance of payments. Standby Credit Facilities (SCF), on the other hand, provide short-term financial assistance to developing countries experiencing short-term needs in their balance of payments. Finally, Rapid Credit Facilities (RCFs) are intended to provide fast concessional financial assistance, with limited conditionality, to developing countries facing urgent balance of payments requirement (IMF 2017c). The objective of ECF, SCF and RCF is "to support low-income countries in their efforts to achieve and maintain a stable and sustainable macroeconomic stance that is compatible with poverty reduction and strong economic growth" (IMF 2017b). These three assistance formula were all created as part of the Poverty Reduction and Growth (PRGT), focusing on the goals of poverty reduction and country growth (IMF 2017e). They were also initiated as part of a wider movement within the IMF, which aimed to allow its financial assistance to improve in flexibility and responsiveness to the diverse needs of low-income countries, particularly in crisis times. The IMF also issues Special Drawing Rights (SDRs),[3] which are an international reserve asset that can supplement official reserves of member countries and can be voluntarily exchanged for currencies among countries (IMF at glance 2018b). In 2009 the Group of Twenty (G20) agreed to increase borrowed resources available to the IMF by tripling its lending resources and complementing its quota resources by up to $500 billion from about $250 billion before (IMF Financial Information 2016a).

The most important New Arrangements to Borrow from the IMF, in millions of SDRs as of April 30, 2016 were granted to the US for SDR 69,074 billion, Japan for SDR 65,953 billion, China for SDR 31,217 billion, Deutsche Bundesbank for SDR 25,37 billion, France for SDR 18,657 billion, The United Kingdom for SDR 18,657 billion, for a total of SDR 369,997 billions,[4] (IMF Financial Information 2016a, p. 21). Besides financial assistance, the IMF also monitors member country policies through a formal system known as surveillance and provides "technical assistance

[3] "The SDR is a reserve asset created by the IMF and allocated to participating members in proportion to their IMF quotas to meet a long-term global need to supplement existing reserve assets. […]. The SDR is not a currency, nor is it a liability of the IMF; instead, it serves primarily as a potential claim on freely usable currencies" (IMF Financial Information 2016a).

[4] Before the payments for quota increase under the Fourteenth Review in February 2016, the NAB (New Arrangements to Borrow) was rolled back from SDR 370 billion to SDR 182 billion.

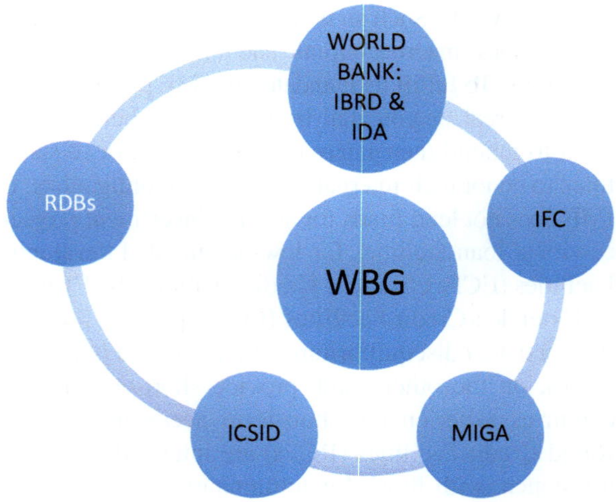

Fig. 3.1 The World Bank Group, WBG

and training to help member countries build better economic institutions and strengthen related human capacities" (IMF at glance 2018b).

The World Bank Group, WBG

The International Bank for Reconstruction and Development (IBRD) is the first international development bank to be established by the Bretton Woods Agreement. It was subsequently developed into the World Bank Group (WBG). The IBRD was from the outset mandated by the Bretton Woods Agreement to promote the long-term economic development and poverty reduction, and was declared to be responsible for the provision of technical and financial assistance to countries in shortage. The WBG is to include, in addition to the IBRD's four international financial institutions, all those aiming to assist developing countries in their development initiatives by granting them or facilitating leveraged loans. The WBG turns out to be the largest development bank in the world today, and has observer status to the United Nations Development system. Figure 3.1 summarizes the constituencies of the World Bank Group. The Bank of International Settlements (BIS), established in 1930 to handle war reparations among European countries, was subsumed subsequently into the Bretton Woods framework, but does not make part of this study, given its limited direct role in development assistance. The World Bank Group, composed by five constituencies, as represented in Fig. 3.1, has been given the mission of achieving two main goals: ending extreme poverty and building shared prosperity among all countries (World Bank[5]).

[5] http://www.worldbank.org/en/who-we-are

As indicated in Fig. 3.1, the five constituencies of the World Bank Group discussed are the following.

International Bank for Reconstruction and Development (IBRD)

The International Bank for Reconstruction and Development (IBRD) is the main constituency of the World Bank Group, established in 1944, with the main mandate of promoting the world economic development, both globally and sustainably, for the sake of reducing the global poverty. The IBRD fulfils its mandate in several ways: first, by granting loans to developing countries; second, by making available to them facilitating borrowing guarantees; and third, by allowing them access to appropriate technical assistance for specific projects and economic reform programs (IBRD_FY_2016_AR). Over the 2011–2015 period, the IBRD reports in its financial statements, development assistance commitments an amount of $107,69 billion, representing an annual average of $21,54 billions (IFC_FY_2016_AR, p. 23). As mentioned previously, IBRD's activities are complemented by four affiliated organizations.

The International Development Association (IDA)

The International Development Association (IDA) is the arm of the World Bank that assists the world's poorest countries in their development initiatives. Overseen by 173 shareholder nations, it was established in 1961 with the specific mandate of granting loans to developing and poor countries on highly favourable terms, aiming to reducing poverty by providing loans and grants under multiple favourable forms (World Bank, IDA).[6] The IDA grants concessional loans and also offers guarantees to the poorest countries for the funding of their development programs.; provides the poorest countries with technical assistance through its fee-based advisory services; offers the poorest countries strategic advice and knowledge transfer services, including country-by-country economic studies; supports member countries with a disaster risk insurance program to contribute to their financial protection in the event of a disaster; and provides or facilitates the financing of development actions through trust fund partnerships with bilateral and multilateral donors.

The IDA support to country members is conditional on a number of requirements, such as the income level of recipients, their performance in already ongoing IDA-financed projects, and their overall economic performance. The lending terms of the IDA are highly concessional, meaning that the loans are granted at very low rates, i.e. carrying little or no interest charges. It is the beneficiary's level of devel-

[6] http://ida.worldbank.org/about/what-ida

opment, expressed in several indicators, as its overall risk of insolvency, its solvency with the IBRD, and its GNI/GNP per capita level, that often determines its borrowing conditions. Usually beneficiaries with a high level of risk of insolvency receive all the financial assistance accorded in the form of grants, while beneficiaries with a medium level of risk of insolvency receive only 50% of assistance in the form of grants. Other beneficiaries receive IDA support in the form of 25–38 year loans. "Since 1960, IDA has provided some $345 billion for investments in 113 countries" (World Bank, IDA).[7] Annual commitments have increased steadily and averaged about $18 billion over the last 3 years.

International Finance Corporation (IFC)

The establishment of the International Finance Corporation (IFC), as a World Bank institution, dates back to 1956. It was conceived under the urgent need to provide funding to private enterprises, operating in developing environments and facing chronic shortage of equity, for their development. Clearly recognizing that development is also a private business endeavour, IFC founders set its goal to be the assisting of growth of profitable private enterprises in developing country members. It quickly became the largest global development institution focused exclusively on the private sector in developing environments, providing private sectors with unsecured loans on market terms and even taking part in equity capital issues, without control purpose, in mind (IFC).[8]

The IFC designs its financial assistance in a way that meets client-specific needs in different industries, especially infrastructure, manufacturing, agribusiness, financial services and financial markets. The IFC's assistance is offered in the form of loans, usually for terms of 7–12 years, but can also be granted in the form of equity participation (IFC_FT_2016_AR). When participating in growth capital issuance by private firms in need of capital in developing countries, the IFC also provides development support. Similarly, when IFC financial support is provided for risk management purposes or for expanding access to domestic and international capital markets, it invests (IFC_FT_2016_AR). These investments are, however, made exclusively in developing countries and in for-profit projects and at market rates. The IFC actually intervenes in different ways to support private companies to cope with their lack of equity (IFC_FT_2016_AR), for instance, by investing in expanding shareholding through public offerings. In doing so, it participates at the same time in the improvement of local capital markets by taking part in syndicated loans, where other financial institutions are involved. In 2016, for instance, syndicated loans accounted for 70% of the funds mobilized by the IFC and nearly half of that was granted to IDA borrowers—by offering to clients trade and commodity financ-

[7] http://ida.worldbank.org/about/what-ida

[8] http://www.ifc.org/wps/wcm/connect/corp_ext_content/ifc_external_corporate_site/about+ifc_new

ing, in the form of payment commitments to approved financial institutions, and through financing options, such as financing derivatives for hedging purposes or merging concessional donor funds into IFC commercial financing.

The IFC's Annual Report for the fiscal year 2016 shows a volume of financial facilities of more than $68 billion for the fiscal year 2016 and a cumulative amount of $320 billion over the 5-year period 2012–2016. The institution's outstanding loans have steadily increased during this period, with the exception of a slight decline in the fiscal year 2015, compared to 2014 level. For the fiscal year 2016, the IFC participated in 344 projects, broken down as follows: (1) long-term investments for an amount of $11.99 billion, (2) investment portfolios for an amount of $51.99 billion and (3) syndicated loan participation for an amount of $16.55 billion, of which more than half was spent on infrastructure (IFC_FY_2016_AR, p. 31).

Multilateral Investment Guarantee Agency (MIGA)

The Multilateral Investment Guarantee Agency, MIGA was established in 1988, as the World Bank constituency, having the specific mandate to facilitate and encourage the funding of productive investment in developing member countries. MIGA provides foreign investors with business insurance against certain non-commercial risks that might be encountered during transactions in or with developing countries, such as risks of transfer restrictions, expropriations, breach of contract, war and civil unrest, non-compliance with sovereign or private financial obligations. In summary, MIGA provides new and existing cross-border investments from any MIGA member country to any developing member country (MIGA_FY_2016_AR, Management Discussion and Analysis, p. 2), and this is achieved either through the provision of non-commercial risk guarantees to foreign private investors, particularly of a political nature, for their investments in MIGA's developing member countries, or through guarantees to help holders access more financing and better terms (MIGA_FY_2016_AR).

The International Center for Settlement of Investment Dispute (ICSID)

The International Centre for Settlement of Investment Dispute (ICSID) is one of the five constituencies of the World Bank Group, and it provides arrangements for conciliation and arbitration purposes, in the case of international investment disputes. The ICSID offers mechanisms specifically tailored for the resolution of international investment disputes between investors and governments. Two main instruments are used in the process of dispute resolution: first, the ICSID Convention and second, the ICSID Additional Facility.

The ICSID Convention is a treaty ratified by 153 Contracting States, establishing an independent, impartial and self-contained system, whose proceedings are delocalized from domestic procedures, meaning that local courts do not intervene in the ICSID process.

The ICSID Additional Facility, on the other hand, requires two steps to start arbitration: first, a party must request and obtain the ICSID's approval of an agreement to access the Additional Facility and second, the party must submit a request for arbitration to the ICSID. These two steps can be taken at the same time, in one document, or separately. This framework is supplemented by detailed Regulations and Rules. The ICSID does not itself make procedural rulings or decide the outcome of the dispute; its intervention is limited to arbitration. (ICSID, Process Overview[9]).

World Bank Trust Fund

The World Bank Group also manages funding packages, involving one or more donors, to finance a wide range of projects and activities. These are trust fund appeals, which can be independent or programmable, as they can be country-specific, region-specific or even global in scope. They can easily be tailored to meet client needs in crisis situations and where other solutions may not be usable. A percentage of funds is retained by the Bank for its oversight and analysis services. The Bank plays various roles in these funds, ranging from a limited financial role of trust, to the implementation of entire fund activities (World Bank 2017a). The IBRD/IDA Project Finance Fund, for instance, implemented in medium and low-income countries, is overseen by both the local representations of the Bank and IDA. These funds represent 35% of the Bank's trust funds and are disbursed through three types of funds. The first of these are Bank Executed Trust Funds (BETFs), which are executed by the Bank and whose purpose is to support the Bank's program. They usually focus on knowledge transfer, advice and technical assistance. The second are Recipient Executed Trust Funds (RETFs), which are transferred by the Bank to a third party recipient. Here, the Bank plays an operational role, such as the evaluation and supervision of funded activities. The third and final type are Intermediate Financial Funds (IFFs), where the Bank acts as a Financial Trustee and whose purpose is to support development initiatives and partnerships. This is the fastest growing category of funds, representing the majority of trust funds (World Bank 2017a).

These funds represented, during the 5-year period from 2011 to 2015, some $19.93 billion of the World Bank's fund activity and an annual average of almost $5 billion. The majority of financing comes from sovereign donors, and funds were in constant growth, except for fiscal year 2015, which suffered a slight decrease. In the fiscal year 2014, there were 982 trust funds, scoring a total of $30.09 billion and in fiscal 2015, $3.98 billion of new funds were committed, an increase of 37.04% over fiscal 2011, but a decrease of 18.56% compared to fiscal year 2011 (IFC_FY_2016_AR, p. 23).

[9] https://icsid.worldbank.org/en/pages/process/overview.aspx

Collaboration across IBRD, IDA, IFC, and MIGA has grown over time, and covers a range of activities "at the regional, country, sector, and thematic levels" (World Bank_FY_2017_AR). Further, in a response to the challenge of the world economic integration, the Bretton Woods institutions initiated first-time regional development banks (RDBs), which are, by order of date of establishment, the Inter-American Development Bank (IaDB), the Africa Development Bank (AfDB), the European Bank for Reconstruction and Development (EBRD) and the Asian Development Bank (AsDB), to be discussed in later chapter. In fiscal 2017, the World Bank committed in development funding some $42.1 billion, including $22.6 billion committed by the International Bank for Reconstruction and Development (IBRD) and $19.5 billion by the International Development Association (IDA) (World Bank_FY_2017_AR).

The Bretton Woods Institutions Financial Models and the Multiplicative Factor

The IMF and the World Bank Group have three main sources of revenue. First, their lending operation revenues, mainly the interest and fees charged to their borrowing country clients; second, their income earned from their investment activities on the financial markets; and third, the contributions collected from their membership. Net loan income and investment returns are used to cover administrative expenses, as well as to build up balance sheet reserves and, in the case of IBRD and IFC, to fund annual transfers to IDA.

At the heart of the function of BWFIs, is the multiplicative factor (MF) they are able to create. This is a factor that is inherent to the financial intermediation of all multilateral institutions. It is meant to help them to increase their capital base for development assistance purpose. MP allows a dollar collected by a regional bank to generate more than it original value and the final outcome to become usable for development assistance purpose. The limited resources of BWFIs are maximized in this way and their impact multiplied. The effectiveness of this leverage effect is made possible because of two factors. The first is the sovereign credit quality recognized to BWFIs debt issues, given their multilateral status, allows them to capitalize on the solvency of their individual member states (mainly the rich non-borrowing members) and consequently offers lenders the same credit assurance, as sovereign credit. The second is the fiduciary credibility inherent in BWFIs debt securities, securing them high fiduciary credibility, (World Bank 2016a).

The International Monetary Fund, IMF Financial Model

As indicated by Fig. 3.2, the IMF is composed of several main departments, namely the General Department, the Concessional Lending & Debt Relief Trusts, the SDR Department, and Other Accounts. Each department also contains several accounts.

Fig. 3.2 IMF main departments

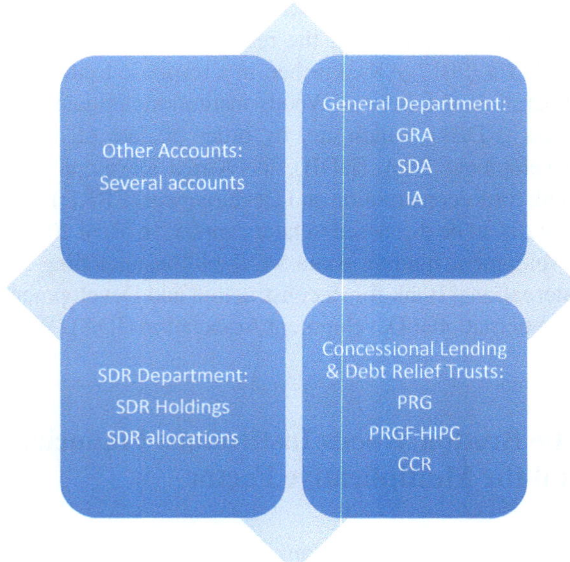

Source: The (IMF _FY_2016_Financial Operations)

The General Department, for instance, includes the General Resource Account (GRA), the Special Disbursement Account (SDA) and the Investment Account (IA). The Concessional Lending & Debt Relief Trusts Department covers the Poverty Relief & Growth (PRG), PRG facility-heavily indebted poor countries (PRGF-HIPC) and trust and catastrophe containment & relief trust (CCR) while the SDR Department covers the SDR Holdings and SDR allocations. Other Accounts department also includes several accounts, depending on the need.

The IMF provides financial support in reserve currency to its country members in need for their operations, through separate channels. These are the regular non-concessional General Resource Account (GRA) loans, the PRGT Concessional Loans and the SDR Department facilities.

Regular lending and concessional operations involve the provision of financial assistance to member countries under IMF conditions. Regular financing facilities are comparable to traditional lines of credit, at commercial banks. Their use is required in the majority of IMF loan agreements in pursuit of economic stabilization objectives (IMF_FY_2016_Financial Operations, p. 7). The IMF also provides PRGT Concessional Loans through the Poverty Reduction and Growth Trust, better tailored to the diversity and needs of low-income countries. PRGT has three concessional lending windows: The Extended Credit Facility (ECF[10]), the Standby

[10] Sustained medium- to long-term engagement in case of protracted balance of payments problems (IMF).

Table 3.1 IMF income statement of the General Department (SDR billion [As of December 29, 2017, SDR 1 = $1.424130. At: https://www.imf.org/external/np/fin/data/rms_sdrv.aspx], as of April 30, 2016) (as of February 5, 2018, SDR1 = US$1.454700)

Operational income	SDR bill
Interest and charges	1.327
Interest on SDR holdings	0.009
Net income from investments	(0.020)
Service charges and commitment fees	0.120
Total operational income	1.436
Operational expenses	
Remuneration	0.012
Interest expense on borrowings	0.018
Administrative expenses	0.951
Total operational expenses	**0.981**
Net operational income	0.455

Source: Finance Department, International Monetary Fund

Credit Facility (SCF[11]), and the Rapid Credit Facility (RCF[12]) (IMF[13]). The IMF can also create international reserve assets by allocating SDRs to members who can use them, to obtain foreign currency from other members. The use of SDR is unconditional, although a market-based interest rate is charged to the borrower (IMF_FY_2016_Financial Operations, p. 7).

The IMF charges fees to its borrower countries and also pays compensation to members on their deposits. When a member country borrows from the IMF, as part of the general account, it pays several fees, non-refundable commitment fees, service fees and interest on outstanding credits. Generally, charged to borrowers, interest rates are 1% point above the rate paid to members' holding deposits with the Fund, and IMF members with exceptional credit are charged interest rates on prevailing market conditions (IMF_FY_2016_Financial Operations). As rule, rates must be sufficient to fully cover interest payments to creditors.

The IMF, however, also pays compensation to members on their deposits in the General Resources Account, with the exception of a small portion. The rate of pay is monitored by the IMF's Articles of Agreement, providing for a rate of pay that is neither higher than the SDR interest rate nor less than 80% of that rate. Currently, this rate of pay is equal to the SDR interest rate. Whenever the IMF has borrowing arrangements, it also pays interest on outstanding loans normally at the interest rate of SDR (IMF_FY_2016, Financial Statements).

Table 3.1 reproduces IMF's income statement for the fiscal year 2016, in billions of SDRs.

[11] Financing for low-income countries with actual or potential short-term balance of payments and adjustment needs (IMF).

[12] Rapid unconditional financial support as a single up-front payout for low-income countries facing urgent balance of payments needs (IMF).

[13] http://www.imf.org/en/About/Factsheets/IMF-Support-for-Low-Income-Countries

Table 3.2 IMF financial position statement of the General Department (SDR billion, as of April 30, 2016) (Nota bene: Data for the fiscal year ending April 30, 2017 are very similar to those of the fiscal year ending April 30, 2016)

Assets	2016 SDR	2016 in %	Liabilities, reserves and retained earnings	2016 SDR	2016 in %
Currencies			Other liabilities	0.811	0.15%
Usable currencies	360.036	68.66%	Employee benefits	0.508	0.10%
Other currencies	65.575	12.51%	Special contingent account	1.188	0.23%
Credit outstanding	47.798	9.12%	Borrowings	31.671	6.04%
SDR holdings	31.842	6.07%	Quotas, represented by:		0.00%
Investments	14.968	2.85%	Reserve tranche positions	45.967	8.77%
Gold holdings	3.167	0.60%	Subscription payments	425.601	81.16%
Other assets	0.283	0.05%	Total quotas	471.568	89.93%
			Reserves of the general resources account	18.438	3.52%
			Retained earnings of the investment account and resources of the special disbursement account	0.199	0.04%
Total assets	524,383	100.00%	Total liabilities, reserves, retained earnings, and resources	524.383	100%
	523.669	0.998638		524.383	100%

Source: Finance Department, International Monetary Fund

During fiscal year 2016, the IMF recorded operating income totalling SDR 1,436 billion, consisting of SDR 1.277 billion of interest and commission revenue, SDR 9 million of interest revenue on SDR holdings and a net loss on investments of SDR −20 million (IMF FY_2016_Financial, p. 106). In contrast, total operating expenses of the IMF for fiscal year 2016 amounted to SDR 981 million, consisting of administrative expenses of SDR 951 million, interest on borrowings of SDR 18 million and compensation for SDR 12 million, leaving the Fund with a profit of SDR455 million.

The IMF's net profit is used in part to help distribute dividends to member countries, as well as to accumulate precautionary reserves, in the form of retained earnings. This ensures that the value of member positions protects the IMF's financial mechanism as whole. In the fiscal year 2016, apart from the distribution of outstanding gold profits, no other distributions were made by the IMF.

Table 3.2 reproduces the balance sheet of the IMF's General Department for the financial year 2016 in billions of SDRs. A look to the IMF's financial position statement shows that with 89.93% of resources, corresponding to SDR471.57 billion, quotas are at the heart of the IMF's financial situation. The reserve tranche positions of member countries, resulting from initial quota payments and changes due to the use and receipt of foreign exchange in the IMF's financial operations, amounted to

SDR 46.0 billion. Loans outstanding were SDR 31.7 billion, or 6.04% of resources. The addition of reserves, the profit carried forward with 0.04%, plays only a very limited role in the financial structure of the IMF. With the addition of some minor elements, the liabilities and other assets of member countries of the General Department amount to SDR 524.4 billion in resources.

On the assets side, the currencies that could be used for IMF lending and repayment operations, amount to SDR 360 billion, representing 68.66% of total assets at the end of the 2016 financial year. Non-usable currencies (other currencies) accounted for 12.51% of all assets and amounted to SDR 65.7 billion. The other major component of the IMF's assets is the outstanding credit, which is the value of IMF financing to its members, and which amounted to SDR 47.8 billion at the end of the fiscal year 2016, that is 9.12% of its total assets.

Gold reserves, valued at SDR 3.2 billion, constitute a relatively small share of total IMF assets. The only interest-bearing asset held by the GDA other than its credit being acquired is represented by its SDR holdings of SDR 31.8 billion at the end of 2016, or 0.06%. The investments account for SDR 15.0 billion and generate additional revenue for the Fund. In the fiscal year 2016, an amount of SDR 3.98 billion new funds were committed, representing an increase of 37.04% over fiscal year 2011, but a decrease of 18.56% over fiscal year 2011 (IFC_FY2016_AR, p. 23).

As of April 30, 2017 the IMF managed over SDR 527 billion in assets in the General Department, SDR 34 billions in the SDR Department and SDR14 in the Concessional Lending and Debt Relief Trusts (IFC_FY2017_AR).

World Bank Group, WBG Financial Model

The World Bank, including its trust funds, is legally and financially independent, having its own separate assets and liabilities, and is only responsible for its own operations and not for those of other partner institutions (WBG_FY_2016_AR, P. 6). The World Bank and constituencies of the WBG also have their own business model.

The International Bank for Reconstruction and Development (IBRD)

As the primary institution of the World Bank Group, IBRD provides medium- and low-income countries with loans, guarantees and advice to support their development initiatives and programs. The IBRD strives to generate enough revenue to carry out its operations and to accumulate enough reserve funds, not only to strengthen its financial situation, but also to support the IDA's special development mission. The IBRD's income statement for the fiscal year 2016 shows that its main

Table 3.3 IBRD key financial indicators, fiscal years 2012–2016 as of and for the fiscal years ended June 30, in $ billions, except ratios which are in percentages

	2016	2015	2014	2013	2012	2012–2016
	$	$	$	$	$	$
Total assets	371.26	343.23	358.88	325.60	338.18	
Net loans outstanding	167.64	155.04	151.98	141.69	134.21	
Net investment portfolio	51.76	45.11	42.71	33.39	35.12	
Borrowing portfolio	178.23	158.85	152.64	135.00	129.68	
Usable equity	39.42	40.20	40.47	39.71	37.64	
Net income/(loss)	0.495	−0.786	−0.978	0.218	−0.676	−1.727
Allocable income to IDA	0.497	0.650	0.635	0.621	0.608	3.011

Source: IBRD_FY_2016_AR, p. 7

source of revenue comes from the contributed capital by its member countries, but also from the net interest margin earned on the loans granted and on the income received from its investment portfolio and from other development activities, such as consulting (IBRD_FY_2016_AR).

Given its large bargaining power, insured by its size and international status, the IBRD is able to borrow on favorable market terms and usually transfers its savings to its borrowing members. Such financial intermediation activity is decisive for the achievement of the objectives of development assistance. The IBRD issues its financial securities, either through global offerings or through specific bond issues that are related to the particular needs of a country or investor (IBRD_FY_2016_AR). These bonds are offered in various currencies, maturities, markets, and with fixed and variable terms. Further, in order to open new markets to international investors, the IBRD often offers them new financial products in the currencies of several emerging markets. Funds not used for loan purposes, in a given year are maintained in the IBRD's investment portfolio and provide liquidity for its operations (IBRD_FY_2016_AR, p. 9). Table 3.3 reproduces selected of IBRD key financial variables, for the period 2012–2016.

Table 3.3 indicates that the IBRD's annual funding volumes varies from year to year, and its total assets have reached in the fiscal year 2016 the amount of $371.26 billion, which is a 9.2% increase over 2015's level and a 9% increase for the whole period of 2012–2016. The IBRD's consolidated net lending reached an accumulated amount of $750.56 billion over the 2012–2016 period. The IBRD's lending increased in in the fiscal year 2016 by 8.1%, reaching $168 billion. Borrowing demand remained strong in the same fiscal year, as evidenced by the steady increase in commitments: they had increased by 24.8% over the period 2013–2016. The loan portfolio had registered a total of $754.40 billion for the full year 2012–2016, and $178.23 billion for the fiscal year 2016 alone, which is $20 billion more than its 2015 level. The IBRD also committed $51.76 billion in 2016 in its investment portfolio, which grew by 21.28% compared to its 2015 level and by 55% since 2012.

In fiscal year 2016, IBRD issued debt securities in various currencies to institutional and private investors for an amount of $178.23 billion, registering an annual increase of 12.2%, for the entire period 2012–2016 and 37.74% for the year 2016. The IBRD issues its securities through global offerings and bond issues, in various currencies, maturities, and markets, and at fixed and variable terms, through diverse investors as asset managers, insurance companies, pension funds, central banks, corporations, and bank treasuries from around the world. It often opens new markets for international investors by issuing new products or bonds in emerging market currencies (World Bank_FY_2017_AR). Finally, the usable capital in the fiscal year 2016 totalled $39.4 billion, an average increase over the 2012–2016 period of 4.14%. The IBRD has recorded a total loss of $1727.00 billion over the whole period of 2012–2016 and only reconnected with profitability in 2016, by scoring a net profit of $495.00 billion.

For the fiscal year 2016, IBRD's earnings amounted to $497 million, and an amount of $3.01 billion was transferred to IDA on the Board's recommendation (IBRD_FY_2015_AR, p. 8). The IBRD's loans are financed by its equity and its borrowing activities on the capital markets.

International Development Agency (IDA)

The second largest international financial institution, member of the World Bank Group and also its concessional window, is the International Development Agency (IDA). This is an institution that plays an interface role within the global development assistance system and complements the work of the other constituencies of the WBG. The resources available to the IDA for funding its development assistance activities reflect its commitment capacity and come from a variety of backgrounds like the contributed capital by its 173 country members and transfers from the IBRD and the IFC. The 17th replenishment of IDA17,[14] for instance, includes indicative IBRD transfers of $1.9 billion; concessional loans made by members; internal resources, including repayments of outstanding loans; and investment income. Contributions from the governments of its member countries, however, represent the major financial source, and donors meet every 3 years to replenish IDA resources and review its policy framework (World Bank, IDA). At the IDA17, the board of governors approved, for the first time, members' concessional loans as an additional contribution facility. As a result, the IDA has entered into concessionary loan agreements with some of its members for a total of $4.4 billion.

Table 3.4 gives Five-Year Summary of Selected Financial Data, for the 2012–2016 period. It shows that the IDA has maintained an average of $170.10 billion in total assets for the period 2012–2016 and an amount of $178.68 billion for the fiscal year 2016, a 2.6% decrease from 2015 level and a 9.9% increase over the period 2012–2016. IDA equity totalled $154.70 billion in the fiscal year 2016, an increase

[14] The Final IDA17 Replenishment Meeting took place in Moscow, Russia in December, 2013. The IDA18 replenishment is the largest in the IDA's 56-year history and heralds a significant step change in its policy and financing framework (World Bank n.d.-c, IDA 18).

Table 3.4 IDA 5-year summary of selected financial data in $ billions, as of and for the fiscal year ended June 30, and the period 2012–2016

	2016	2015	2014	2013	2012	2012–2016 average
	$ billion	$ billion	$ billion	$ billion	$ billion	$ billion
Total assets	178.68	183.45	165.81	160.03	162.54	170.10
Total equity	147.149	153.749	143.46	137.55	136.42	143.66
Net development credits outstanding	126.76	132.01	121.16	116.88	118.37	123.04
Commitments of development credits, grants and guarantees	18.97	22.24	16.3	14.75	16.7	17.79
Transfers from affiliated organizations and others	0.99	0.99	0.88	0.96	0.86	0.94
Grants	−1.23	−2.32	−2.65	−2.38	−2.06	−2.13
Investment revenue, net	0.514	0.631	0.099	1.006	0.305	0.511
Revenue from development credits and guarantees	1.068	1.015	1.021	0.914	0.897	0.98
Net income (loss)	−0.731	−1.612	−1.752	−0.21	−2.332	−1.33
Net investment portfolio	28.418	28.3	27.487	26.333	24.872	27.08
Net loans outstanding	0.03	0.13	0.13	0.12	0.12	0.11

Source: (IBRD and IDA Financial statement 2016, p. 133)

of 5.1% over 2015 level and 12.4% over the 2012–2016 period, an average of $143.66 billion a year for the whole period 2012–2016. The IDA's outstanding net development credits scored $126.76 billion in 2016 and an average of $123.04 billion for the period 2012–2016, but a 5% decrease from the 2015 level. The IDA's commitments in development loans, grants and guarantees totalled $18.97 billion in 2016, a decrease of 14.7% from 2015 and an increase of 13.5% over the year 2012.[15]

Transfers to the IDA from affiliated institutions and others amounted to $4.69 billion, of which $3.011 billion came from other World Bank constituencies, an average of almost $1 billion a year. Net Income on Development Loans and Guarantees provided the IDA with a total of $4.915 billion over the 2012–2015 period and an amount of 1.68 for the year 2015 alone (IDA_ FY_2016, income statement).

The IDA's administrative costs are largely covered by its service fee revenue billed to users and set at 75 basis points on loan balances (IDA_FY_2016, income statement). It is, however, supplemented by commitment fees and interest charges on certain loans. Commitment fees are traditionally set annually by the Board of Directors and are payable on unused and undisbursed loan balances, and usually vary between 0 and 50 basis points (IDA_FY_2016, income statement). The IDA

[15] In the fiscal year ending June 30, 2017, the IDA commitments totalled $19.5 billion, of which 17% was provided on grant terms. New commitments in FY17 comprised 261 new operations. Since 1960, the IDA has provided $345 billion for investments in 113 countries. Annual commitments have increased steadily and averaged about $18 billion over the last 3 years (World Bank n.d.-d, what is IDA?).

accumulated total loss reached −$6.637 billion, but the IDA nevertheless ended the fiscal year 2016 with a net profit of $371 million, compared to a net loss of −$731 million for the previous fiscal year. By comparing the 2016 numbers to averages of the period 2012–2016, we can see that except for net loans outstanding, the tendency in the IDA's financial activities is to the increase. The Eighteenth Replenishment of IDA (IDA18) is considered the largest replenishment in the IDA's 56-year history, and it "heralds a significant step change in its policy and financing framework" (IDA_FY_2017). The IDA 18 intends to enable countries to implement the ambitious development program that calls for "a world free of poverty and hunger; a world that is peaceful and equitable [...]" (IDA_FY_2017).

International Finance Corporation, IFC

The International Finance Corporation (IFC) is the third member institution of the World Bank Group, with a strong focus on helping with the funding of the private sector in developing countries. However, its membership is open to IBRD member countries only. It uses part of its resources to invest in country members' equity, mainly for development purposes. It does not, however, seek to secure strategic control positions or holdings in investee companies. The IFC's investments are made through the purchase of shares in companies (IFC_FY_2016_AR, Vol 2, p. 56). The IFC has a wholly owned subsidiary called Asset Management Company, LLC (AMC), which invests in the capital stock of third-party companies, like the IFC. While these investments have a positive impact on the development of the countries in which they are invested, they also allow external investors to benefit from the IFC's expertise and achieve high returns. For the fiscal year 2016, the IFC's consulting services portfolio registered an amount of $1.3 billion.

To diversify its accesses to financing and reduce its borrowing costs, the IFC borrows in a variety of currencies and uses different debt instruments. Under certain current loan agreements, the IFC is not, however, permitted to mortgage or grant a security on its assets. (IFC_FY_2016_AR, Vol 2, p. 58). The IFC mobilizes funds from commercial banks and other participating financial institutions. It also provides financial guarantee facilities to various clients to enhance the quality of their credit to their investors and suppliers. The warranties offered may be partial or whole. (IFC_FY_2016_AR, Vol 2, p. 57). Lastly, the IFC provides consulting services to its clients and collaborates with companies and foundations that strongly support its action in development. These collaborative organizations have committed up to $219 million, during the fiscal year 2016.

The IFC's main resources come from equity investments from member countries and contributions from partners. The IFC is currently collaborating with more than 30 governments in multilateral and institutional partnerships; Table 3.5 provides some key financial elements of the IFC's financial position for the period 2012–2016, in billions of dollars. It shows that the IFC funds its activities through a range of financial sources, obtained from such diversified horizons as participating gov-

Table 3.5 IFC financial highlights, in $ billion, for the year ended June 30

	2016	2015	2014	2013	2012	2012–2016 average
	$	$	$	$	$	$
Net income (loss) attributable to IFC	−0.033	0.445	1.483	1.018	1.328	0.8482
Grants to IDA	0.33	0.34	0.251	0.34	0.33	0.3182
Total assets	90.434	87.548	84.13	77.525	75.761	83.0796
Loans, equity investments and debt securities, net	37.356	37.578	38.176	34.677	31.438	35.845
Long-term investment commitments	11.117	10.539	9.967	11.008	9.241	10.3744
Total investment commitments	18.856	17.672	15.109	17.512	14.137	16.6572
Total investment disbursement	14.382	12.075	11.094	12.113	10.568	12.0464
Total committed portfolio	68.544	65.732	66.993	63.25	56.445	64.1928
Advisory services program expenditures	0.2206	0.2021	0.234	0.2319	0.197	0.21712

Source: IFC_FY_2016_ AR, p. 31

ernments, various donors, retained earnings from its operations, fees received from service recipients, as well as from budget. (IFC_FY_2016, Vol 2, p 100). The IFC had achieved a net income of $4,2 billion over the period 2012–2016, with a loss of $33 million in 2016. Its net incomes are significantly used to subsidize IDA operations and what is left is used as retained earnings.

The IFC's annual report for the fiscal year 2016 shows total assets of $90.43 billion and equity loans and investments of $37.36 billion, with equity investments at $37.35 billion (IFC_ FY_2016_AR, p. 31). IFC guarantees are generally granted in local currency, but if executed, the customer is required to repay the IFC in dollars. An amount of $3.478 billion in guarantees was released during the fiscal year 2016 and spending with clients amounted to $221 million, focusing on strategic priority areas.

During the fiscal year 2016, AMC, a wholly owned subsidiary of the IFC, managed 12 funds, with an amount of total assets under management of $8.9 billion. Investors in funds managed by AMC include sovereign wealth funds, national pension funds, international financial institutions, etc. The comparison of 2016 numbers to the averages of the period 2012–2016 shows substantial progress in all financial statement components.

Multilateral Investment Guarantee Agency (MIGA)

The Multilateral Investment Guarantee Agency (MIGA) is the constituency of the World Bank Group that plays the decisive role of encouraging and maintaining private investment flows to developing countries. In fulfilling its mandate, the MIGA

Table 3.6 MIGA key financial indicators, fiscal years 2012–2016, as of and for the fiscal year ended June 30, $ billion, unless otherwise stated

	2016	2015	2014	2013	2012	2012–2016 average
	$	$	$	$	$	
Total shareholders' equity	0.989	0.971	0.974	0.911	0.905	0.95
Total assets	2.34	2.07	n/a	n/a	n/a	
Gross guarantee exposure	14.19	12.54	12.41	10.76	10.35	12.05
Net premium income	0.0864	0.079	0.0725	0.0663	0.0617	0.07318
Investment income	0.0229	0.0241	0.0534	0.0336	0.0369	0.0268
Administrative expenses	0.0481	0.0449	0.0456	0.0471	0.0439	0.04592
Operating income	0.0383	0.0341	0.0269	0.0192	0.0178	0.02726
Administrative expenses/net premium income	56%	57%	63%	71%	71%	0.636

Source: MIGA FY_2016 Management's Discussion and Analysis, p. 8

seeks to operate in a financial environment that is both sustainable, but that also generates sufficient revenue for its guarantee and investment portfolios to cover its operating expenses and to contribute to its growth. The MIGA's revenues come from gross premiums generated by its guarantee portfolio, less reinsurance premiums, commissions and brokerage fees. The net income allows the MIGA to increase its unallocated and reserve portfolio reserve and strengthen its ability to cope with existing and future exposure (MIGA FY_2016_AR).

Table 3.6 provides an overview of the MIGA's Key Financial Indicators, for the period 2011–2016 in billions of dollars. For the fiscal year 2016, the MIGA managed an amount of total assets of $2.34 billion, which represents an increase of 13% over the level registered the previous year. Its total equity reached $989 million this same year, compared to $905 million for the fiscal year 2012, and $950 million average for the period 2012–2016.

During the fiscal year 2016, MIGA's gross exposure in collateral toped a record $14.2 billion, scoring a 13% increase, over 2015 fiscal year, and a $12.05 billion average for the whole period considered. Net premium income increased in the fiscal year 2016 by 9%, to reach $86.4 million. Earnings from operations, defined as net premium income, net of administrative expenses, were $38.3 million for the fiscal year 2016, an increase of 12% from the prior year. By comparing 2016 financial figures to the average of the period 2012–2016, we can see an increase trend in MIGA activities.

Summary of the World Bank Group Development Assistance

Table 3.7: gives an overview of the World Bank Group Cumulative assistance to development for the period 2012–2015, in billions of $ dollars. The overall World Bank Group cumulative assistance to development for the period 2012–2017 scored

Table 3.7 World Bank Group development cumulative assistance for the period 2012–2017, in $ billions

Commitments	2017	2016	2015	2014	2013	2012	2012–2017 average
IBRD	22.611	29.729	20.58	15.25	18.6	23.53	21.72
IDA	19.513	16.171	14.75	16.3	22.24	18.97	17.99
IFC	11. 85 4	11.117	10.54	9.97	11.01	9.24	8.65
MIGA	4.842	4.258	2.66	2.78	3.16	2.83	3.422
Recipient-Executed Trust Funds	2.962	2.91	3.914	4.225	4.897	3.988	3.82
Total World Bank Group	49.928	64.185	52.444	48.525	59.907	58.558	55.60

around $333 billion (around $55.6 billions annually for the period 2012–2017), most of which came from the IBRD and the IDA, with contributions of $130.3 billions and $107.944, respectively. The IFC and the MIGA contributed, respectively, 51.877 billion and $20.53 billion and the Recipient-Executed Trust Funds $22.89 billion.

The World Bank Group Cumulative assistance, however, decreased by 14.7%, in 2017, from its level of 2012. All constituents of the World Bank Group are showing the same upward trend, with the exception of the IBRD, which registered a small loss over the fiscal year 2012, and Recipient-Executed Trust Funds. Comparing the 2017 figures to the period average, we can see an increasing trend in the overall World Bank Group activities for the period, except for Recipient-Executed Trust Funds, which suffered a significant decline.

Conclusion

When designing the Bretton Woods financial institutions, the institutions' crafters relied on the possibility that the market might not always operate efficiently and that potential dysfunctions would inevitably lead to serious economic and financial crisis. Further, economic retraction would inevitably make it difficult to generate the necessary funds for economic recovery. However, they were far from expecting that the institutions they proposed to establish would become so sophisticated and so impactful over time. They were acting with the firm conviction of the need for a collective and global action, in favour of economic stability and development, similar to the United Nations, which had been founded on the conviction of the need for global political stability. In the end, together the BWFIs cover the entire spectrum of development finance and devote significant amounts of funding to global development. Their action as main provider of development assistance is, however, seriously challenged.

Chapter 4
Governance of Bretton Woods Financial Institutions

Understanding the governance of Bretton Woods Financial Institutions (BWFI) may help illuminate their role in funding global development and fighting poverty, and may allow the assessment of their effectiveness in fulfilling their mandate. The number of votes to which each member country is entitled in the decision making of the BWFIs is crucial to the institutions' current operations, and to their future. The governance of BWFIs is constantly subject to harsh critics, specifically and most seriously the so-called 15% rule, where only 15% of votes are required to be owned by any member to block any decisions at institutions Board meetings. Not any country member is, however, permitted to own such a number of shares, and many country members have tried unsuccessfully. Consequently, decision-making at BWFIs is structurally monopolized by a club of a handful members. This situation has made reform of the governance of institutions, a constant demand, aim to give more voice to poor and emerging economies, which are constantly underrepresented, despite their growing weight within the global economy.

This chapter discusses the governance structures of BWFIs, including their voting systems. The first section introduces the *issue* of Bretton Woods governance. The second section provides a brief overview of the current governance structure of the IMF. The third section examines the current governance structure of the World Bank Group. Section four examines the connection of the BWFI and the OECD. Section five discusses the Calls for Reform at the governance of the Bretton Woods Institutions. Section six concludes the chapter.

The Issue of Bretton Woods Governance

The founders BWFIs "aimed to build a framework for economic cooperation that would forestall the kinds of economic policies that contributed to the Great Depression of the 1930s and the global conflict that ensued" (IMF, Financial

A. Naciri, *The Governance Structures of the Bretton Woods Financial Institutions*, SpringerBriefs in Economics, https://doi.org/10.1007/978-3-319-97906-9_4

Information 2016a). BWFIs dominate the international development financial system and play a decisive role in development assistance management. In addition to resorting to them for funding, governments tend to use BWFIs to design and support economic policies, and select institutional frameworks that are supportive of their economic growth and development. International aid donors often opt for the Bretton Woods financial framework as a basis for making decisions about their development assistance programs. BWFIs, including the regional development banks, also place their financing and development support activities within the context created by BWFIs. Ultimately, their financial assistance is often perceived by other bilateral and multilateral institutions as a signal to initiate or expand their own assistance programs, and, as countries develop, their decisions also become impacting signals to markets for private funds. BWFIs governance systems are, however, subject to strong criticism.

Emerging countries dislike seeing the BWFI decision-making bodies continuously under the full control of rich economies, allowing rich countries to retain significant power over the global macroeconomic governance, particularly at the level of the IMF, the WBG and RDBs (Villafranca 2014). Faced with poor countries' dissatisfaction and insistent claims, advanced economies seem today to privilege new global decision making systems, ones that are likely to escape the BWFIs' framework, and that are embodied in smaller networks, like the OECD, the G7 and the like. Although it is often tempting to put all institutions of the global financial system under the same banner, each institution has its own particularities, which the following sections will detail.

The IMF Current Governance Structure

The IMF's governance has evolved under the pressure of changes in the global economy, allowing the Fund to retain a central role within the international financial architecture (IMF[1]), without, however, bargaining any of its original decision-making structure. Several jurisdictions contribute to the decision-making at the IMF, as summarized in Fig. 4.1.

As expected, the Board of Governors (BG) at the IMF, is the highest decision-making authority; each member country is entitled to appoint a governor and alternate governor to the Fund's Board of Governors, and these are usually finance ministers or central bank chairman. However, the BG at the IMF delegates most of its powers to a chosen executive board (EB), while retaining key decisions, such as quota approval and/or increase, special drawing rights allocations, admission of new members, compulsory withdrawal of members, and any modifications to the statutory regulations of the Fund. Further, the Board of Governors "is the ultimate judge on issues related to the interpretation of the IMF's Articles of Agreement" (IMF Regulations 2016b). There are two ways to vote at the IMF's BG, either on the

[1] https://www.imf.org/external/about/govstruct.htm

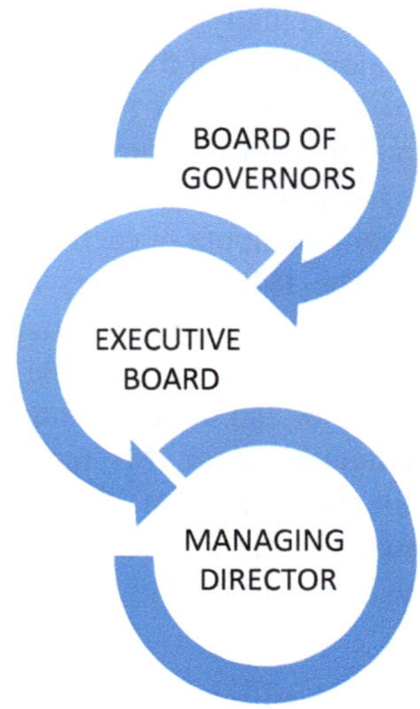

Fig. 4.1 International Monetary Fund decision-making structure. Sources: Established from the International Monetary Fund Chart, 2017

spot or remotely through a secure e-voting system. Unless otherwise specified in the IMF's Articles, decisions of the BG are to be taken by majority vote. In its decision-making, the BG of the IMF is supported by two ministerial committees: the international monetary and financial committee (IMFC) and the Joint IMF-World Bank development committee (DC).

The IMFC is composed of 24 members, coming from the 189 governorates, representing all IMF's member countries. With its 24 constituencies, the IMFC's structure reflects the executive board structure. The IMFC meets twice a year, during the IMF and the World Bank General Meetings, to discuss the management of the international monetary and financial system, along with the Executive Board's proposals for eventual amending the IMF's chart or any other question of common interest, concerning the world economy. After each meeting, the IMFC issues minutes summarizing its views, and eventually provides guidance for the IMF's work program. Its decisions are usually made by consensus, not by formal votes (IMF 2017g).

In contrast, the development committee (DC) is a joint IMF-World Bank committee. It is currently composed of 25 World Bank governors (IMF Financial Information 2016a), and it is entrusted with the advising of the boards of governors of the IMF and the World Bank on issues related to economic development in emerging and developing countries. The DC serves primarily as a forum for reaching intergovernmental consensus on critical development issues (IMF 2017g).

The executive Board (EB) of the IMF is composed of 24 members[2] and chaired by the Managing Director of the IMF. The EB is responsible for managing the day-to-day activities of the IMF and for exercising the powers delegated to it by the board of governors of the IMF and those conferred upon it by the IMFs' Articles,

[2]The Executive Board consisting of 24 elected Executive Directors is maintained and the number of directors is supposed to be reviewed every 8 years (IMF Financial Information 2016a).

and it actually ends up discussing all operations and all aspects of management and policy issues of the Fund. As rule, decisions of the executive board are also reached by consensus, but formal votes are occasionally taken. Meetings of EB can be formal or informal: formal meetings give rise to a report, while informal meetings are mostly held to discuss complex political issues, that are at a preliminary stage. Here again the quota of each member determines its voting power (IMF 2017g).

The IMF Governors appoint the Managing Director (MD), who is both the Chairman of the Executive Board and the Chief of Staff of the IMF. The MD is appointed for a renewable 5-year term and is assisted by a first Deputy Managing Director and three Assistant Deputy Managing Directors. Governors and Executive Directors of the IMF may designate nationals of any member country of the Fund for the position of Managing Director. Although such a choice can be made by a majority of the votes cast, past appointments have been made by consensus, and, up to now, a European national has always been promoted to the position.

Voting Power at the IMF

When a country becomes a member of the IMF, it is allocated an initial quota in the same proportion of existing comparable country quotas in terms of size and economic characteristics, plus one additional vote for every SDR 100,000. The IMF relies on a quota formula to help assess the relative position of its members, and each IMF member country is finally allocated a quota, largely based on its relative position in the global economy (IMF 2017c). A new member must pay in full its quota, at the time of joining the IMF, up to 25% in Special Drawing Rights contribution or in widely accepted foreign currency with the rest being paid in its own currency.

The quota is determined according to the following formula (IMF_FY_2016 financial operations).

$$\mathrm{CQS} = \left(0.5^{*}\,\mathrm{Y} + 0.3^{*}\mathrm{O} + 0.15^{*}\,\mathrm{V} + 0.05^{*}\,\mathrm{R}\right)\mathrm{k} \tag{4.1}$$

where:

CQS is the calculated quota share;

Y represents a blend of GDP converted at market rates and purchasing-power-parity (PPP) exchange rates averaged over a 3-year period (the weights of market-based and PPP GDP are 0.60 and 0.40, respectively);

O is the annual average of the sum of current payments and current receipts (goods, services, income, and transfers) for a recent 5-year period;

V represents the variability of current receipts and net capital flows (measured as a standard deviation from the centred 3-year moving average over a recent 13-year period);

R is the 12-month average over a recent year of official reserves (foreign exchange, SDR holdings, reserve position in the IMF, and monetary gold); and k is a compression factor of 0.95. The compression factor is applied to the uncompressed calculated quota shares, which are then rescaled to sum to 100.[3]

The quota formula includes four variables: GDP, openness, variability, and reserves, expressed as shares of the global totals and assigned weights totalling to 1,0 (IMF 2016c). The formula also includes a compression factor that reduces dispersion in calculated quota shares. (IMF_FY_2016 financial operations, p. 41). However, since seats at the Executive Board of Directors are allocated according to the quotas, some member countries end up representing only themselves, which is the case for the United States, Japan, China, Germany, Russia, France, Saudi Arabia and the United Kingdom, while others, represent several countries. Sub-Saharan Africa, for example, has only two Executive Directors for 46 countries. Quota plays a fundamental function in IMF operating:

1. The quota determines the maximum amount of financial resources that an IMF's member must provide to the institution in order to become member;
2. The quota determines the repartition of the seats at the executive Board of Directors of IMF, among members;
3. The quota determines votes at the executive Board, which are usually kept to a minimum, because decision-making is usually made by consensus. Nevertheless, in case of voting on substantive issues 85% approval is required, making the US, with its 16.46% quota, the effective decision maker.
4. The quota also determines the amount of funding a member can get from the IMF. For example, under Stand-By (SBA) and Extended Arrangement (EA), a member can borrow up to 145% of its quota annually and 435% cumulatively. However, in exceptional circumstances access may be higher. SBA is designed to help countries address short-term balance of payments problems and disbursements are made conditional to achieving these targets. EA, on the other hand, is designed to help countries address longer-term balance of payments difficulties, requiring reforms (IMF_FY_2016 financial operations, p. 41).

Articles of Agreement of the IMF require the institution to review its quotas every 5 years to make sure the distribution of votes is linked to the economic weight of member countries. The amendment to the recent reform of the Executive Board of January 26, 2016, introduced the election of the Board. Previous to the reform, member countries that held the six largest quotas were each entitled to appoint their own executive director, while the remaining member countries were electing the 19 executive directors left. The reform also reduced by two the number of Executive Directors representing advanced European economies (IMF Financial Information

[3] The current quota formula is a weighted average of GDP (50%), openness (30%), economic variability (15%), and international reserves (5%).The formula also includes a "compression factor" that reduces the dispersion in calculated quota shares across members (IMF_FY_2016 financial operations, p. 41).

Table 4.1 Total of eligible Fund votes 5,031,614, July 23, 2017, IMF's General Department and Special Drawing Rights Department

	Quota		Vote			Quota		Vote	
Member	Millions of SDRs	Percent of total	Number	Percent of total	Member	Millions of SDRs	Percent of total	Number	Percent of total
US	829,942	1746	831,407	1652	Canada	110,239	232	111,704	222
Japan	308,205	648	309,670	615	Spain	95,355	201	96,820	192
China	304,829	641	306,294	609	Mexico	89,127	187	90,592	180
Germany	266,344	560	267,809	532	Netherlands	87,365	184	88,830	177
France	201,551	424	203,016	403	Korea	85,827	181	87,292	173
United Kingdom	201,551	424	203,016	403	Australia	65,724	138	67,189	134
Italy	150,700	317	152,165	302	Belgium	64,107	135	65,572	130
India	131,144	276	132,609	264	Switzerland	57,711	1.21	59,176	118
Russian Federation	129,037	2.71	130,502	259	All 189 members	4,754,729	1000	5,031,614	1000
Brazil	110,420	232	111,885	222					

Source: IMF Members' Quotas and Voting Power, and IMF Board of Governors (IMF 2018a)

2016a). Table 4.1 shows the quotas and voting rights distribution of IMF members with 1% or more of votes. After the coming into effect of the recent IMF Reform of January 26, 2016, quotas and voting rights have gradually changed, as members pay their quota increases.

Table 4.1 provides a clear picture of the current distribution of votes at the IMF's General and Special Drawing Rights Departments and allows a number of conclusions:

1. The United States, with 16.52% of all the votes, exercises an effective right of veto on all the decisions at the IMF;
2. The European Union, as a group, is also in a position to exercise a veto vote on the decisions of the IMF;
3. The other two main IMF voters are Japan in second position and China in third, but both neither individually, nor even together, are they able to block any IMF decision.
4. The other emerging country among the ten first economies in voting power, and ranking eighth, is India, coming after Germany, France, the United Kingdom and Italy.
5. The six IMF members outside China—The United States, Japan and the four largest European countries—hold 40.5% of the total vote.
6. The other three emerging countries excluding China—India, Russia and Brazil—hold, only 8.64% of the total votes; and
7. Other developed countries hold 11.50 of the vote.

Indeed, rich countries of America and Europe have an effective veto right on the IMF's decisions, while developing countries retain only insignificant voting power. The disequilibrium in voting at the IMF is so disturbing that a country like India, for instance, with its 1.324 billions of population, can only exercise 2.64% of the total vote, twice as much as Belgium, with only 0.0113 billion population, i.e. less than 1% (0.85%) of the population of India. It should be noted, however, that awareness is making some progress and that, for instance, following the latest IMF reform, European members committed themselves to reducing the number of their representatives at the Executive Board of the IMF in favour of emerging and developing countries. The voting structure described in Table 4.1, combined with a lack of resources, may have eventually diverted the IMF from its original role of providing balance of payments crisis financing (Globalization for All 2002) and fighting poverty.

The Governance Structure of the World Bank Group

The predecessor of the World Bank Group (WBG), the International Bank for Reconstruction and Development (IBRD), was established in 1944, and has evolved into a group of five development institutions (IBRD included). Originally, assistance of the IBRD, was intended to help rebuild the European countries devastated by the Second World War, but, over time, it has shifted from reconstruction initiative to

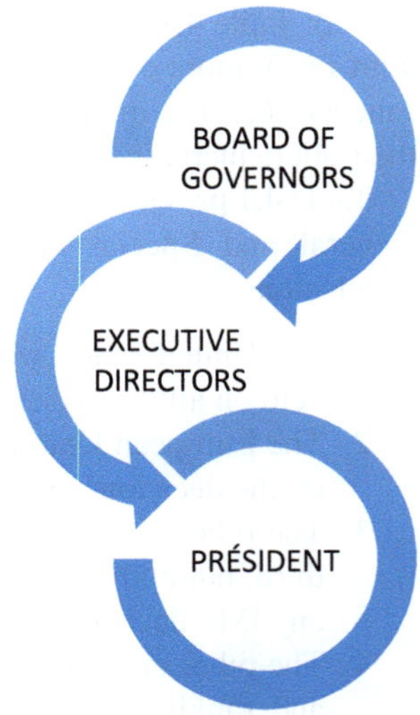

Fig. 4.2 WBG, Simplified Organizational Chart, effective June 9, 2017. Sources: Established from the WBG's Organisational Chart, 2017

development initiative. Consequently, the emphasis has shifted to the support for development infrastructure investments such as dams, road networks, irrigation systems, and so on. The World Bank secured itself a funding window for lending to private companies and financial institutions in developing countries, with the establishment of the International Finance Corporation (IFC) in 1956. The establishment of the International Development Association (IDA), in 1960 allowed the Bank to focus more on assisting the poorest countries of the world, and consequently the goal of eradicating poverty became one of its main goals. The subsequent launching of the International Centre for Settlement of Investment Disputes (ICSID) and the Multilateral Investment Guarantee Agency (MIGA) has complemented and reinforced the Bank Group's capacity to link global financial resources to the needs of developing countries.

To become a member of the Bank, under the IBRD's Agreement, a country must first join the IMF. Actually, the memberships at IDA, IFC and MIGA, are also subordinate to the IMF's membership, additional to IBRD adhesion. Further, the accession process and information on the status of country members, including membership lists, are coordinated and updated by the General Secretariat of the World Bank in collaboration with the IMF and in consultation with other members of the World Bank Group. The Boards of Governors of the WBG and the IMF meet traditionally once a year, as already mentioned, at annual meetings of the World Bank and the IMF, to discuss activities of their respective institutions. Annual meetings are held in September or October, in Washington for two consecutive years and in another member country, in the third year (IMF 2017h).

The global economy has undergone major changes since 1944, and many country members feel that the WBG has failed to adjust accordingly. Consequently, increasing voices have been demanding changes to its governance that would adapt to the changes. Figure 4.2 summarily describes the decision-making structure at the World Bank Group, with great similarity to the IMF's decision-making structure.

Several jurisdictions interact in the governance structure of the WBG, governed through the its Board of Governors and Executive, making all decisions within the institution.

"The World Bank Group, WBG can be regarded as a kind of cooperative, made of 189 member countries," (WB leadership) and governed by a board of governors, which is the ultimate decision-maker organ. The WBG is composed of affiliated organizations, also owned by member countries, who retain the ultimate decision-making power within each and every constituency, and on all issues, including policy, finance or membership issues. Each country member appoints governors and alternates, who also serve as governors and alternates on the boards of governors of IBRD, IFC, and IDA. Unless otherwise stated, they also sit on the Boards of ICSID. Governors and alternates at MIGA are appointed separately (WB, leadership). The Board of Governors of the WBG refers therefore to four separate governing bodies, namely the BG of the IBRD, the BG of IDA, the BG of the IFC, the BG of MIGA. Each board is responsible for the general operations of its respective organization. As for the IMF, the governors of the WBG are finance ministers of the member country members, its minister of the economy, its central bank chairman, and the like. The governors meet once a year at the Annual Join Meetings of the WBG and IMF (World Bank n.d.-g, leadership).

The Board of governors appoints the 25 executive directors composing the Executive Board and delegate specific tasks to them. Executive directors are said to be residents, in the sense that they work permanently at the institution's headquarters in Washington. Until recently, the five largest shareholders each appoint an executive director, while the other member countries are represented by elected executive directors (World Bank n.d.-g, leadership).

Executive Directors of the World Bank constitute the resident Executive Board of the IBRD and IDA, which normally meets at least twice a week to oversee the Bank's current activities, including approval of loans and guarantees, new policies, administrative budget, country assistance strategies, borrowing and financial decisions. They are representatives of member countries' viewpoints on the Bank's activities (World Bank_FY_2017_AR, p. 10). Executive Directors are not individually entitled to represent the Bank unless specifically authorized by the Board to do so. The executive directors of IBRD are automatically members of the IFC and IDA and separate elections are held for the Board of Governors of MIGA. In accordance with the articles of the Bank, the Executive Directors appoint the President of the World Bank that presides over the Executive Board, without having, however, the right to vote, except in case of a split vote of the Board, where his vote becomes decisive (WB leadership). Nominations for the Presidency of the World Bank are subject to confirmation by the Board of Governors and are for a renewable 5-year term. Until recently, however, the President of the World Bank Group was always a US citizen, appointed by the United States,[4] in their capacity as the largest shareholder.

[4]The current president of WBG is Korean-American and the former president of Dartmouth College.

For years, the BWFIs' effectiveness was compromised because it was seen, in part, "as a tool of western governments and their countries' financial and corporate sectors" (The Guardian 2012). Should US and Europe continue to insist on controlling the selection process for the IMF managing director and the World Bank chairman roles, it is the BWFIs themselves that would suffer. The year 2011 saw a slight change in the way the managing director of the IMF is to be selected, with the Board adopting a new selection process that is supposed to be "open, merit-based and transparent". The next appointment of the managing director of the IMF will constitute a test to such change. The most important borrowers from the Bank, as of the year 2018 are Indonesia $16.8 billions; Brazil $16.3 billions; Mexico $14.8 billions; China $13.9 billions; India $12.8 billions; Turkey $12.3 billions; Columbia $9.9 billions; Poland $8.5 billions; and Egypt $7.7 billions (World Bank Finance).[5]

Voting Powers at the WBG

The voting power of each member country at the World Bank Group depends on the number of shares the member country holds. However, they are allocated differently in each constituency of the WBG, resulting in different voting powers by institution (Institutions web sites):

1. At the International Bank for Reconstruction and Development, for instance, each member country receives votes consisting of one vote per share, i.e. one vote for each share in the capital of the Bank held by the member, plus basic votes, equal to 5.55% of the sum of basic votes and votes of all members.
2. At the International Finance Corporation each member receives votes consisting of one vote for each share of the IFC's capital held by the member, plus one basic vote, calculated as for IBRD, so that the sum of all basic votes equals 5.55% of the sum of basic votes and votes for all members.
3. At the International Development Association, each member receives the IDA replenishment credits in accordance with the rules established in each IDA replenishment resolution. The votes consist of subscription votes and member votes.
4. At the level of the Multilateral Investment Guarantee Agency, each member receives votes consisting of one vote for each MIGA's share of capital held by the member, plus a joint vote calculated so that the total number of category-1 and category-2 members is the same. Indeed, members can choose the category they want to join at the time of membership. Category-1 members were originally defined as developed countries and category-2 members as developing countries.

[5] https://finances.worldbank.org/Loans-and-Credits/IBRD-Countries-by-Borrower-s-Obligation/2akt-uau7/data

Table 4.2 World Bank Group, voting power of directors, FY_2017

Directors appointed by	IBRD, % of the total	IFC, % of the total	IDA, % of the total	MIGA, % of the total	FIFs, % of the total
United States	16.32	20.9	10.21	15.02	16.32
Japan	7.04	6.01	8.45	4.22	7.04
Germany	5	6.01	6.23	4.2	4.12
France	3.86	4.77	5.46	4.03	3.88
United Kingdom	3.8	4.8	3.81	4.03	3.86
China	4.55	2.3	2.2	2.64	4.55
Total appointed	40.57	42.94	26.15	34.14	35.91
Total elected	59.43	57.06	73.85	65.86	64.09

Source: http://www.worldbank.org/en/about/leadership/votingpowers

5. At the level of the Financial Intermediary Funds (FIF) of the World Bank, each contributor receives votes, corresponding to its contribution to the FIF.

Table 4.2 provides an overview of the voting power in different constituencies of the WGB.

Examination of Table 4.2 allows a number of interesting observations:

1. Depending on the institution considered, the voting power of the top 6 contributors varies between 42.94% for the IFC and to 26.5% for the IDA, resulting in similar percentages of appointed/elected directors.
2. The United States dominates the vote in each institution, holding 20% of the total vote in the IFC's decision-making, 16.32% for the IBRD and the Financial Intermediate Funds (FIF) of the WBG.
3. Other major contributors to the establishment of the WBG are Japan, followed by Germany, France, the United Kingdom and China.

As for the IMF, the US retains a veto over the decisions of the WBG. Members of the EU as a group are also in position to block any decision of the World Bank. The other two main voters, Japan and China, cannot block IMF decisions, not even jointly.

The World Bank presents itself as a vital source of financial and technical assistance to developing countries around the world and its constituencies seem themselves to suggest that they may have not only contributed to reducing poverty and improving the standard of living in developing countries, but also that their sustainability seems to be vital to the economic prospects of the less developed countries (WB leadership). They are, however, often subject to criticism of their inefficiency and unfairness toward poor countries, due to attributed weaknesses in governance.

The BWFI-OECD Connection

The IMF and the WBG closely through the joint IMF-World Bank committee, the so-called Development Committee (DC), composed of 25 World Bank governors (IMF Financial Information 2016a). The DC advises the boards of governors of the

IMF and the World Bank (IMF 2017g). BWFIs also collaborate with the Organization for Economic Cooperation and Development (OECD), mainly on development issues and policy matters, such as financial regulation, international investment, tax issues, etc. The IMF participates as a full member of the Development Assistance Committee's working group on Aid Effectiveness and Donor Practices and participates as an observer in more than 30 OECD instances (OECD n.d.-c, Global Relations). The International Tax Dialogue, for example, is another collaborative movement, between the World Bank, the IMF, the regional development banks, the OECD and the United Nations. It aims to encourage and facilitate dialogue between national tax authorities, international organizations and other stakeholders. In addition, the IMF has been an important partner for the OECD's work on financial regulation and market efficiency, particularly in the countries of Europe in transition. Cooperation and information-sharing between the OECD and the IMF are facilitated by the strong participation of the IMF in official OECD bodies. Similarly, the World Bank is a key partner for the OECD's cooperation with non-member countries. It contributes effectively to this activity, thanks to its wide presence in various countries and its experience with policy applications in very different contexts and sectors. The World Bank is indeed believed to combine intellectual and financial support for its borrowers, with a commitment to building their capacity (OECD n.d.-c, Global Relations). The World Bank also participates as an observer in more than 30 OECD bodies and takes part as a full participant in the DAC Working Group on Aid Effectiveness and Donor Practices and International Dialogue. It also provides strong support for OECD global forums and regional events.

Previous sections suggest a complete appropriation of global financial decision-making by a limited number of rich countries and the badly felt refusal to grant poor countries voting power in decisional instances of BWFIs, which would be at the level of their rights and aspiration. It also raises the fear that the reinforced collaboration between the OECD and Bretton Woods Institutions may further even lead to the weakening of poor countries' voices in global financial and development issues. It is not surprising, therefore, that calls for reform continue to be heard.

Calls for Reform at the Governance of the Bretton Woods Institutions

Regardless of the institution examined, all BWFIs show a governance structure that favours rich countries: the voting power of the top 6 contributors ranges from 42.94% for the IFC to 26.5% for the IDA, translating into as much percentages of appointed governors and executive directors. The United States dominates the vote in each institution, with 20% of the total vote in the IFC's decision-making, 16.32% in the IBRD and the Financial Intermediate Funds (FIF) of the WBG. Other major contributors to the WBG constituencies are Japan, followed by Germany, France, the United Kingdom and China. Despite periodic adjustments, this situation seems to have continued without interruption since 1944. Occasional limited changes in the balance of power have not prevented developed countries from maintaining a "controlling interest" or using the BWFIs, as a fee for their overall policy (Katasonov 2014). Calls for changes in the governance of the Bretton Woods Institutions are persistent. In addition to decrying unfair voting in decision making, inefficiencies in operating institutions are also commonly evoked:

1. It is, for instance, recalled that the voting power in BWFIs appears to be a historical anachronism imposed by the victorious countries of the second world war (Stiglitz 2017). The BWFIs created in another era and, to a certain extent, for different purposes, are increasingly under pressure to take account of the change that has occurred since 1944, in order to have a chance to survive (Villafranca 2014);
2. The inequitable distribution of voting power is also reflected in the number of Executive Directors. Such distribution, however, seriously compromises the strength of the developing countries' voices in BWFIs operating (Griffith-Jones 2002);
3. The very location of the secretariats of institutions is considered a challenge. Since they are mainly headquarted in the metropoles of rich countries, they contribute to the increase in their capacity to influence national policies and make them more responsive to rich countries' views, and financial markets' requirements than to the needs of people struggling with underdevelopment (Stiglitz 2017);
4. In addition, the responsibility of BWFIs, which is left to finance ministers, can be worrying (Stiglitz 2017), as senior officials are ministries of finance, and—being rather absorbed by the immediate financial problems of their government—they can easily be kept away from the interests of the poor (Globalization for All 2002, p. 66), not to mention the often lacking required competency for the job; and
5. The neglected fact that "increasing the voice and vote of developing countries in BWFIs governance would increase their appropriation of their advocated policies, as well as the relevance and impact of their policies to development (Griffith-Jones 2002).

Conclusion

The Bretton Woods Institutions formally established in 1945 were based on the need for economic freedom and global security. Their crafters saw trade and investment as ways of achieving global prosperity and stability and were convinced that if economic growth could not be shared through employment, their aim would not be reached (Globalization for All 2002, p. 8.). In general, decision-making at the level of the BWFIs is dominated by the developed countries and even when they are under some pressure to change, they continue to dodge reforms by resorting to the

OECD to impose their will. As we know, the OECD's activity, in which BWFIs are deeply involved, obeys its own governance rules, and in every case emanates 100% from wealthy countries.

For many, the governance of BWFIs may have kept them from fully attaining the objective of Breton Woods. Their governance seems to be historically geared towards the hegemony of the few, which belongs to rich developed economies. "Today some major shareholders, especially the US exercise influence that is out of proportion to their current costs" (Birdsall 2000). For a long time, it has also been noted that the BWFIs are wielding enormous power over developing country governments, despite severe shortcomings in their legitimacy and effectiveness (Bretton Woods Project 2003). Consequently, the rebalancing of their board composition and voting power was required as well as the making transparent of their governing bodies, the opening of their leadership selection, and the reversing of their mission (Bretton Woods Project 2003). The usual defence of the BWFIs for the inequitable vote distribution is that it is simply a result of historical circumstances (Griffith-Jones 2002). However, there is no reason for unfairness not to be corrected. Whatever reforms of BWFIs are chosen, long-term expected progress will be difficult to achieve as long as the vision of development has not been changed.

The biggest challenge may not, however, be only in the institutions' governance but also in the mentalities (Stiglitz 2017), which must accept that the poor have a say in the decisions that affect them and should be allowed take hold of their destiny. Unfortunately, the institutions may have ended up reflecting the mentalities of those to whom they are accountable (Stiglitz 2017), neglecting the interests of those they are supposed to serve.

Chapter 5
Regional Development Banks Within the International Financial Architecture for Development

Regional development banks (RDBs) were established based on the World Bank's business model and have been assigned a similar objective of assisting development with particular emphasis on the respect of regional particularities and needs. In addition to main donor countries, the shareholders of RDBs are regional member countries. Overtime two distinct categories of regional development banks have come into being: the group of World Bank obedient RDBs and the group of those with a weaker affiliation to the World Bank. The accelerating trend of creating new, competing regional institutions makes it eventually essential to reconsider the role of the whole RDB system.

This chapter discusses the historical development of RDBs and highlights their respective roles within international financial system for the fight of poverty and in the enhancement of development. The first section introduces regional development banks; the second section discusses their lending windows; the section third gives an overview of RDB's resources; section four discusses regional development banks of group one; section five discusses regional development banks of group two; section six gives an overview of the RDBs' role; and finally, section seven concludes the chapter.

Introduction to Regional Development Banks (RDBs)

Regional development banks provide a range of services for the benefit of their low- and middle- income member countries, within specific countries and regions, for development purposes. RDBs are independent multilateral international institutions not affiliated to the United Nations system, but they must nevertheless comply with the guidelines agreed to by the United Nations Security Council. Most RDBs have observer status to the United Nations, without being subjected to the decisions of its General Assembly or the decisions of any of its affiliate organizations (Nelson

A. Naciri, *The Governance Structures of the Bretton Woods Financial Institutions*, SpringerBriefs in Economics, https://doi.org/10.1007/978-3-319-97906-9_5

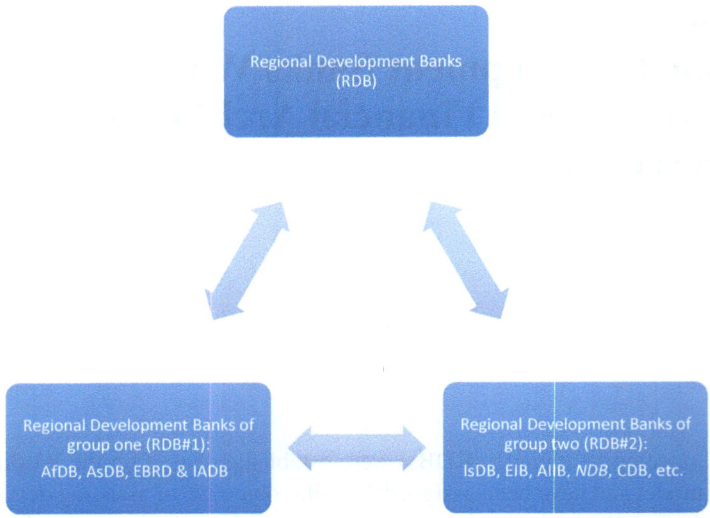

Fig. 5.1 The two groups of regional development banks

2015). All RDBs aim to support partner countries in achieving their development plans through financial assistance, and strategic advice. The mission of RDBs was defined the day the World Bank was established more than seven decades ago, and most of them chose to comply with this mission, which can be summarized through two objectives: first providing financial assistance to poor and developing countries, allowing them to deal with underdevelopment problems, and second providing them with technical assistance and strategic advice for development.

Although each RDB has its own legal and operational framework, they all share the same goal and maintain a high level of cooperation. As a group, RDBs are present on all continents, gather several hundreds of member countries, sometimes the same countries, and employ tens of thousands of people. In addition, the strategic advice they provide helps developing countries to eventually attract and manage the funds needed to support their sustainable development. The business models of RDBs seems well suited to their quest for funds. In the year 2016 alone, more than $600 billion was granted in Official Development Assistance (ODA) and other types of aid (WBG_FY_2016_AR), (See Appendix 5.1 to the chapter). Figure 5.1 summarizes the main grouping of RBDs.

As underlined in Fig. 5.1, there are currently two distinct groups of regional development banks: those of World Bank obedience, in this book called regional development banks of group one (RDBs#1) and those with weaker affiliation to the WBG, which are called RDBs of group two (RDBs#2).

RDBs#1 maintain closer links to the WBG than RDBs#2, as well as within themselves. RDBs#2, on the other hand, have fewer ties to the WBG and are relative newcomers to development assistance. RDBs#2 include the Asian Infrastructure Investment Bank (AIIB) or the New Development Bank (NDB), that was seemingly established in reaction to some dissatisfaction with the World Bank Group governance. They are discussed later in the chapter. All regional development banks try, however, to closely align their rules, procedures and practices to those of the WBG, both to reassure reluctant shareholders to support them financially and also to secure favourable credit ratings in the three As′ range, commonly held by other institutions.

Lending Windows and Development Assistance of RDBs

The main objective of the RDBs is to assist developing countries, through financial support for their major development initiatives, generally subject to conditionality, as policy reforms, economic improvement and increased accessibility to national and international financial markets. Support to member countries usually takes the form of some dominant scenarios, such as:

1. Assisting member countries' domestic financial markets in mobilizing local capital for development purposes;
2. Helping member countries improve sustainable accessibility to international financial markets;
3. Assisting member countries in mitigating of pro-cyclical behaviour by private sources of financing; and
4. Assisting member countries in improving their capacity to generate and disseminate knowledge and best practices.

To fulfil their mandate, most regional development banks, whether RDBs #1 or RDBs #2, usually use two windows of intervention. A non-concessional loan window is generally used for financial assistance under market conditions. This may take the form of loans, equity investments or guarantees. The non-concessional window is usually reserved for middle-income economies, some solvent economies in the low-income group and private-sector firms in developing economies. The other window for development assistance is the so-called concessional window, because it is used for the granting of assistance on more advantageous terms than those prevailing on the market, using specific development funds. With few exceptions, each regional development bank literally has its own development fund dedicated to concessional loans funded directly through specific contributions from wealthier donors and usually replenished periodically for terms up to 10 years.

Some RDBs transfer part of their excess net income from non-concessional activities to concessional aid (Ottenhof 2011). The cost of accessing WBG and RDB resources is usually determined as a function of the London Interbank Offered Rate (LIBOR) plus 40 or 60 base points, depending on the institution (Chervalier 2015).

Overview of RDBs' Resources

Some key financial indicators concerning RDB activity are given in Appendixes 5.1 and 5.2 of this chapter. Data are expressed in US dollars unless otherwise specified, in which case the monetary unit used is specified. For instance, some data are expressed in currencies, as Euro (€), Islamic Dinars (ID), or African drawing right unit (AU). Columns 5 and 6 of Appendix 5.1 provide an overview of the main source of funding available to RDBs, their capital. In order to be able to offer loans, RDBs use first the contributions to their equity made by their country members. Although only a small portion, usually 5–10%, of the value of capital shares is actually paid to RDBs (as "Paid-up capital"), the remainder called, "Authorized Capital", represents what each member is committed to paying in case of need, and actually serves as a guarantee that an RDB can use to get to advantageous conditions, when borrowing at the international financial market. An RDB can, however, only call on the authorized capital when its resources are exhausted and it is still in need of funds to repay its debt. To date, however, no RDB has had to resort to its authorized capital. The reading of the columns 5 and 6 in Appendix 5.1 allows for a number of observations:

1. First, for the fiscal year 2016, total RDB authorized capital had reached a maximum of $1,086 billion, of which an amount of $451,78 billion went to group one regional development banks, representing 41% of the total, and another amount of $634,38 billion went to group two regional development banks, representing 58.5% of the total. Of this amount, $99,76 billion was actually paid-in capital, $28.03 billion (or 28%) was paid to RDB#1, and $71,73 billion (or 72%) to RDB#2. This means that group two of the RDBs dominates largely in terms of capital.
2. Among group two regional banks, the Inter-American Development Bank benefits from more capital by cashing an amount of $170,92 billion, and was followed by the Asian Development Bank with $142,70 billion. The African Development Bank and the European Bank for Reconstruction and Development come in in third and fourth positions, with $103,14 and $35,02 billions of capital, respectively.
3. With regard to the capital of the regional development banks of group two, the European Investment Bank, with a capital of $243,28 billion, was "at the head of the pack", followed by the Islamic Development Bank with $230,87 billions of capitals. These two banks' capital accounted for more than 43% of total capital of RDBs#2.

RDBs are able to provide financial support to developing country members, only because of the financial commitments of their more prosperous country members. The United States, for example, is a major contributor to IBRD and IaDB capital, and is, along with Japan, the largest contributor to AsDB capital and the second largest donor to the AfDB. Several regional members are also major contributors to the capital of certain regional banks. China and India, for example, are major contributors to AsDB's capital; Nigeria, Egypt, Algeria and South Africa are major contributors to the AfDB; Argentina, Brazil and Venezuela are major contributors to the IaDB's capital; and Russia is a major contributor to the capital of the EBRD.

The other source of funding available to RDBs is debt they borrow from international capital markets. Further, because of the financial support of their member governments, they are able to borrow on the most advantageous terms, usually under the same conditions at which advanced economies governments would borrow within their own national borders. This allows RDBs to lend to their members at much lower interest rates than members would generally pay for similar loans. As a rule, RDBs' non-concessional development support is self-financing and even generates net positive revenues.

Funds obtained from various sources, as paid-up or subscribed capital, indebtedness, as well as margins earned on non-concessional loans, are used by RDBs to financially support their assistance programs and to cover their operating costs. Most regional development banks transfer some of their net income from their non-concessional windows to their concession window, in order to partially finance loans and grants on favourable terms. For the fiscal year 2016, for instance, the Special Operations Fund (FSO) of the Inter-American Development Bank approved $247 million in development assistance (IaDB_FY_2016_AR). The African Development Fund has committed, for development purposes, a cumulative amount of $45 billion over a 40-years period. Most of the funds come from the United States, Japan, the United Kingdom, Germany, France, Canada, Italy, the Netherlands, Switzerland, Sweden, and Belgium. In 2016, the Asian Development Fund approved a total of $3,1 billion, of which $2,6 billion was provided in the form of loans and $518 million in the form of grants (AsDB Fund_FY_2016_AR). Of RDB#2, only the Islamic Development Bank seems to have specialized funds for concessional financing, such as its Waqf Fund. When the resources of a concessional fund are exhausted, donors meet and eventually decide on their replenishment. Contributions from borrowing countries to development funds are generally more symbolic than substantive, with the exception of BID-FSO, where Brazil, Argentina, Mexico and Venezuela are important contributors.

Regional Development Banks of Group One (RDBs # 1)

These are regional development banks with strong ties to the WBG, and three of the four RDBs #1 were founded in the 1950s and 1960s and one in the 1990s. The Inter-American Development Bank, or IaDB, for instance, was founded in 1959 and currently employs over 2000 people. The IaDB establishment was followed by the African Development Bank, or AfDB, which was established in 1964 and currently employs over 1500 people. In third position is the Asian Development Bank, or AsDB, founded in 1966 and today employing over 2800 people. Finally, and only established more recently, in 1991, is the European Bank for Reconstruction and Development, or EBRD, which already employs over 1541 people. Together regional development banks of group one employ more than 10,000 people worldwide and their headquarters are spread across all continents. They all use the same formula to finance their activities, presented in the previous paragraph. They also get some extra financing from member donations.

Inter-American Development Bank (IaDB)

Within the regional development banks of group one, the Inter-American Development Bank (IaDB), stands out as the oldest and largest RDB of this group, and as the first to be launched—as early as 1959. The IaDB becomes a group in late years, with headquarters in Washington D.C. The inter-American development bank group (IaDBG) is composed of the inter-American development bank (IaDB), the Inter-American Investment corporation (IaIC), and the multilateral investment fund (MIF). The inter-American group offers flexible financing solutions to its member countries in Latin America and the Caribbean region, allowing them to support their economic and social development. The IaDBG belongs to its 46 member countries, 26 of whom are borrowing countries from the Latin American and the Caribbean, and the 20 others of whom are non-borrowing countries, including the United States, Japan, Canada, 16 European countries and Israel (IaDB_FY_2016_AR).

The IaDB obtains its resources, which are made available to borrowers, through its regular paid-in capital and retained earnings, its special operations fund, its financing facilities, and various trust funds established by individual groups of countries (IaDB, Lending and Grants[1]). The IaDB is, indeed, the main source of sovereign and non-sovereign financing for the social and economic development of the Latin American region. Its Inter-American Investment Corporation (IaIC) affiliate focuses exclusively on the establishment, the expansion and the modernization of small and medium private enterprises in the region. Its Multilateral Investment Fund (MIF) works with the private sector to develop, finance and implement innovative business models that should benefit poor and low-income entrepreneurs and households. The IaDBG's financial assistance, in addition to loans, grants, guarantees and equity investments, also includes the funding of national and regional technical cooperation programs in areas ranging from institution building to knowledge transfer (IaDB, Lending and Grants).

The IaDBG has two windows for development assistance in Latin America and the Caribbean region. Appendixes 5.1 and 5.2, at the end of this chapter, provide a summary of some of the key financial indicators of the IaDB for fiscal 2016. The IaDB recorded total assets of $113 billion and a total equity of $26,46 billion. It also approved a total amount of $81,42 billion of loans. The IaDB's top five borrowing countries for fiscal 2016 are Mexico, with $1.995 billion in loans from the bank; Brazil, with $1.197 billion; Argentina, with $1.127 billion; Colombia, with $0.950 billion and Panama with 0.602 billion; these numbers account for 22.12%, 13.27%, 12.49%, 10.53%, 6.67% and 7.6% of loans, respectively (IaDB_FY_2016_AR).

[1] https://www.iadb.org/en/fin

The African Development Bank (AfDB)

Based in Abidjan, Côte d'Ivoire, the second regional development bank, by date of establishment, is the African Development Bank (AfDB), which established in 1964 with the mandate of contributing "to the economic development and social progress of its regional member countries" (AfDB 2004). The assumption made was that Bank's support for economic development would also reduce poverty. The AfDB later become the African Development Bank Group (AfDBG), composed of the AfDB and the African Development Fund (AfDF). As of the year 2015, AfDBG membership has been formed of 80 member countries, 54 of them African countries and 26 of them non-African countries. For a non-African country to become a member of the AfDB, it must first be a member of the AfDF, established in 1973, as a window of concessional lending. The resources of the Fund are contributed mainly by non-African members, and are replenished every 3 years by the donor countries. The African Development Fund currently comprises 29 contributing member countries and 38 beneficiary member countries. During its four decades of operation, the Fund has made a cumulative investment of (African unit of account) UA29.4 billion, which is equivalent to $45 billion. Concessional activities of the Bank are also complemented by those of the Nigerian Trust Fund (NTF), financed by the Nigerian Government and administered by the AfDB. Its initial capital of $80 million has been replenished several times and recently extended for an additional 10 years (AfDB_AR_FY_2016).

Appendixes 5.1 and 5.2 to the chapter give an overview of the financial activities of the African Development Bank for the FY_2016. The AfDB was managing total assets of around UA30 billion, equivalent to some $40 billion. Its loans to members amounted to UA 15.9 billion, an increase of 17% over FY2015 level. Its borrowings amounted to UA 2.8 billion and equities to UA 6.6 billion, of which an amount of UA4.9 billion is capital paid (AfDB_AR_FY_2016). The top five borrowing countries of the AfDB for the fiscal year 2016 are, by volume of grants, Nigeria, UA 1.3104 billion; Kenya, UA 0.6124 billion; Tunisia, UA 0.5095 billion; Morocco, UA 0.4266 billion; and Cameron UA 0.323 billion, representing percentages of 30.8%, 14.4%, 11.96%, 10.01% and 7.6% of loans, respectively (AfDB_AR_FY_2016).

Asian Development Bank (AsDB)

Headquartered in Manila, Philippines, the third largest bank within RDB#1, the Asian Development Bank (AsDB), was initiated in 1966 as an Asian-based multilateral financial institution, dedicated to the promotion of economic growth and cooperation in Asia. The AsDB has 67 members, 48 originating from Asia and the Pacific region. It has also two development assistance intervention channels, a non-concessional window and a concessional window, embodied in the Asian Development Grant Fund (AsDF), established in 1973.

Like the World Bank, and unlike the Inter-American Development Bank, the original mandate of the AsDB is focused on the financing of large infrastructure projects, rather than directly funding social projects or poverty reduction actions. Like the AfDB, the AsDB does not have a separate vehicle for the financing of private sector projects; however, it provides assistance to the private sector through its non-concessional window. The AsDB provides loans, as well as technical assistance using the capital provided by its member countries, as well as resources obtained through bond issues in the global capital markets. AsDB offers its assistance for low and middle income countries on near-market terms, and starting in 2017 to low-income countries at very low interest rates (AsDB_AR_FY_2016).

Appendixes 5.1 and 5.2 to the chapter give an overview of the financial activities of the AsDB for the FY_2016. It was managing total assets of $125.85 billions, with shareholders' equity of $17.4 billion, a slight decrease of −1.5% over 2015 level. The subscribed capital amounted to $142 billion, $7 billion of which had been paid. Non-concessional lending of ordinary capital resources amounted to $67.6 billion, an increase of 9% over 2015 level (AsDB_AR_FY_2016). Loans and grants to the Asian Development Fund (AsDF) reached $3.1 billion, with loans for $2.6 billion and grants for $518 million. Technical assistance increased by approximately 20%, to register $170 million in 2016. The AsDB's top five borrowing countries for the fiscal year 2016 are, by level of loans, China with $15.62 billion or 24.8% of the total, India with $13.33 billion or 21.2% of the total, Indonesia with $8.7 billion or 13.8% of the total, the Philippines with $5.9 billion or 9.4% of the total and Pakistan with $4.5 billion or 7.3% of the total (AsDB_AR_FY_2016).

European Bank for Reconstruction and Development (EBRD)

Headquartered in London, UK, the European Bank for Reconstruction and Development (EBRD) was founded in 1991 as the last established of the RDBs#1. Its mandate consists of facilitating the transition to market economy of former communist countries of Central and Eastern Europe. Its members, numbering 65 countries, are, however, scattered across the five continents. The European Union and the European investment bank, are also members of the bank. The EBRD is distinct from other regional development banks in three fundamental characteristics: First, it has an explicit political mandate of supporting democratic construction activities; second, it does not have a concessional window; and third, its financial support is heavily focused on the private sector, although it also lends to governments of the former Soviet Union.

Appendixes 5.1 and 5.2 to the chapter give an overview of the financial situation of the EBRD, in billions of UK pounds (£1 = $1.27). At the end of the FY 2016 it was managing some €56.15 billion of assets and had a subscribed capital of €29.703 billion, of which €6.2 billion had been paid and no less than €9.224 billion in reserves and retained earnings. The EBRD had also an amount of outstanding loans of €9.91 billion, down 18% from the 2015 level. The EBRD's five largest borrowing countries for the fiscal year 2016 are, by loan level, Turkey, €5.09 billion; Ukraine, €2.39 billion; Russia, €7.3 billion; Poland, €1.54 billion; and Serbia, €1.27 billion, i.e. 22.0%, 10.3%, 7.5%, 6.6%, and 5.4% of total loans, respectively (EBRD_AR_FY_2015).

Regional Development Banks of Group Two (RDBs # 2)

A number of other regional banks have been established outside the direct circle of influence of the World Bank Group, and these are RDBs of group two (RDBs#2), which were set up to contribute to the harmonization of economic growth and development of member countries and to promote economic cooperation and integration in specific regions, while, at the same time, giving special attention to the needs of less developed members. RDBs#2 consist of the European Investment Bank (EIB), established in 1958; the Caribbean Development Bank (CDB), established 1969; the Islamic Development Bank (IsDB), initiated in 1974; the New Development Bank (NDB), established in 2015; and the Asian Infrastructure Investment Bank (AIIB), launched in 2016; the Corporación Andina de Fomento (CAF); the Central American Bank for Economic Integration (CABEI); the Council of Europe Development Bank (CEB); the Eurasian Development Bank (EDB); and other small multilateral development institutions.

The European Investment Bank (EIB)

Headquartered in Kirchberg, Luxembourg, the European Investment Bank (EIB) was established in 1957 by the Treaty of Rome, as a political bank whose shareholding is composed of member states of the EU. All the 28 EU member countries are indeed also members of the EIB. It is, in a way, the home bank of the European Community. The EIB's operations are mainly oriented toward the promotion of European integration and the enhancement of European social cohesion. As an institution of the European Union, the EIB works to promote the objectives of the EU by providing Europeans with sound long-term funding for investment purposes (EIB_AR_FY_2016). Two fundamental principles are at the heart of its action: First, the achievement of the EU's objectives, geared towards the promotion of sustainable development within the EU and elsewhere in the world, and second, the funding of projects that, while economically and socially viable, may carry levels of risk that may make them unattractive to private investors. The EIB draws its sources of funding from three horizons: its equity, consisting of contributions from its members; its issues of debt securities on the European and international financial markets; and its retained earnings.

Appendixes 5.1 and 5.2 to the chapter give an overview of the financial situation of the European Investment Bank at the end of the fiscal year 2016. Some €573 billion of assets were managed by the EIB in the fiscal year 2016, a slight growth of less than 0.4%, compared to 2015 level. It granted an amount of €311,94 billion in outstanding loans, a slight decrease of less than 1% compared to 2015 level. Its subscribed capital amounted to €43.28 billion, of which the portion paid was €21.7 billion (EIB_AR_FY_2016).

The EIB is by far the largest and most profitable regional development bank, and it is also the largest borrower and the most important multilateral lender in the world. In FY_2016, it issued, on the international capital markets, an amount of €66.4 billion of bonds, compared to €62.4 billion for the FY_2015, and of this, an amount of €3.8 billion was green bonds, i.e. climatically responsible bonds. The EIB's issues are aimed at investors who would not normally invest in Europe but who, by investing in the Bank's bonds, contribute indirectly to European projects. The five main EIB borrowing countries for the fiscal year 2015 are Spain with €91.40 billion Euros or 15.75%; Italy with €67.64 billion Euros or 12.01% of the total loans; France with €55.27 billion Euros or 9.64% of total loans; Germany with €46.84 billion Euros or 8.96% of total loans; and the United Kingdom with €46.37 billion euros, or 8.56% of all loans (EIB_AR_FY_2016, p. 41).

The Caribbean Development Bank (CDB)

Headquartered in Saint-Michel, Barbados, the Caribbean Development Bank (CDB) was established in 1969 to contribute to the growth and economic development and cooperation and integration of member countries, with particular attention given to the needs of the least developed members (Article 1 of the CBD Agreement). Toward this end, CDB established in 1970, its Special Development Fund (SDF), offering loans to poor members, on more affordable terms than those applied in the ordinary activities of the Bank, namely longer maturities, grace periods and lower interest rates (CBD_AR_FY_2016).

Appendixes 5.1 and 5.2 to the chapter, provide an overview of the financial situation of the Caribbean Development Bank, in billions of dollars. For FY_2016, the CBD's assets totalled $1.6 billion and its subscribed capital of $1.72 billion, the paid-in capital $0.34 billion, its outstanding loan amounted to $1.02 billion, its borrowings for the same year totalled $1.02 billion (CBD_AR_FY_2016). The CBD's top three borrowing countries for the fiscal year 2016, receiving approximately 40% of the committed loans, are Jamaica with $0.21 billion dollars or 20.86% of the total; Barbados $0.11 billion or 11.02% of the total; and Saint Vincent and the Grenadines, with $0.092 billion or 9.09%, for a total of $1.016 billion (CBD_AR_FY_2016).

The Islamic Development Bank (IsDB)

Headquartered in Jeddah, Saudi Arabia, the Islamic Development Bank (IsDB) was established in 1973, with the primary goal of contributing to the development of its 56 Muslim country members, as well as Muslim communities in general and some non-member countries. Contributions are to be made in accordance with to Shari'ah, the Islamic law. IsDB quickly became a group of five entities (IsDBG). The constituencies of the IsDBG are (IsDB _AR_FY_2015):

1. The Islamic Research and Training Institute (IRTI), established in 1981, as the arm of IsDBG research and training. It plays an important role in transforming the Group into an international knowledge based organization. Fundamentally, IRTI aims to encourage and support the development of a "vibrant and comprehensive Islamic financial services sector", which works for the socio-economic development of member countries. IRTI undertakes many activities: it conducts training, performs research, provides advisory services, and enhances and builds the capacity of Islamic economies and finance at both substantive and applied levels.
2. The Islamic Corporation for the Insurance of Investment and Export Credit (ICIEC), was established in 1994, with the aim of increasing the scope of member countries' trade transactions, facilitating foreign direct investment and providing reinsurance services to credit bureaus within these countries.
3. The Islamic Corporation for the Development of the Private Sector (ICD) was created in 1999 with the objective of financing the development of the private sectors of member countries, in accordance with the principles of Shari'ah, and it also advises and encourages governments and private organizations to modernize their private sectors and facilitate their growth.
4. The International Islamic Trade Finance Corporation (ITFC) was created in 2007 as an autonomous entity with the aim of improving the economic conditions and livelihoods of citizens throughout the Muslim world.

The IsDB Group also has specialized funds and programs, including the Waqf Fund, the Awqaf Properties Investment Fund (APIF), the Waqf World Foundation, the Islamic Solidarity Fund for Development, the Special Assistance Program, the Scholarship Program, Fund/Specialized Trust Programs (Al-Aqsa and Al-Quods), and the Special Program for Africa's Development (IsDB _AR_FY_2015).

Appendixes 5.1 and 5.2 to the chapter, give an overview of the financial situation of the IsDB for the FY_2015 (the most recent year available to date), in billions of Islamic Dinar (ID) (ID 1.00 = $1.54). By the end of the FY_2015 the group was managing some ID 16,10 billion, which corresponds to $24. 8 billion, an increase of 6.8%, over the previous year. The issued capital had scored an amount of ID 7.85 billion, of which ID 4.94 billion had been paid. Outstanding loans were recorded at ID 1.85 billion, while financial support in the form of equity investments in customers had reached ID10.41 billion. Shareholders realized a return of 3.19% (IsDB _ AR_FY_2015). The top five recipient countries receiving IsDB support for the fiscal year 2015, sharing 87% of total loan approval, are: Egypt with ID 1,42 billion or 31.31% of total loans; Bangladesh, with ID 0.9058 billion or 20%; Turkey ID 0.8361 billion or 18.50%; and Pakistan ID 0.7685 billion or 17%, for a total of ID 4.5181 billion (IsDB_AR_FY_2015).

The Asian Infrastructure Investment Bank (AIIB)

Headquartered in Beijing, China, the Asian Infrastructure Investment Bank (AIIB) started its operations in 2016, with a membership of 57 countries, from Asia and Europe, despite early resistance from the United States. This Euro-Asian cocktail was further reinforced by an increase to 80 member countries, as soon as the date of its first annual meeting in June 2017. Only the US and Japan, among the major economies, are not members of the AIIB, which has the mandate of supporting and building the Asia-Pacific region infrastructure. At the beginning of operations, the Bank signed a co-financing framework with the World Bank and memoranda of understanding to collaborate on joint project financing with other regional development banks like the AfDB, the EBRD and the EIB (AIIB_FY_2016_AR). By doing so, the AIIB shows an attachment to international cooperation and a desire to work within the existing multilateral funding framework. These are two fears that were commonly expressed by opponents to its establishment (https://www.aiib.org/en/index.html).

Appendixes 5.1 and 5.2 to the chapter give the financial overview of the AIIB at the end of the FY_2016, its first year of operation. Its capital approaches $100 billion, of which $18.07 billion are released, and represents 2/3 of the capital of its direct competitor in the region, the Asian Development Bank and about half that of the World Bank. During its first year of operation, the AIIB approved $9.55 billion in funding, to the benefit of nine infrastructure projects in seven member countries, and all projects meet high environmental and social standards, and high quality and recognized international practices (AIIB_FY_2016_AR). Six of the projects are co-financed with other multilateral development banks, such as the World Bank, AfDB and IBRD.

The New Development Bank (NDB)

Based in Shanghai, China, the New Development Bank (NDB) was created in 2013 by the five largest emerging economies: Brazil, Russia, India, China and South Africa, the so-called BRICS, with the specific mandate of supporting public and private projects in member countries through loans, guarantees, equity participation and other financial means, and also strengthening cooperation between BRICS countries. The NDB also aims to contribute to the international collective commitment to achieve the goal of strong, sustainable and equitable growth by complementing the efforts of other multilateral international and regional financial institutions for development.

Appendixes 5.1 and 5.2 provide an overview of the financial position of the NDB for its first year of operation, in billions of dollars. Its total assets amount to $10.05 billion during the first year of operation. Only $10 billion out of its subscribed capital of $100 billion had been paid. However, its commitments for the year are still not significant.

The Corporación Andina de Fomento (CAF)

Headquartered in Caracas, Venezuela, with offices in Asuncion, Bogota, Brasilia, Buenos Aires, Mexico City, Panama, La Paz, Lima, Madrid, Montevideo, Port of Spain and Quito, the Corporación Andina de Fomento (CAF) started operations in 1970, when it was established as a multilateral development institution. Its member countries are subdivided into different country groups:

1. Member countries holding Series "A" and "B" shares, which are Argentina, Bolivia, Brazil, Colombia, Ecuador, Panama, Paraguay, Peru, Trinidad and Tobago, Uruguay and Venezuela, and
2. Member countries holding "C" series shares, which are Barbados, Chile, Costa Rica, Dominican Republic, Jamaica, Mexico, Portugal and Spain.
3. In addition, the membership includes 13 banks that are Series B shareholders.

The objective of CAF is to support sustainable development and economic integration in Latin America and the Caribbean by providing financial support to member countries, to diversify their economies, to become more competitive and to adapt to social needs. CAF collects funds to finance its operations, inside and outside its member countries, in the form of stock or bond issuances, and employs outcomes to provide financial and related services to its government members, as well as to their public and private institutions. CAF also undertakes feasibility studies for investment opportunities in shareholder countries. And manages and supervises third-party cooperation funds, owned and sponsored by other countries and organizations, in accordance with its policies and strategies.

Appendixes 5.1 and 5.2 give an overview of the financial capacities of the CAF for the financial year 2016 in billions of dollars. The assets managed by the CAF were close to $34 billion, the subscribed capital exceeded $7 billion, of which $4.78 billion was paid. Outstanding loans and investments totalled $21.98 billion. The CAF's top five borrowing countries for the fiscal year 2016 are Ecuador with $3.32 billion, Venezuela with $3.32 billion, Argentina with $2.84 billion, Columbia with $2.34 billion and Peru with $2.27 billion, for a total loan of $21.98 billion (CAF_FY_2016_AR, p. 25).

The Central American Bank for Economic Integration (CABEI)

Headquartered in Tegucigalpa, Honduras, the Central American Bank for Economic Integration CABEI was established in 1960 as a development bank and Central American financial integration arm. Its mission is to promote economic progress and the integration of the region's economies by supporting their public and private projects and programs that create productive jobs and contribute to improving the productivity and competitiveness of the region's economy recipients. There are two kinds of members of CABEI: member countries holding the "A" series shares, which are only available for the founding countries, and member countries holding "B" series shares, which are not available for non-regional countries (CABEI_ FY_2016_ AR).

Appendixes 5.1 and 5.2 provide an overview of the financial position of CABEI for the FY 2016 financial year, in billions of dollars. CABEI managed assets of $9.26 billion in 2016 and had an authorized capital of $5 billion, of which $0.11 billion was paid. Its outstanding credits amounted to $6.11 billion in 2016. The five major borrowers of the Central American Bank for economic integration, for the fiscal year 2016 are Costa Rica with $1.43 billion, Honduras with $1.3 billion, Guatemala with $20 billion, El Salvador with $1.04 billion, for a total of 6.12 loans (CABEI_FY_2016_AR).

Council of Europe Development Bank, CEB

Based in Paris, France, the Council of Europe Development Bank (CEB) was created in 2007 by 19 member countries as a multilateral development bank providing various financial services, loans and guarantees to countries in central and eastern Europe, their governments, their regional authorities and their financial institutions.

Appendixes 5.1 and 5.2 give an overview of the financial situation of the CEB for the fiscal year 2016, in billions of euros. In 2016, the CEB managed assets totalling €25.5 billion and had a subscribed capital of €5.47 billion, of which only €0.104 billion had been paid. Outstanding loans for 2016 amounted to €16.5 billion. The five largest borrowers are Spain with €1.91 billion, Poland with €1.74 billion, France with €1.48 billion, Turkey with €1.43 billion, Hungary with €0.869 billion, for a total of loans of €13.71 billion (CEB_FY_2016_AR, p. 39).

Eurasian Development Bank (EDB)

Based in Almaty, Kazakhstan, with branches in St. Petersburg, Russia and representative offices in Astana, Bishkek, Dushanbe, Minsk, Moscow and Yerevan, the Eurasian Development Bank (EDB) is an international financial organization established to reach several aims: the promotion of the economic growth of its member countries; and the strengthening of commercial and economic links between them and support for economic integration in Eurasia. Initiated in 2006, the EDB currently consists of six member countries: Russia, Armenia, Belarus, Kazakhstan, Tajikistan and Kyrgyzstan.

Appendixes 5.1 and 5.2 provide an overview of the EDB's financial situation for the FY_2016 in billions of dollars. The EBD was managing $3.5 billion of assets and had a subscribed a capital of $7.00 billion, of which $1.5 billion had been paid. Its 2016 outstanding loans amounted to more than $1.6 billion, while its borrowing also exceeded $1.61 billion. The top five borrowing countries of the Eurasian

Development Bank for FY_2016 are Belarus with $0.456 billion, Armenia with $0.510 billion, Kyrgyzstan with $0.360 billion, and Tajikistan with $0.110 billion, for a total of 5.54 (EDB_FY_2016_AR).

Other Multilateral Development Institutions

In this group, we can mention the Bank of the South and the Inter-American Investment Corporation. The Bank of the South (BS) was created with an initial capital of $20 billion, by the countries of South America, Argentina, Venezuela and Brazil, each having pledged $4 billion, and Uruguay, Ecuador, with Paraguay and Bolivia, which contributed smaller amounts. The intention of the bank is to lend money to the countries of the Americas for the construction of social programs and infrastructure. The BS would like to position itself as an alternative to borrowing from the IMF and the World Bank. In 2015, the bank only existed on paper. The Inter-American Investment Corporation (IaIC), on the other hand, has set itself the goal of promoting the economic development of its member countries by encouraging the establishment, expansion and modernization of private enterprises in the region, preferably those of small and medium size, as a way to complement the activities of the Inter-American Development Bank.

An Overview of RDBs

More than a dozen regional development banks are currently operating across the world and their impact on the global economy continues to grow. Appendixes 5.1 and 5.2 to the chapter detail the extent of the financial strength of RDBs and the importance of their role within global financial development architecture, based on selected financial variables such as assets, equities, outstanding credits, subscribed capital, authorized capital, indebtedness and return on equity. A number of interesting conclusions can be drawn from the data of Appendixes 5.1 and 5.2:

1. First, an impressive volume of assets is managed by the regional development banks: it reached $1,150 billion in the fiscal year 2016;
2. Second, regional development banks equity recorded for the FY 2016 an amount of $181 billion dollars;
3. Third, their outstanding loans amounted to $640.60 billion;
4. Their subscribed capital had reached $1,086.16 billions of which only $99.76 billion had been paid;
5. Fourth, borrowings from regional banks amounted to $542.74 billion; and
6. Sixth, in general, RDBs had a positive return on their development assistance operations: 0.38% for the African Development Bank and 12% for the Corporacion Andina de Fomento.

Although policy is rarely absent from their mandate, RDBs are, however, far from forming a homogeneous group, and a few of them dominate the rest. Among the RDBs#1, AsDB and IaDB largely dominate their group, holding $125 billion and $113 billion, respectively, out of the total group assets of $345.57 billion. At RDBs#2 level, the EIB manages alone some $676.41 billion of all assets managed by its entire group i.e. $804.46 billion. The predominance of the Asian bank and the inter-American bank within the RDBs#1 and that of the European Investment Bank within the RDBs#2, is also confirmed at the level of RDBs' outstanding loans. Indeed, of the total of $203.03 billions of the RDBs#1 outstanding loans for the FY 2016, an amount of $81.42 billion was granted by the Inter-American Bank and $67.6 billion by the Asian Bank. Regarding the RDBs#2 of regional banks for the same period, the European Investment Bank alone provided $368.09 billion, out of $437.8 billion in outstanding loans. The Asian Infrastructure Investment Bank and the new Development Bank, given their current membership, should significantly improve their position in the future.

Apart from the development financing granted by RDBs#1 and by the European Investment Bank of RDBs#2, the contribution of the other RBDs, although very helpful, remains rather marginal. They are barely responsible for $120 billion in development loans, out of a total of $1,150.02 billion. RDBs#1, with a strong affiliation to the WBG, provide some $345.57 billion in development assistance, compared to $128 billion for group two, when the European Investment Bank is excluded ($804.46 – $676.41).

The assistance of Regional Banks focuses on three areas of development: social inclusion and decreasing inequality, sustaining productivity and innovation, and encouraging economic integration. Since the creation of the first RDBs, questions remain about how they will fit into the existing international financial architecture. This question is even more acute today with the accelerated creation of new institutions outside the fold of the World Bank. No matter the answer, however, it is seeming inconceivable today to imagine a global financial system without the new RDBs; they are increasingly covering the global financial field and there seems to be no way to exclude them.

Opponents of new RDBs see recent newcomers as challenging to the political leadership of the existing multilateral system and express concern about whether these new institutions would undermine former institutions under the US control and whether they would be able to comply with internationally recognized "best" practices in the world regarding governance, procurement and environmental and social safeguarding (Nelson 2015). Proponents of the new institutions argue, however, that:

1. They can present many advantages: They may, for instance, help meet the financing needs of developing countries and increase the representation of emerging markets in the global economy.
2. They might be better positioned to help solve local problems, requiring a close regional approach and coordination. RDBs provide, each in their region, an added value, and one that is distinct from that provided by the WBG. This

is rendered possible by their better knowledge of regional problems and their easier adaptation to the customs of their clients (Hind 2002).

3. It is far more preferable to work with them to ensure the quality of operation and to increase their cooperation, particularly with the institutions of the WBG. Coordination, however, may involve the division of responsibilities, although circumstances may vary so much from one situation to another that the distribution of these responsibilities should be pragmatic. (Hinds 2002).
4. Despite the fact that basic problems of underdevelopment are common to all developing countries, financial scarcity tends to have different causes and different regional impacts. Latin American economies, for instance, may tend to be more volatile and prone to crises than African or Asian economies. In Africa, problems result mainly from lack of access to international markets and tend to be more serious. In Asia, however, it is the insufficiency of investment in infrastructure that orients the need for financing. Income levels are also different across regions, and this explains the wide divergence in funding issues (Morris 2017).

The success of the new RDBs may not, however, be only financial, and should also be measured by the capacity of new RDBs to bring about changes in the existing international financial architecture. Given the political dimension of some newly established RDBs, such as the Council of Europe Development Bank, the Asian Infrastructure Bank, the new Development Bank, the Eurasian Development Bank, it is also necessary to go beyond their current performance, to consider what their recent creation may mean for the Bretton Woods financial system. It could even help shape a new global approach to such a system by imposing a new division of labour or even forcing some long-sought institutional innovations (Morris 2017).

The World Bank Group will, however, always retain the significant comparative advantage of allowing the sharing of knowledge and experiences between regions. For this reason, excessive formal division of development assistance between the RDBs and the institutions of the World Bank Group may not be desirable, after all. Instead, further collaboration should be more beneficial, despite the fact that certain overlap of tasks appears to be unavoidable and may even be desirable, as it is likely to stimulate creativity by mixing global and regional approaches and introducing a healthy competition of points of view (Morris 2017).

Conclusion

The dozen RDBs worldwide manage over $1 trillion in assets for development purposes. They operate in a similar way to the model originally drawn by World Bank, as they provide non-concessional financial support to medium-income economies and highly concessional aid to the poorest countries. The basic model of financing for development introduced at the World Bank for MDBs continues to be the rule (Morris 2017), and it is reproduced by all the previously and the newly established

RDBs. The World Bank, in collaboration with its allied regional development banks, continues to be the dominant player in the development finance system. Some RDBs work closely with the Bretton Woods institutions in providing co-financing to support the development objectives and policy reform efforts of some countries. Others try to operate by collaborating with the Bretton Woods institutions while escaping their direct control. The worse that can happen from the multiplicity of regional banks, if accomplished without cooperation, is a more fragmented system than it is today, the pressure of diverging strategic interests of competing shareholders, and a loss of all sense of the collective purpose of development assistance. One way to avoid such a disastrous situation may be by the establishment of a federation of multilateral financial institutions under the UN auspices.

Appendix 5.1: Regional Development Banks, Some Key Financial Variables, as of FY2016 in ($ Billion)

Regional Development Bank	Total assets	Equity	Outstanding loans	Authorized capital	Paid-in capital	Borrowing	ROE[a] (%)
Group one							
Inter-American Development Bank	113.33	26.46	81.42	170.92	6.02	81.42	3.20
African Development Bank (UA1 = $1.35)	40.14	8.92	27.86	103.14	7.54	15.10	0.38
Asian Development Bank	125.85	17.21	67.60	142.70	7.15	67.60	0.91
European Bank for Reconstruction & Development (€1 = $1.18)	66.26	18.21	26.14	35.02	7.32	9.91	6.38
Total Group one	**345.57**	**70.80**	**203.03**	**451.78**	**28.03**	**174.03**	**10.87**
Group two							
The European Investment Bank (€1 = $1.18)	676.41	52.49	368.09	243.28	21.70	311.94	6.42
The Caribbean Development Bank	1.60	0.90	1.02	1.72	0.34	1.02	0.83
The Islamic Development Bank (1ID = $1.54)	24.79	12.09	12.71	230.87	14.41	12.20[b]	2.0
The Asian Infrastructure Investment Bank	17.80	17.79	9.55	100	18.07	9.55	0.90
The New Development Bank	10.05	9.61	–	50.00	10.00	–	0.23

Regional Development Bank	Total assets	Equity	Outstanding loans	Authorized capital	Paid-in capital	Borrowing	ROE[a] (%)
The Corporacion Andina de Fomento	35.67	10.47	21.98	7.22	4.78	21.98	12.00
Central American Bank for Economic Integration	9.27	2.72	6.12	3.96	0.91	6.12	4.25
Council of Europe Development Bank	25.60	2.87	16.50	5 .47	0.61	16.50	3.73
Eurasian Development Bank	3.26	1.67	1.61	7.00	1.52	1.61	9.81
Total group two	**804.46**	**110.61**	**437.58**	**634.38**	**71.73**	**368.71**	**38.17**
Gran total	**1,150.02**	**181.41**	**640.60**	**1,086.16**	**99.76**	**542.74**	**49.04**

Source: Regional Development Banks, FY2016, annual reports
[a]*ROE* return on equity
[b]Including investment in project

Appendix 5.2: Regional Development Banks, Some Key Financial Variables, as of FY2016 in %

Regional Development Bank	Total assets	Equity	Outstanding loans	Authorized capital	Paid-in capital	Borrowing	ROE[a] (%)
Group one							
Inter-American Development Bank	9.9	14.6	12.7	15.7	6.0	15.0	6.5
African Development Bank (UA1 = $1.35)	3.5	4.9	4.3	9.5	7.6	2.8	0.8
Asian Development Bank	10.9	9.5	10.6	13.1	7.2	12.5	1.9
European Bank for Reconstruction & Development (€1 = $1.18)	5.8	10.0	4.1	3.2	7.3	1.8	13.0
Total Group one	**30.0**	**39.0**	**31.7**	**41.6**	**28.1**	**32.1**	**22.2**
Group two							
The European Investment Bank (EIB) (€1 = $1.18)	58.8	28.9	57.5	22.4	21.8	57.5	13.1
The Caribbean Development Bank	0.1	0.5	0.2	0.2	0.3	0.2	1.7
The Islamic Development Bank (1ID = $1.54)	2.2	6.7	2.0	21.3	14.4	2.2	4.1

Regional Development Bank	Total assets	Equity	Outstanding loans	Authorized capital	Paid-in capital	Borrowing	ROE[a] (%)
The Asian Infrastructure Investment Bank	1.5	9.8	1.5	8.3	18.1	1.8	1.8
The New Development Bank	0.9	5.3	0.0	4.6	10.0	0.0	0.5
The Corporacion Andina de Fomento	3.1	5.8	3.4	0.7	4.8	4.0	24.5
Central American Bank for Economic Integration	0.8	1.5	1.0	0.4	0.9	1.1	8.7
Council of Europe Development Bank	2.2	1.6	2.6	0.5	0.6	3.0	7.6
Eurasian Development Bank	0.3	0.9	0.3	0.6	1.5	0.3	20.0
Total group two	**70.0**	**61.0**	**68.3**	**58.4**	**71.9**	**67.9**	**77.8**
Gran total	**100.0**	**100.0**	**100.0**	**100.0**	**100.0**	**100.0**	**100.0**
Group 2 (excluding EIB)	11.1	32.0	10.8	36.0	50.2	10.5	64.7

[a]*ROE* return on equity

Chapter 6
Governance Structure of Regional Development Banks

Most of the regional development banks (RDBs#1 and RDBs#2) share many of the same features. All provide loans and grants at favourable and on market term conditions to various developing countries and sectors (Ottenhof 2011). They also face similar criticisms to those expressed with regard to BWFIs, in particular that their decried governance models lead to an "unfair" voting system (Carrasco et al. 2009). Eventual weaknesses in governance of the RBDs' decision making can affect their efficiency in managing development assistance. Two key questions come to mind: First who, within RDBs, controls the allocation of funds? And second, whether funds' allocation decisions could be made in a more democratic way?

This chapter provides an overview of the current state of governance of Group 1 and 2 of RDBs and explains their governance structures and policies. Section one discusses the governance structure and voting power within the regional development banks of RDB#1; Section two deals with the governance of Group 1 of regional development banks; Section three deals with the governance of other regional development banks or group 2; and Section four concludes the chapter.

The Governance Structure and Voting Power Within Regional Development Banks of Group One (RDBs#1)

All Regional Development Banks belong to government members, having participated in their capital, as shareholders. Regional members are often borrowers, but not always, while non-regional members are mostly lenders. Brazil, Mexico, Venezuela and Colombia, for instance, are regional members of the Caribbean Development Bank, but in their role of lenders, and the same situation can be encountered at the Islamic Development Bank or at the European Investment Bank, where regional members are also lenders. The number of votes and the level of representation on the Boards of Governors and Executive Boards of the RDBs are essentially

A. Naciri, *The Governance Structures of the Bretton Woods Financial Institutions*, SpringerBriefs in Economics, https://doi.org/10.1007/978-3-319-97906-9_6

Table 6.1 Voting shares of the five more important shareholders, by RDB of the group one, as of FY_2016

AfDB		AsDB		EBRD[a,b]		IaDB	
Nigeria	8.88	U.S.	15.57	U.S.	10.3	U.S.	30.00
U.S.	6.44	Japan	15.57	Japan	8.76	Argentina	11.81
Japan	6.49	China	6.43	France	8.76	Brazil	10.76
Egypt	5.14	India	6.32	Germany	8.76	Mexico	6.93
South Africa	4.56	Australia	5.77	Italy	8.76	Venezuela	5.76

Source: Institutions' annual reports
[a]Russian Federation (4.13%), Canada (3.51%), European Community (3.10%) and European Investment Bank (3.10%), are the 6th, 7th, 8th and 9th shareholders, respectively
[b]U.K. detains also 8.76% of the total votes

determined by the size of the member country's economy, and are often reflected in the importance of its financial contributions to the institutions. Although all the powers of RDBs are entrusted to their boards of governors, they usually delegate their management powers to their executive boards, which effectively provides for operation and supervision of the regional banks, often through specialized committees.

Table 6.1 shows the number of voting shares held by the five largest shareholders of the four regional development banks of group one (RDBs#1).

Examination of Table 6.1 allows a number of interesting observations:

1. The US is the largest shareholder of three out of the four RDBs#1, they retain 30% in IaDB votes, 15.5% in AsDB, 10.3% in the EBRD. Only the AfDB escapes such control rule and where the United States still hold the second vote, with 6.44%, after Nigeria with 8.88% of all votes.
2. The other major shareholder of the AsDB, the EBRD and the AfDB, is Japan, holding respectively 15.57%, 8.76% and 6.49% of the votes.
3. Once the vote of Japan is added to that of the United States, it is a question of 12.93% of the votes held by these two countries. It is also 31% of the capital of the AsDB and beyond 30% of the capital of the IaDB.
4. The largest shareholders of the African Development Bank, after the United States and Japan added, are in order of importance Nigeria, Egypt, and South Africa.
5. China, India and Australia are the largest shareholders of the AsDB.
6. France, Germany and Italy are the largest shareholders of the EBRD.
7. Finally, Argentina, Brazil and Mexico are the largest shareholders of the IDB.

The shareholding of RDBs#1 seems not only to translate the economic power of country members, but also to express their will to defend their own interests. Recently efforts have been made by RDBs, seeking the adjustment of their mission to maintain their institutional relevance in their respective regions. The governance of RDBs#1 is very similar to the one in use at the WBG, where the contribution made to the RDB determines the number of shares that country member holds in the RDB, and this holding also determines the voting rights at the Board of governors and Executive Board. The Board of Governors of RDBs is also the supreme authority: it appoints the members of the Executive Board and puts them in charge of conducting general operations and policies of institutions.

Governance Structure and Voting at the Inter-American Development Bank (IaDB)

The IaDB, with its 48 country members, 26 regionals 22 non-regionals, has also two decision-making bodies, namely a board of governors and a board of executive directors. Each of the 48 member countries appoints to the IaDB a governor and a deputy governor whose voting power is proportionate to the number of capital shares subscribed by his country and to whose a voting right is attached.

Each member country has 135 basic votes, plus one vote for each share held. The distribution of subscriptions is currently and approximately as follows: Latin America and the Caribbean, 50% of the shares; United States, 30%; Japan, 5%; Canada, 4%; and other non-borrowing members, 11%. In summary, regional borrowers account for 50% of the shares, and the remaining 50% are provided by non-borrowing regional members (US and Canada) at 34%, and non-regional member countries at 15.98%.

The Board of Directors has five standing committees that review and discuss all of the Bank's affairs. Here again, the governors are usually finance ministers, chairman of central banks or other senior officials of the same rank. They are ultimately responsible for overseeing the activities and administration of the Bank, although in practice they delegate many of these responsibilities to the Executive Board.

The Executive Board of the IaDB is composed of 14 Executive Directors, and 14 alternates Directors, representing 48 member countries, of which 9 are representatives of regional member countries, and the other 5 are representatives of the non-regional member countries. The executive directors of the United States and Canada represent their own country, and all other directors represent groups of countries. Alternate directors have the power to act only when their directors are absent. The executive board usually meets once a week, with the mandate of approving the day-to-day operations, such as loan and guarantee approvals, policy discussions, country strategies, administrative budgets, interest rates fixation, borrowing, and other financial decisions. Remarkably, the IaDB charter guarantees borrowing member countries, as a group, vote majority position. It is also important to note that the IaDB has always maintained a credit rating in AAA.

The president of the IaDB is the legal representative and the general manager of the institution. He is responsible for the day-to-day business of the Bank and manages its operations and oversees its administration. Elected by the Board of Governors, he presides over the meetings of the Executive Board, but does not, however, have the right to vote, except in case of equality of votes and where his vote is called upon to decide. Since the creation of the IaDB, all its presidents have been South American.

IaDB share ownership based on contributions was introduced by the 1959 Agreement, creating the Bank and specifying two groups of members, borrowers and non-borrowers. This has resulted in a particular voting model whose characteristics are as follows (https://www.iadb.org/en):

1. Borrowing countries are required by the IaDB Charter to hold more than 50% of the voting rights of the Bank. Argentina holds 10.7% per cent of total per cent votes, Brazil 10.7%, Mexico 6.9% and Venezuela 5.7%.
2. The group of non-borrowing members, mainly from North America and Europe, holds the remaining 50% of the voting rights, with the United States holding about 30% of the vote, while Japan holds 5% and Canada 4%.
3. The distribution of votes has remained virtually unchanged since the establishment of the IaDB in 1959, with the exception of the arrival of Canada and Japan to the bank as shareholders.
4. Often more than a simple majority of shares is required for most decisions, and some decisions can only be made by an absolute majority of country members, and the Charter also requires higher percentages of the total votes for some specific decisions. This increases even more the power of members who hold the high percentages of voting rights.
5. The United States, holding 30% of the total number of votes, automatically appoints its own director to the Executive Board of the IaDB, while the other directors are appointed by the Board of Governors of the Bank.
6. The quorum of the Board of Governors meetings is an absolute majority of the total number of governors, which represents at least two-thirds of the total number of the votes cast.
7. The modification to the IaDB charter requires two-thirds of the total number of governors, as well as three quarters of the total votes.
8. The President of the IaDB is elected by a majority of the votes of the members and by a majority of the votes of country members.

In any case, any significant action cannot be taken solely by IaDB borrowers alone, and the United States retains the upper hand on the IaDB's decisions.

Governance Structure and Voting Within the African Development Bank (AfDB)

The AfDB is made up of three separate institutions, or lending windows: The African Development Bank, providing facilities at market terms; The African Development Fund (AfDF), providing concessional loans and grants to countries unable to borrow from the African Development Bank; and the Nigeria Trust Fund (NTF), providing concessional financing to low-income borrowing countries. It has two boards of governors: one board for the AfDB window and the other for the African Development Fund.

The AfDB is composed of 80 country members; of these, 54 are regional country members and the remaining 26 are non-regionals. However, for a non-regional country to become a member of the AfDB, it must first register as an African Development Fund (AfDF) member. The AfDB and the AfDF form together the AfDB group (AfDBG). The Executive Board of the AfDB is elected by the Governors and comprises 18 Executive Directors representing all AfDB member countries, 12 executive directors representing African country members and 6 representing non-African member countries. The Executive Board of the African Development Fund has 12 members, who also sit on the Board of the AfDB. It is composed of six Directors of the AfDB's Board, selected by the non-regional member's states, and half of the remaining Directors on the AfDB's Board. Each appointed governor and alternate governor represents his country and exercises a voting right proportionate to the capital subscribed. Governors and Alternate Governors serve for 5-year terms, subject to revocation and renewal by the country members and are de facto governors and alternate governors of the African Development Fund.

The President of the AfDB is the Head Executive of the Bank, while also serving as Chair of its Board of Governors and the Executive Board, and five vice-presidents and all the staff of the bank operate under the authority of this position. The AfDB Board of Governors meets once a year, while the Executive Board meets on a weekly basis at the Bank headquarters in Abidjan to make decisions about projects and policy proposals of the bank and the fund. Each executive director is expected to express his or her opinion on all the proposals and, interestingly, a silence is considered approval. AfDB management and staff attend executive board meetings and are often invited to respond directly to the questions and concerns of Board members. Contributions of members to the AfDB and to the AfDF determine the number of shares that each member holds in the fund, and this number also determines the voting rights he holds on the Executive Board of the fund. The voting model of the AfDB has a number of special features (https://www.afdb.org/en/):

1. All member countries of the AfDB are represented on its Executive Board, in a proportion of 50/50 between African member countries and non-African countries.
2. The AfDB articles of incorporation require a two-thirds majority vote for the decisions of both the Board of Governors and the Executive Board;
3. Where a member country considers that an item on the agenda of any of the boards is of particular interest to it, articles of incorporation allow the country to request that the decision under study be taken at a majority vote of 70%. The AfDB's voting rules are designed to allow regional member countries to "tailor the assistance they receive" from the AfDB based on their interests and needs, rather than on those of donors.
4. The rules allow regional member countries to unite against an eventual unfavourable proposal to them.
5. Unlike for the World Bank, none of the executive directors has enough votes to block the decisions of the executive board of the AfDB or the AfDF.

6. Each of the Executive Directors represents more than one country, with the exception of the United States, which is represented alone by a director. Usually, the various countries represented by the same executive director assume the position by alternation.
7. Further, the allocation of credits at the AfDB is also unique in that it aims to prevent any single governor or director from controlling the outcome of the decision-making process.

The largest regional shareholder of the AfDB is Nigeria with 9.28% and the largest non-regional shareholder is the United States with about 6.5% of total voting stock, followed by Japan with about 5.4%. It is also important to note that the AfDB has always maintained a credit rating in AAA range. Despite all these specific features, and even though non-regional Member States are the minority shareholders in the AfDB, they nonetheless exert considerable influence over its activities, and currently the AfDB Executive Board is dominated by non-African members.

Governance Structure and Voting at the Asian Development Bank (AsDB)

The AsDB's Charter gives all the powers of the institution to its Board of Governors. In 2017, it had 67 country members, represented by 67 governors and as many alternate governors, 48 coming from Asia and the Pacific and 19 from outside the region. Governors or their deputies represent their countries and exercise a voting right proportional to the subscribed capital by their countries. Governors and Alternate Governors are usually ministers of finance, central bank chairs or other senior officials of the same rank. The board of governors delegates its operating powers to an appointed executive board, composed of 12 executive directors and entrusted with managing the general operations of the Bank. The executive board specifically performs functions such as making decisions about Bank policies on loans, guarantees, investments and technical assistance; approving the Bank's borrowings; approving the financial statements of the Bank; and approving the Bank's budgets.

Out of the 12 Executive Directors elected by the Board of Governors, eight are chosen from the Asia-Pacific region. Their voting power amounts to 65.21% of the total votes, and the remaining four, among the member countries outside the Asian region, have 34.789% of the votes (AsDB_FY_2015_AR). The Executive Board is a full-time resident board, operating from the headquarters of the Bank in Manila, Philippines. The President of the AsDB is also the chair of the Executive Board. Up until to today, all AsDB's presidents have been Japanese nationals.

The AsDB has two boards: the Board of Governors and the Executive Board, both of which are composed of regional and non-regional member country representatives. The voting model at the AsBD has a number of features, the main ones being as follows (AsDB)[1]:

1. The preponderance of the vote of the regional member countries of the bank at the level of the two boards;
2. That the Board of Governors is composed of 67 country representatives, 48 designated by regional member countries, and holding 65.040% of the total votes;
3. That Japan is the regional country member with the largest number of votes, holding 12.756%;
4. That the United States, as a non-regional country member, holds the largest number of votes, 12.756%, placing them at the same position as Japan;
5. That China is the second regional country member, far behind Japan, holding 5.442%;
6. That Regional member countries also hold 75% of the total number of votes on the Executive Board, and choose eight of the twelve directors composing the Board; and
7. That an absolute majority at the Board of Governors is required for some situations, when, for instance, the Board of Governors must decide whether a member country should be recognized as a "developed" or "developing" country. In such situations, a two-thirds vote of the total number of Governors is required. The nomination of the AsDB President also requires a majority vote of the total number of Governors, representing, at least, the majority of the total number of votes cast for members.

Here again the structure of the vote favours US control over the decision making of the AsDB. This situation is even further reinforced by the voting rules at the level of the AsDB Board, which simply require "the majority of votes of members present or represented at board meetings". In other words, non-regional members can make the decisions they favour, in meetings where they constitute a majority. This makes the AsDB definitely a development bank under US-Japan control.

Governance Structure and Voting at the European Bank for Reconstruction and Development (EBRD)

The membership at the EBRD is mainly composed of European and Central Asian countries, but also of a small number of non-European countries. Thirty-two members are beneficiary country members and 34 are donor country members, including the EU and the European Investment Bank. Like at other RDBs, the voting power at the EBRD is determined proportionally to the number of shares held by each country member, also appoints a Governor and an Alternate Governor to serve on its

[1] https://www.AsDB.org/sites/default/files/institutional-document/237881/AsDB-financial-report-2016.pdf

behalf. The EBRD is managed by its board of governors, which elects an Executive Board, consisting of 23 Directors and representing 8 recipient country members and 15 other representatives from donor country members. The Chairman of the Executive Board is responsible for the daily operating of the Bank. This includes policy approvals, loan decisions, granting guarantees and loans, and equity interests. The number of votes held by each Executive Director is linked to the number of member countries that person is representing. The president is the chief of staff of the bank and is, under the supervision of the executive board, responsible for the daily management of the bank and chairs the meetings of the executive board, without the right to vote, except in a situation of vote division between executive directors, where the president's vote is called upon and becomes decisive. Since the establishment of the EBRD in 1990, all the presidents have come from European country members, and all have been French citizens. The voting model of the EBRD has a number of special features (http://www.ebrd.com/home):

1. The main shareholders of the EBRD are the United States, with 10% of the votes; the United Kingdom, with 8.5%; Italy, with 8.5%; Japan, with 8.5%; France, with 8.5%; Germany, with 8.5%; and Russia, Spain and Canada, which also have significant voting rights;
2. There is no explicit distinction between borrowing and non-borrowing member countries;
3. The de facto voting power of non-borrowing countries, from Western and non-European countries, far outweighs the voting power held by borrowing countries in Eastern Europe and Central Asia;
4. The Board of Governors elects the President and Executive Board of the EBRD, but the Charter explicitly grants Western European countries majority representation on the Executive Board;
5. The President must be elected by a majority of the Board of Governors, but also by a majority of votes, and there is also an informal agreement within the EBRD that the President will come from France or Germany; and
6. Many of the voting conditions in the EBRD charter favour non-borrowing members. For example, some operational decisions require two-thirds of the vote at the Board of Governors, but three-quarters of the total number of votes cast for members.

The EBRD appears to be an institution under effective control of the Western Europe (European Union), but also under the watchful eye of the United States and Japan. Further, the votes held by member countries from the European Union amount to 57.98%, of which 11.93% is for member countries of the European Community, and the situation is expected to endure, since the EBRD's increases in the authorized capital, although permitted, require that the majority of shares—and therefore voting rights—be insured to member countries of the European Economic Community and Western Europe. The EBRD is a unique among regional development banks in the sense that non-regional members have a significant voting weight in decision-making.

Governance Structure and Voting of Group Two of Regional Development Banks (RDB#2)

A number of new regional development banks have emerged since the Bretton Woods Agreements, and some have been established even very recently. These are the European Investment Bank (EIB), established in 1958; the Caribbean Development Bank (CDB), established in 1969; the Latin American Development Bank (Andean Development Corporation - Corporación Andina de Fomento) (CAF), established in 1973; the Islamic Development Bank (IsDB), established in 2014; the New Development Bank (NDB), established in 2016; and the Asian Investment Infrastructure Bank (AIIB), also established 2016. The advent of the new regional development banks seems to come out of frustration with the BWFIs, but appears also inevitable, due to the inability of existing regional development banks and the World Bank Group alone to cope with the growing financial needs for infrastructure investment in the world. It is hoped, however, that the multiplicity of development institutions will be in the interest of global development and world peace.

Table 6.2 describes the voting shares held by the five largest shareholders in each of the five development banks of group two RDB # 2.

The Board of Governors in all EDBs#2 is also the supreme authority and includes representatives appointed by their member countries, usually finance ministers, or the same ranking government officials. The Board of Governors decides on matters as setting guidelines and policies for loans, approving financial statements, increasing and distributing capital, arrival of new members, appointing the members of the Executive Board, conducting general operations, and deciding on policies of the Bank. The following section, examines the voting structure of each one of RDBs#2.

Governance Structure and Voting at the European Investment Bank (EIB)

At the European Investment Bank (EIB), the Board of Governors is also the highest decision-making authority, and it consists of representatives appointed by each of the 28 member states of the institution, usually finance ministers or other high-ranking individuals. The Board of Governors also appoints executive directors to the executive board, as well as the management team and audit committee members. The Executive Board is composed of one director appointed by each Member State and one by the European Commission, for a total of 29 and 19 substitutes. This means that some executive director positions must be shared among several country members. In addition, and in order to broaden its professional expertise in certain areas, the Executive Board can engage up to a maximum of six experts, as well as three Directors and three Substitutes, to fully participate in its work but without voting rights (http://www.eib.org/).

Table 6.2 Voting shares held in 2017 by the five largest shareholders in each of the five banks of Group 2, RDBs#2

EIB		CDB		IsDB		NDB[a]		AIIB[b]	
Germany	16.170	Spain	13%	Saudi Arabia	24.01	Brazil	20%	China	27.52
France	16.170	Italy	13%	Libya	9.53	Russia	20%	India	7.93
Italy	16.170	Germany	10%	Iran	8.43	India	20%	Korea	3.69
U.K.	16.170	United Kingdom	9%	U.A.E.	7.62	China	20%	Russia	6.25
Spain	9.702	Spain	13%	Nigeria	7.28	South Africa	20%	Australia	3.65

Source: Institutions' annual reports

[a]Unallocated shares 100

[b]Indonesia (3.3443%Turkey (2.6573%), Saudi Arabia (2.5975%), Pakistan (1.2154%), Philippines (1.1651%)

Decisions at the EIB are taken by a majority of at least one-third of the voting members, representing not less than 50% of the subscribed capital and in certain clearly defined situations, not fewer than 18 votes, representing not less than 68% subscribed capital. The Chair of the Executive Board or, in that person's absence, one of the Vice-Chairs chairs the meetings of the Executive board, but does not vote. All the presidents of the EIB, since its establishment, have come from European member countries. The five largest shareholders of the bank are Spain, holding 13% of the votes; Italy, holding 13%; France, holding 11%; Germany, holding 10%; the United Kingdom, holding 9%; Poland, holding 6%; and the rest of the member countries holding 22%.[2] The EIB is a truly a European bank.

Governance Structure and Voting at Caribbean Development Bank (CBD)

At the Caribbean Development Bank (CDB), the Board of Governors also incorporates the highest authority and delegates the supervision of the Bank's operations to an appointed Executive Board. Each member country of the bank appoints a governor and a deputy governor, and each governor is entitled to exercise the votes of the member territory he represents. The Board of Governors also appoints the Chairman of the Executive Board and entrusts him with the day-to-day operation of the Bank, and has him assisted by an advisory management team.

The five main shareholders of the Caribbean Development Bank, as of the end of the fiscal year 2017, are Jamaica, holding 17.14%, of the total votes; Trinidad and Tobago, with 17.14%; Canada, with 9.24%; the United Kingdom, holding 9.24%; and Italy, holding 5.56% (CDB_FY2016_AR[3]). The bank seems to be controlled by Jamaica and Trinidad, but also by the group of three donor countries, Canada, United Kingdom and Italy.

Governance Structure and Voting at the Islamic Development Bank (IsDB)

Each of the 56 member countries of the Islamic Development Bank (IsDB) is represented on the Board of Governors by a representative and an alternate. Each member country has 500 basic votes, plus one vote for each share subscribed. The most important member countries of the Islamic Bank, in terms of voting power are Saudi Arabia, holding 24% of the total votes; Libya, holding 9.53%; Iran, holding 8.43; the United Arab Emirates (UAE), holding 7.62%; and Nigeria, holding 7.28%. As a rule,

[2] http://www.eib.org/attachments/general/reports/en2016en.pdf

[3] CDB_FY2016_AR

decisions are made by the Board of Governors on the basis of a simple majority of the voting rights, present or represented at each meeting. The Board of Governors meets once a year to review the Bank's activities for the previous year and decide on future orientations. At its annual meeting, the Board of Governors appoints a chairperson to hold office until another chair is elected at the next annual meeting of the board. As the highest decision-making body, the Board of Governors delegates certain powers to an appointed Executive Board, and entrusts it with the carrying out of the overall operation of the Bank. Certain matters are only dealt with by the Board of Governors, and these mainly relate to an increase or decrease in the capital of the Bank, the authorization of cooperation agreements with other international and regional organizations, and the election of the Chairman and Directors and their remuneration.

For its part, the Executive Board, in addition to the powers expressly conferred on it by the Statutes, exercises all the powers delegated to it by the Board of Governors. The IsDB Executive Board currently consists of 18 directors, nine of whom are nominated by their respective countries in their capacity as major shareholders, and together they hold around 84.74% of the total voting rights. Moreover, nine other executive directors are elected by all the governors of the other member countries. The term of office of Executive Directors is renewable for a period of 3 years. All presidents of the IsDB, since its establishment, have been representatives of Saudi Arabia, so the effective control of the Islamic Bank would seem to belong to Saudi Arabia.[4]

Governance Structure and Voting Powers at the New Development Bank (NDB)

The New Development Bank (NDB) is one of the most recent establishments within the RDBs, launched in 2014 by five emerging countries: Brazil, Russia, India, China and South Africa, collectively called "BRICS" countries. The NDB aims to mobilize resources for financing infrastructure projects in member countries, as well as in other emerging and developing economies, while complementing the financial support provided by other multilateral initiatives. The Board of Governors of the New Development Bank is the highest decision-making body, currently composed of governors appointed by the five founding member countries. However, some of his responsibilities are delegated to an Executive Board, which also includes representatives of the five founding countries. Headquartered in Shanghai, China. In 2017 the NDB had a staff of 24 employees, including the president, 4 vice-presidents, 19 staff, and 34 consultants (NDB_AR_2016). The five largest shareholders are Brazil, Russia, India, China and South Africa, with 20% of the voting shares each. The NDB would seem under the joint control of the five emerging countries of the BRICS.

[4] http://www.isdb.org/irj/go/km/docs/documents/IDBDevelopments/Internet/French/IDB/CM/Publications/AnnualReports/41st/annrepen1436.pdf

Governance Structure and Voting at the Asian Infrastructure Investment Bank (AIIB)

The other recent development bank is the Asian Infrastructure Investment Bank (AIIB), which began its operations in 2016 with 56 member states, while 24 others states were potential members, for a total of 80 members approved. The Board of Governors of the AIIB is the highest authority and consists of one Governor and one Alternate Governor, appointed by each member country and serving at his discretion. The Board of Governors delegates some of its powers to the Executive Board. In the case of the AIIB, this is a non-resident executive board, which is to say a board whose directors do not work at the head office of the bank in Beijing, but rather elsewhere in the world, each from his place of residency. The Executive Board is responsible for managing the Bank's overall operations, exercising all powers delegated to it by the Board of Governors, including approving the Bank's strategy, annual plan and budget; establishing policies; making decisions about the functioning of the Bank; overseeing the management and operation of the Bank; and, establishing a monitoring mechanism.

The Bank is led by a president elected by the shareholders and supported by a management team, formed of prominent individuals from diverse member countries, "bringing with them years of experience and a wide range of professional expertise",[5] both international and from private sector. The bank also uses the knowledge of an international advisory group of global experts, providing bank management with impartial advice and perspectives to support the President and senior managers on the Bank's strategies and policies, as well as on general operational issues. The advisory group usually meets in parallel with the Bank's annual meeting or at the request of the President. The members of the international advisory group are appointed for 2-year terms and receive a small fee and no salary. The Bank assumes only the costs associated with committee meetings.

Contrary to what happens in most international institutions, the fact that the executive Board of the AIIB is non-resident and that Executive directors cannot meet physically on a weekly basis is likely to reflect the dominant views of the Chinese president. It is believed that it is essential to the good governance of the institution, to have a board that constantly checks day-to-day management. The AIIB would therefore seem under the control of China. The five largest shareholders of the AIIB, in terms of the number of votes, are China, holding 27.52% of the total votes; followed by India, holding 7.93%; Russia, holding 6.25%; Korea, holding 3.69%; and Australia, holding 3.657%. The rest of the member countries share the remaining 51% of the votes. The Executive Board, as of July 3.2017 is composed of Saudi Arabia, Turkey, Thailand, China, Korea, Egypt, Australia, United Kingdom, Russia, Germany, India and Indonesia.

---

[5] https://www.aiib.org/en/index.html

Other RDBs #2 Governance Structure and Voting

The other RDBs#2 are The Corporación Andina de Fomento, CAF, The Central American Bank for Economic Integration, CABEI, Council of Europe Development Bank, CEB, Eurasian Development Bank, EDB, and other multilateral development institutions. Their governance and voting structures are similar to RDB # 2 structures in that they are mainly dominated by majority shareholders.

RDBs' Relations with the OECD

As in the case of major BWFIs, many RDBs maintain a fairly high level of cooperation with Organisation for Economic Co-operation and Development (OECD), especially the regional banks of Group 1. In general, most development institutions have cooperation agreements with the OECD, as they do between themselves. In 2010, for example, the OECD and the Inter-American Development Bank signed a Memorandum of Understanding to develop cooperation in many policy areas. A Letter of Intent was also signed between the OECD and the Asian Development Bank in 2005. The OECD and the European Bank had signed a joint statement in 2009 outlining a number of areas where cooperation will be developed and / or strengthened, such as support for small and medium-sized enterprises, urban development, investment, corporate social responsibility, corporate governance and climate change (OECD n.d.-c, Global Relations). Some observers argue that the OECD, whose membership is made up mostly of developed or donor countries, could be the means by which major economies effectively strengthen their control over the decision-making of regional development banks, especially those belonging to Group 1, and perhaps wisely allows them to monitor voting within RDBs.

Summary of the Governance Structure of Regional Development Banks

Governance structures of RDBs are mostly similar and entirely reflect the WBG model. In addition, RDBs maintain a high level of collaboration and engagement among themselves and with the WBG. More than 100 inter-RDB working groups can be inventoried (Morris 2017). The RDBs shared governance structure is one that is overseen by a Board of Governors, which delegates most of its powers to a Board of Executive Directors. There are essentially two Boards of Governors and two Boards of Directors in almost each regional group of Development Banks: one for non-concessional financing on market-like terms and one for non-concessional financing on more favourable terms. The Board of governors in each RDB is the highest decision-making body. It consists of a governor and a deputy governor, who are usually finance ministers or a ranking equivalent, elected for 5-year terms, or sometimes three, and subject to a one-term renewal. The Board of Governors meets annually and generally at the institution's headquarters, but video conference scan be held more frequently and, when needed, votes can be taken by correspondence.

While the Board of Governors in each regional bank retains its authority over major fundamental decisions, day-to-day operational authority is usually delegated to a board of executive directors. These are directors that usually work on site, at the head offices of the institutions. The executive Board of each institution is generally much smaller than its board of governors. The number of directors varies between 7 and 20 directors, depending on the institution involved, and each member country is represented on the Executive Board by an executive director. Countries retaining a high percentage of shares of an institution are often represented by their own director as is the case with the United States, Japan, UK, France or Germany, for RDBs#1, and Saudi Arabia, China, etc., for RDBs#2. The other shareholders are usually represented in groups by the same executive director.

Each RDB is also headed by a chairman, who is the legal representative. Elected by the Board of Governors on the recommendation of the Executive Board, the president of the bank is also its managing director and as such manages its operating activities The presidents of regional banks are responsible for the general management of institutions and at the same time chair their boards of governors and executives. Decision-making within the RDBs is done by vote, and the number of voting rights allocated to each member country is linked to its cumulative financial contributions and its commitments to the institution. Decisions on matters of general policy are usually made by a majority of the two-thirds of the total number of votes, held by all member countries participating in the vote. Decisions on all other issues may only require a simple majority of the votes held by all member countries participating in the vote. However, this is not necessarily the case for votes on concessional windows of RDBs. In the majority of cases, donor countries appear to have comfortable majority votes in the concessional windows of the RDBs (Nelson 2015).

As can be seen, the governance structures of RDBs are strongly inspired by the governance structure of the World Bank Group. Many of their projects, as well as their lending policies, are often jointly funded in collaboration with the World Bank and other donors, especially in the case of RDB # 1. Most RDBs rely on macroeconomic research and analysis undertaken by the Bank.

Discussion of the Governance of RDBs

RDBs are subject to a plethora of criticisms regarding the quality of their governance, which has become a source of worry for many observers. The felt limitations observed in RDBs' governance may also have prompted the emergence of new recent regional development banks.[6] This section highlights a number of potential issues of governance of RDBs.

The first concern comes from the shareholding structure that is dramatically tilted toward a very small number of shareholders, creating a dilemma of corporate democracy. Globally, the United States is the largest shareholder of the IaDB, AsDB and the EBRD. It is also the largest shareholder of the AsDB, at the same rank as Japan. At the AfDB, the United States is also the second largest shareholder, after Nigeria. Among the regional members, China and India contribute significantly to the AfDB; Egypt and South Africa are major contributors to the AfDB; Argentina, Brazil and Venezuela are major contributors to the IaDB; and Russia is a big contributor to the EBRD. As the largest shareholder, the United States holds a seat on the executive board of many RDBs. Actually, decision-making authority in most RDBs #1 is firmly in the hands of non-borrowing members, except in institutions such as the Inter-American Development Bank, where borrowing members have a majority of 51% of the votes. At RDBs#2, large regional contributors hold the key to decision making, and once they become vote majority holders, they become reluctant to embrace any attempt at change because of the need to protect their acquired rights. In fact, this is the main reason why most attempts to increase the institutions' capital have failed (Morris 2017). Even in the few cases where non-regional donors do not hold a majority of the votes on executive boards of regional banks, their influence, particularly, through the process of replenishing funds, would be persuasive at any time. It is, indeed, at the level of the replenishment of the Funds where operational priorities, strategic orientation and funding levels are determined.

The second governance concern that comes from the structural deficit that appears within RDBs, in addition to the democratic deficit (Nye Jr 2003), as borrowing member countries have comparatively fewer means and less power to control the policies of their RDBs. At the AfDB, for example, representation had to be further strengthened to avoid the marginalization of African voices. At the IaDB, many important decisions require support from the United States or another non-Latin American country. The United States, Canada, and Japan control a sizeable share of voting rights in the IaDB, but, being non borrowers, are not subject to loan conditionalities. At the AsDB, some majority requirements do not allow regional member countries to vote meaningfully, as a majority bloc. Notably, the AsDB president has always come from Japan, although the AsDB Charter allows for diversification. The power of the EBRD to make important political decisions rests with its non-borrowing members, who decide which projects to fund and determine the terms of their funding.

The third governance concern relates to the way chairpersons are nominated to the position. It seems that the main contributor to always have the last word in the decision of nominating a chairman to institutions is usually a national of the main contributor.

[6] Some see the benefit in this multiplicity of institutions, if only as an improvement in the competition within the sector. On the contrary, others see a harmful segmentation, inevitably leading to an undue relaxation of financing conditions and financial crises.

The fourth major governance issue facing RDBs lies in the tendency that main contributors often show to use their voting power for geopolitical purposes, prioritizing funding requests coming from countries deemed to be "politically correct" or "geopolitically important", which ignores the fundamental reason for the RDBs' existence.

The fifth governance concern that arises when examining the governance of regional development banks stems from their chronic need of funds, which often makes them constantly at the mercy of their rich country members. Their funds are mostly derived from the financial resources obtained largely from these developed member countries membership. Often non-regional wealthy countries join regional development bank memberships, largely because of their financial contributions, constituting a dominant share of the capital of most RDBs. These non-regional holdings in RDBs make an impact, not only because they bring the most of the capital to RDBs, but also because their multiplier has a significant effect on the capacity of RDBs to access the international financial market. Such a funding structure of RDBs leads inevitably to the control of the regional banks by the contributing rich countries. However, critics argue that such contributor-controller systems, duplicated both internationally and regionally, do not reflect the new global economic realities (Carrasco et al. 2009).

The sixth concern stems from the fact that RDBs' assistance is often made in the name of so-called "national interests", usually conditional to commercial requirements. The hundreds of billions of dollars made yearly available to RDBs, and awarded in contracts, make every contributing developed country look at having its "fair" share. Some contributing countries have even instituted their own protection rules. The US Congress, for instance, exercises oversight over U.S. participation in the RDBs through legislative mandates and hearings, directing the U.S. Executive Directors to the RDBs to advocate certain policies and ways to vote on various issues. Congress also issues reporting requirements for the Treasury Department on issues related to RDBs' activities. Congress has also tied RDBs funding to specific institutional reforms (Nelson 2015). The Foreign Commercial Services of the United States (US_FCS) has even representatives at the RDBs, who are responsible for the protection and the promotion of American commercial interests at institutions (Nelson 2015). Other main economic powers contributing to RDBs also have their own similar protective mechanisms.

The seventh concern comes from the fact that some developed country members of RDBs are simultaneously shareholders and customers of institutions. This dual role may contribute to a conflict of interest. To address such an issue, the introduction of predefined limits to the proportion of capital that can be held by any member country at RDBs is usually suggested. The imposition of such limits, may, however, affect only high-income countries' influence; I may leave unaffected the risk of seeing some large regional shareholders meddling with RDBs funding processes.

The eighth governance issue has to do with competency and training. Some designated governors, Finance Ministers, and the like would simply lack the required training or would not be given the sufficient institutional resources to carry out their work with RDBs, and this dynamic could be repeated at the level of the executive board. There are, for instance, situations in which funder representatives may have more information about projects in a certain borrowing countries than the executive directors representing these countries.

The ninth concern with RDB governance has to do with the fact that policy-based loans from RDBs are often developed and co-financed in collaboration with the World Bank and the IMF, and are usually granted to countries that have ongoing programs with the IMF and the Bank, such as the Poverty Reduction and Growth Facility (PRGF) and a Credit for the Poverty Reduction Strategy. The economic conditions often associated with these programs and policy loans seem often to have exacerbated poverty in some countries. This has been recently acknowledged by a recent report by the IMF's Independent Evaluation Office (IEO), which states that although PRGF countries have generally experienced positive economic growth, the proportion of people living in poverty has not decreased.

The tenth concern is related to the fact that most RDBs' policies seem to be based on decisions made privately by their boards of governors or executives and internal documents are generally not made public (Ottenhof 2011).

The eleventh concern comes from the fact that overall ability of RDBs to stimulate economic development is often disputed, and it is argued that RDBs focus much more on the means of obtaining funds than on achieving development goals, and the funds granted are totally outside the control of donors. They are virulently criticized particularly in relation to transparency. RDBs are generally not part of international treaties that may subject them to external regulation and submit them to appropriate disclosure. There seems also to be a lack of independent review mechanisms within RDBs that would allow parties directly affected by their decisions to express their grievances. The lack of quality disclosure can prevent constructive criticism that could be issued against RDBs (Carrasco et al. 2009).

Fortunately, there are those who think that RDBs' action is the right thing to go by, because it has helped developing countries in recent decades to make tangible progress in their fight against poverty. They also point out that support from the RDBs is important for the mobilization of funds, both at the level of the financial market, as well as from other bilateral donors; RDBs' actions can ultimately prove to be a prerequisite to any good economic or political reform (Nelson 2015).

Conclusion

Despite the plethora of criticisms they are subject to (Nye Jr 2003; Carrasco et al. 2009), RDBs present the great advantage of providing development assistance on a larger scale than many other bilateral agencies, and generate additional sources of funding, leading to significant economies of scale in terms of financial and intellectual capital. Some RDBs#2 had apparently been launched in a protest to the governance failure within RDBs#1, where the US has decisive voting rights. The founders of some RDBs#2 seem, however, to be accurately replicating the contested governance system of RBDs#1, where the main contributors also secure themselves decisive voting powers. The voting system of RDBs voting seems, however, to have some bias towards the developed economies, through a biased vote distribution and various appointments to key positions, which are closely linked to distribution of votes. At the Inter-American development bank, for instance, the United States constantly controls its destiny. At the Asian Development Bank, Japan and the United States are major shareholders, and have traditionally maintained Japanese presidents at the head of the ASDB (Carrasco et al. 2009). In other regional development banks, China, Saudi Arabia, the European Union have always applied the rule of "the one who brings the funds controls the vote" and names the chairman. One can, however, wonder if this could be otherwise, since non-borrowing members are among the largest contributors to regional development banks, and their contributions are critical to the operating survival and missions of RDBs. Indeed, could those who provide funding to RDBs waive their vote right? Could they give up wanting to monitor the way their funds are used? Could they give up trying to ensure that their contributions get them what they consider a "fair share" in RDBs contracts? The answer to all these questions, when we place ourselves in a purely financial framework, can only be no. But this also means giving up, in the first place, the spirit of Bretton Woods that led to the creation of the RDBs. Adopting a pure financial logic for development assistance would only lead to the contradicting of the spirit of Bretton Woods.

Chapter 7
Development Assistance Movement Within the International Financial Architecture for Development

The early 1930s witnessed several reactions to the misery in the world and to the financial crisis caused by the Great Depression. It was not until the end of the Second World War, however, that the urgency of fighting poverty and stabilizing the international financial system prevailed and with it the desire to keep past mistakes from surfacing again. Such a desire ultimately led to the Bretton Woods Conference, originally and mostly looking for setting the rules for trade and financial relations between the signatory countries; it has, however, paved the way for a more ambitious project of a new international financial architecture, which favours development assistance and collaboration. Although the Bretton Woods movement was originally aimed at rebuilding the European economies destroyed by war, it quickly took the form of a fight against poverty and underdevelopment in countries newly escaping colonial yoke. This movement culminated with the advent of the Official Development Assistance (ODA) program, introduced by the Development Aid Committee (DAC) of the OECD. Though trillions of dollars were spent by the international community on development assistance for the fight against poverty, the results appear to be mitigated.

This chapter will mainly concentrate on ODA analysis. Section one gives a brief history of official development assistance; section two introduces the Development Assistance Committee (DAC) of the OECD; section three gives an overview of development assistance; section four discusses Official Development Aid (ODA); section five discusses Official Development Flows **(ODF); section six discusses the** other official flows (OOF); section seven discusses official and private flows (OPF); section eight introduces to the Aid for Trade (AFT) movement; section nine gives a summary of official development aid; section ten discusses official development assistance conditions; section eleven discusses some causes of inefficiencies; and section twelve concludes the chapter.

A. Naciri, *The Governance Structures of the Bretton Woods Financial Institutions*, SpringerBriefs in Economics, https://doi.org/10.1007/978-3-319-97906-9_7

Brief History of Official Development Assistance (ODA)

Official development assistance (ODA) was actually preceded by a famous ancestor aid program, the US-sponsored economic stimulus package for Europe, better known as the Marshall Plan (MP). This is a major initiative, launched by the US in 1947 and considered to be the first major foreign aid initiative in history. The MP consisted of granting concessional loans to 16 European countries heavily affected by the Second Great War. Later, in the 1950s, the United States was again stimulating foreign aid under their "Mutual Security Act," designed to channel funds to foreign governments whose participation in the anticommunism crusade they wanted to secure (Fuhrer 1996). During the same period and in response to the success of the national liberation movements across the globe, former colonial powers of Europe reconfigured their imperial funds to monitor closely their newly independent old colonies. Thus, the British Colonial Development Corporation was created in 1948, and it metamorphosed in the mid-1960s into the Commonwealth Development Corporation, and the French "Fonds d'investissement économique et social des territoires d'outremer" (FIDES) created in 1946 became in 1960 the Fund for Aid and Cooperation "Fonds d'Aide et de Coopération (FAC)" (Sogge 2002). These two organizations would later be respectively transformed into the Commonwealth of Nations[1] and the "Organization Internationale de La Francophonie (OIF)".[2] Such strategies are mainly aimed at keeping the imperial upper hand on the former colonies. It was not until 2012 that Russia also structured its development aid by launching its RusAid agency.

Foreign aid programs of the US, France and the UK during the 1950s and 1960s accounted for more than 75% of total ODA (OECD/DAC). Throughout the 1960s, Cold War imperatives had continued to shape the aid agenda, with the United States alone accounting for more than half of bilateral ODA and also occupying a dominant position in BWFIs and DAC. Foreign aid seems to be mainly motivated by the political objectives of the donors, rather than the development needs of recipients.

Development Assistance Committee (DAC)

The spirit of Bretton Woods as well as the awareness of the damages of the extreme world poverty scourge paved the way for the advent of the international development assistance movement. This assistance encompasses different international categories of support, offered by governments and other agencies to developing countries to back up their development initiatives. International development assistance was first structured by the establishment, by the Organization for Economic Co-operation and

[1]The Commonwealth of Nations is an intergovernmental organization composed of 52 member states, most of which are former territories of the British Empire.

[2]The OIF comprises 57 member states and governments, 3 associate members and 20 observers.

Development (OECD) in 1969, of its Development Assistance Committee (DAC). This is a forum created by ministerial resolution, and consisting of the largest aid-donating countries, whose aim is to discuss issues surrounding aid, development and poverty reduction in developing countries, and to coordinate development assistance amongst the rich nations. The DAC set up a list of countries that qualified for development assistance. The World Bank, IMF, UNDP, as well as RDBs are DAC observers. The DAC has currently 30 member countries, listed in Appendix 7.1.

Membership at the DAC is based on a number of prerequisites, such as the existence in the member country of appropriate strategies, policies, and institutional frameworks to demonstrate its relevance, ability to put in place a development cooperation program, and the existence of a monitoring and evaluation system for development assistance.[3] DAC meetings are, however, open beyond DAC membership, to all countries active in development assistance. Countries such as Brazil, China, India, Indonesia or South Africa take part in DAC meetings. President Harry Truman of the United States spelled out the rationale for U.S. development aid in his inaugural address of 1949, which also announced the founding of NATO by stating, as reported by *Kanbur (*2006*)*:

> *"[...] More than half the people of the world are living in conditions approaching misery. Their food is inadequate. They are victims of disease. Their economic life is primitive and stagnant. Their poverty is a handicap and a threat both to them and to more prosperous areas".*[4]

Overview of Development Assistance

Development assistance can be seen as the product of the Bretton Woods movement, stemming from the ashes of the Second World War. It refers to resources made available to poor and developing countries on favourable terms, by more fortunate and economically advanced countries, for the aim of promoting their development and well-being. DAC keeps statistics on major categories of international development assistance summarized in Fig. 7.1. Here each category is discussed in more depth. These categories are:

1. Official Development Aid, ODA, defined as the assistance to countries on the list of ODA recipients and to multilateral institutions;
2. Official Development Financing, ODF, measured for recipient countries only, defined as the sum of their receipts of bilateral ODA, and other bilateral official flows unrelated to trade, in particular loans to refinance debt;
3. Other Official Flows, OOF, which are transactions by the official sector (not private) that are neither "development-motivated" nor concessional. The

[3] http://www.oecd.org/dac/dacmembers.htm#members

[4] *For the first time in history, humanity possesses the knowledge and skill to relieve the suffering of these people.*

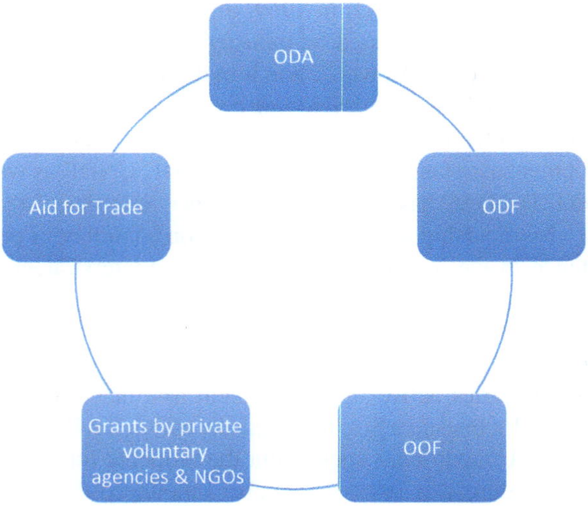

Fig. 7.1 Major categories of official development assistance

main items in OOFs are export credits, official sector equity and portfolio investment, and debt reorganisation;

4. Private Flows, which consist mostly of investment by transnational corporations and private banks, and export credits given by industries. The figures for Private Flows and OOFs are quite volatile from year to year because they represent a balance between positive and negative flows;
5. Net Private Grants. or aid mostly from private sources such as NGOs;
6. Aid for trade, which is a joint OECD and WTO assistance initiative offered to developing countries to help them to address trade-related infrastructure constraints.

Figure 7.1 summarizes the multiple sides of ODA, which fall into different categories.

Figure 7.1 indicates that official development assistance can take diverse forms and can have different origins, to be discussed in the following.

The Official Development Aid (ODA)

DAC defines ODA as "those flows to countries and territories on its list of ODA recipients and to multilateral institutions, provided by official agencies, including state and local governments, or by their executive agencies", and respecting two conditions: "first, that each transaction is administered with the promotion of the **economic development and welfare of developing countries,** as its main objective; and second, that it is **concessional in character** and conveys a grant element of at least 25% (calculated at a rate of discount of 10%)".[5]

[5] http://www.oecd.org/dac/stats/officialdevelopmentassistancedefinitionandcoverage.htm

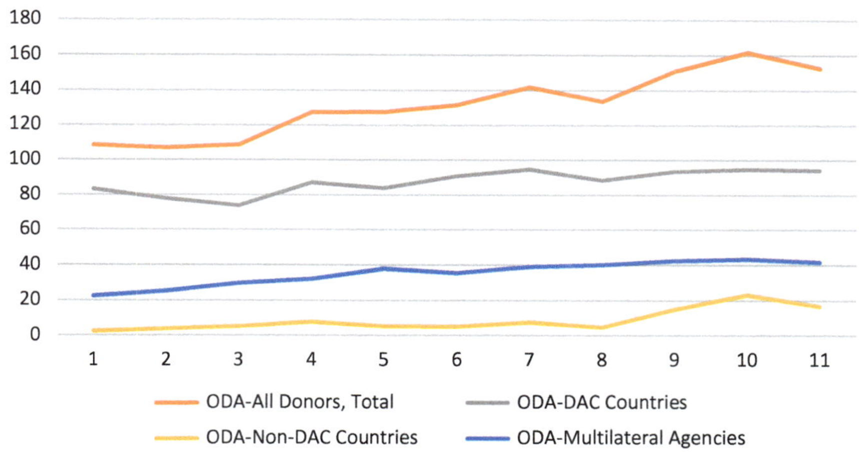

Fig. 7.2 Official development aid, as registered by DAC of the OECD (2005–2015) in $ billion

Official development assistance is therefore a measure of government-contributed assistance, compiled by the DAC of the OECD. It includes developmental and humanitarian aid, with the humanitarian side being much smaller. ODA can take several forms: "grant funds, grants in kind, services or concessional loans that have at least 25% grant component" (DAC). It can be provided bilaterally, as it can be channelled through a multilateral development agency such as the United Nations Development Program (UNDP), the World Bank, the European Commission or the regional development banks, ODA can come from a single donor country, in which case it is described as bilateral, as it can come from several donors at the same time, and it is described as multilateral. Since 1970, the United Nations has recognized the "great value" of ODA as a mean of transferring resources to developing environments (UN General Assembly).[6]

The best-known target in international aid is 0.7% of donors' national income. This figure grew out of an earlier suggestion to transfer 1% of donor countries' incomes to developing countries. **In 1970**, the 0.7% ODA/GNI target was first agreed upon and has been repeatedly re-endorsed at the highest level at international aid and development conferences.[7] The weighted average of DAC members' ODA has, however, never exceeded 0.4% of GNP.[8]

Figure 7.2 plots total ODA made by all donors for the period of 2005–2015, classified by DAC countries, non-DAC countries and multilateral agencies. These data are an excerpt from **ODA disbursements to countries and regions [DAC2a].** The DAC computes ODA from data submitted by its member states. It also collects some data on other countries' aid donations, which are significant. OPEC dona-

[6] UN General Assembly Resolution 2626 (XXV), October 24, 1970, para, 43, 45–47.

[7] http://www.oecd.org/development/financing-sustainable-development/development-finance-standards/the07odagnitarget-ahistory.htm

[8] http://www.oecd.org/dac/stats/ODA-history-of-the-0-7-target.pdf

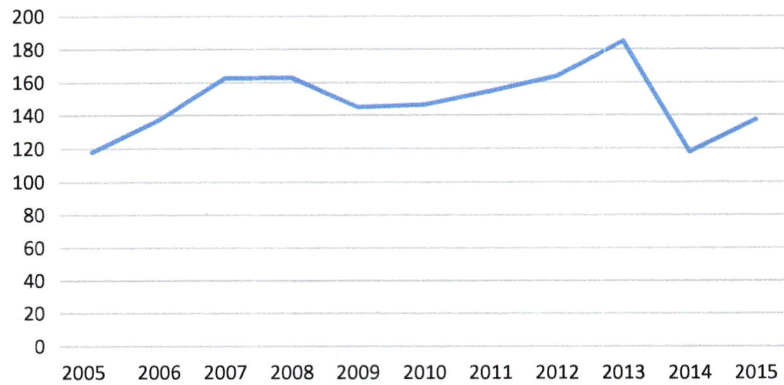

Fig. 7.3 Official development flows, ODF (2005–2015) in $ billions. Source: Data from OECD, Official and private flows

tions, for instance, are currently about twice that of the DAC countries, as a fraction of donor gross national income.[9]

Total ODA-All Donor assistance scored $108.54 billion in 2005, and toped $152.73 billion in 2015, an overall increase of 40.70%. ODA-DAC countries' contribution slipped from 77% of the total of ODA-All Donors in 2005 to 62% in 2015, a 15% decrease over the period of 2005–2015. ODA-Non-DAC countries' contributions increased by 8%: from 3%, its 2005 level, to 11% in 2015. Similarly, ODA-Multilateral Agencies' contribution improved by 6%, from 21% in 2005 to 27% in 2015.

Official Development Flows (ODF)

When two other assistance components are added to ODA, they sum up to what is named by the DAC as official development flows (ODF). These added components are according to *data of OECD*: Grants and concessional and non-concessional development lending by multilateral financial institutions, and Other Official Flows for development purposes, including refinancing Loans which contain too low a Grant Element to qualify as ODA.[10]

ODF measured for recipient countries only is defined as the sum of three elements: their receipts from bilateral ODA, their receipts from concessional and non-concessional resources from multilateral sources, and their receipts from bilateral other official flows, made available for reasons unrelated to trade, in particular loans to refinance debt. Figure 7.3 plots official development flows for the period of 2005–2015, in $ billions.

---

[9]According to DAC figures, Arab countries gave some $2.50 billion in 2006, which represented 0.81% of their GNI.

[10]https://data.oecd.org/drf/other-official-flows-oof.htm

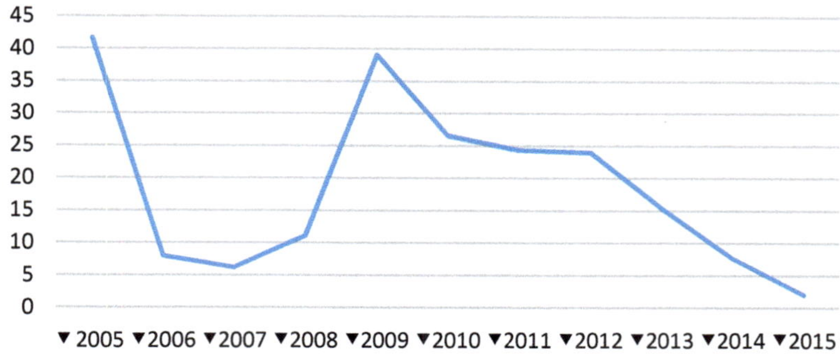

Fig. 7.4 Total other official flows, OOF (2005–2015), in $ billion. Source: Data from OECD, Official and private flows

Official development flows oscillated during the period of 2005–2015 from between $118,033 billions in 2005 to $185,06 billions in 2012, only to drop to $118,033 billions in 2014, and again to increase to $137.398 billion in 2015.

Other Official Flows (OOF)

DAC also collects data on other official flows (OOF), defined as official sector transactions that do not meet official development assistance criteria. OOF include several components *(data, OECD):*

1. Grants to developing countries for representational or essentially commercial purposes;
2. Official bilateral transactions intended to promote development in developing countries, but having a grant element of less than 25%; and,
3. Official bilateral transactions, whatever their grant element, the purpose of which is primarily export-facilitating for developing countries. This category includes, by definition, export credits extended directly to an aid recipient by an official agency or institution; the net acquisition by governments and central monetary institutions of securities issued by multilateral development banks at market terms; subsidies (grants) to the private sector to soften its credits to developing countries; and, funds in support of private investment.[11]

Figure 7.4 plots DAC countries' contributions to OOFs for the period of 2005–2015.

Numbers in Fig. 7.3 are Other Official Flows (OOF) in $ billion constant prices, using 2014 as the base year. The total OOF fluctuated tremendously during the

[11] https://data.oecd.org/drf/other-official-flows-oof.htm

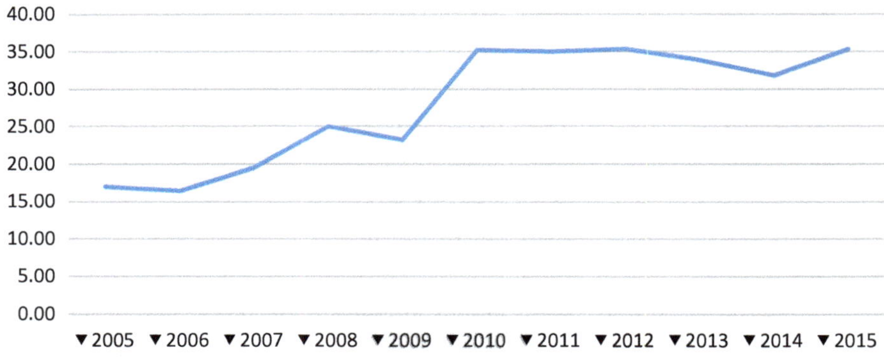

Fig. 7.5 DAC Countries, total grants by private agencies and NGOs in $ billion, 2005–2015. Source: Data from OECD, Official and private flows

period of 2000–2016. After scoring a maximum of $41.69 billion in 2005, and $39.08 billion in 2009, it ended the period with as low as $2.10 billion.

Grant by Private Voluntary Agencies and Non-government Organisations (GPV)

DAC also collects data on Grants offered by voluntary private agencies and non-government organisations (NGOs), in cash, goods or free from charge services. Here, the private sector referes to corporations, households and non-profit institutions. This group is becoming more significant and includes private foundations, which play an increasing role in finding innovative ways to promote development assistance; non-government organisations; and the for-profit private sector. Voluntary private development assistance is measured in million US$ constant prices, using 2014 as the base year. Figure 7.5 plots total grants by private agencies and NGOs in $ billion, from 2005 to 2015. Data are from the OECD Detailed aid statistics (Official and private flows).

The total grants by private agencies and NGOs has increased by 107% over the period from 2005–2015. From its level of 2005 of $17,05 billion, it toped $35,38 Million in 2015 and it is characterized by its steady increase.

Official and Private Flows, OPF

DAC collects data on total official and private flows, defined as the sum of official development assistance, other official flows and private flows (OPF) to a recipient country. Total OPF incorporates the sum of concessional and non-concessional flows to developing countries, including export credits, which have a primarily

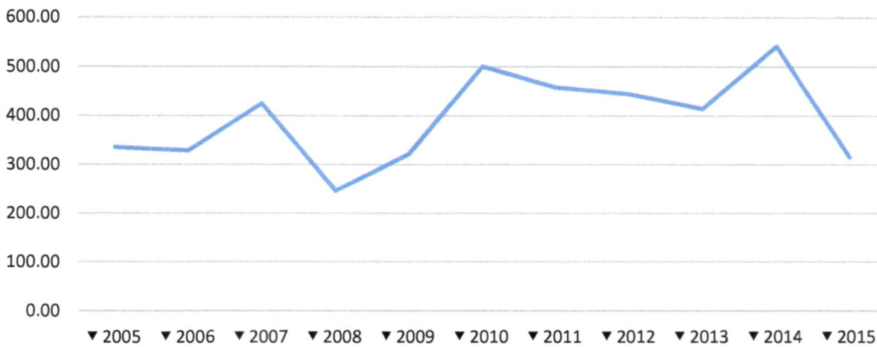

Fig. 7.6 DAC Countries, total official and private flows in $ billion US dollars (2005–2015). Source: Data from OECD, Official and private flows

commercial motive. Private flows are defined as flows at market terms and financed out of private sector resources and private grants. OPF is measured in $ million constant prices, using 2014 as the base year (DAC). Figure 7.6 plots total official and private flows in $ billion US dollars for the period of 2005–2015. Data are obtained from OECD Detailed aid statistics (Official and private flows).

OPF have oscillated between $336,34 billion in 2005 and $542,51 billion in FY 2014, dropping to $315,58 billion in FY 2015, which represents a slight decrease of 6.25%, compared to the 2015 level, but a 62% increase, compared to the FY 2000 level.

Aid for Trade (AfT)

A new aid initiative, worth mentioning here, is the "Aid for Trade" initiative (AFT), launched in 2005, jointly by the OECD and the World Trade Organization (WTO), addressing the trade-related infrastructure constraints that often hamper developing countries' exports and their effective participation in global trade. The AFT initiative aims to encourage both physical connectivity and digital connectivity, within and outside boundaries of developing countries (OECD/WTO 2017). It is believed that while physical connectivity may enable the movement of goods and services in local, regional and global markets, digital connectivity, on the other hand, can be of a larger scope and may enhance developing countries' internal and global trade—and offers greater opportunities for growth (OECD/WTO 2017). Yet Internet connection remains unavailable to 3.9 billion people in the world, many of whom live in the least developed countries (LDCs) (OECD/WTO 2017). Table 7.1 gives total and average aid for trade grants for indicated period and year 2005–2015.

Around $500 billion has been disbursed as AFT support since its launch, an annual average of $35.33 billions and $53.88 billions for the single year of 2015. According to Aid for Trade at a Glance (2017), some 146 developing countries have received AFT: 41.5% in Asia and 38.7% in Africa, with 27% of the total going to

Table 7.1 Aid for trade in $ billion

Period/year (average)	Total $	Average $
2002–2005	93.24004	22.3101
2006–2008	88.0314	29.3438
2009–2011	114.8436	38.2812
2012–2014	144.5841	48.1947
2015	53.8788	53.8788
Total	494.57794	35.32699

Source: OECD-DAC/CRS aid activity database. (OECD/WTO 2017)

less developed countries. More than 75% of total disbursements were allocated to four sectors: transport and storage (28.6%), energy generation and supply (21.6%), agriculture (18.3%), and banking and financial services (11.1%).

Summary on Official Development Aid

Appendix 7.1 to the chapter provides, in addition to the list of DAC members, their official development assistance commitments for the period 2012–2015. These are firm engagements made by governments or official bodies, supported by the provision of, or making available to a developing country, funds at specific terms and conditions. Commitments are considered made on the date of the signing of loan or grant agreement. For fiscal year 2015, a total of $153.25 billion was committed by DAC members in the fight against poverty and development, an increase of 21.62% over the 2012 fiscal year. The main contributors for the year 2015 were the United States with $34.34 billion dollars (22.41%), Japan with $22.055 billion dollars (14.39%), Germany with $21.26 billion dollars (13.88%), the United Kingdom $13 billion, and France $12 billion (8.47%), Since the 1970s, oil-exporting countries have joined the ranks of major donors of development aid, particularly for transport and energy projects in developing countries funding. For fiscal year 2015, $37.17 billion was transferred from DAC member countries to multilateral development agencies, with the EU receiving the largest portion or $11.81 billion, followed by the World Bank Group of $8.5 (mainly IDA), United Nations agencies and regional development banks, respectively, received from DAC countries $4.1 billion and $3.16 billion respectively, for the fiscal year for 2015.[12] The EU receives more transfer from DAC than United Nations agencies and regional development banks combined.

Overall, official development assistance is well diversified and involves large amounts of capital, but remains not very significant in its contributions to developing country finance. The UNDP assesses foreign aid to account for 0.5% of the GDP

[12] http://www.oecd.org/dac/stats/statisticsonresourceflowstodevelopingcountries.htm

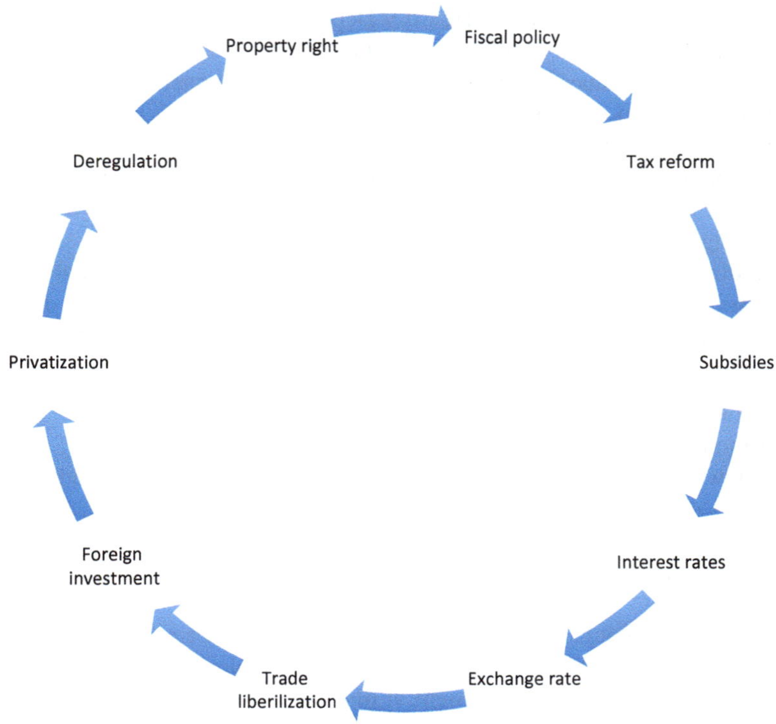

Fig. 7.7 The Washington Consensus

of developing countries. Aid is, however, volatile and therefore does not appear to be suitable for long-term development. Its short-term nature makes it difficult to use in long-term projects funding. By contrast, private flows, mainly foreign direct investments, account for 3.5% of the GDP of developing countries, and only the world's very poorest countries now receive significant amounts of official development assistance (Globalization for all 2002).

Official Development Assistance "Conditionalities"

Despite the relatively easy assistance period of the 1970s, development assistance seems to be somehow drying and seems to have failed to achieve the promised development objective. It is even blamed for having ultimately contributed to an uncontrolled accumulation of third-world debt. This has probably provided fuel for those who would like to attach yet more political conditions to development assistance, as suggested by the so-called Washington consensus, WC. This is a set of ten economic policy prescriptions considered fundamental to economic reform for poor countries, by BWFIs, and the US Treasury Department. The IMF exercises in low-income countries' capacity-building activities focused largely on how they can "boost domestic revenues, manage public finances and monetary policy, regulate the financial system, and develop statistical systems" (IMF 2017f). The sought objective is to help them implement sound policies and good practices. Accordingly, for developing countries to access international aid, they may be required to agree to a specific reform package of economic policies, summarized in WC, as represented in Fig. 7.7:

According to Washington Consensus, countries seeking international development assistance, must first demonstrate having adopted their fiscal policy discipline and the broadening of their tax base. This can be shown by undertaking specific actions like:

1. Avoiding large fiscal deficits, relative to their GDP;
2. Simultaneously diminishing the subsidies of their public spending;
3. Allowing the market to regulate commodity prices, interest rates and exchange rates;
4. Liberating import and foreign direct investment;
5. Eliminating quantitative restrictions and any trade protection to be provided by law;
6. Abolishing regulations that impede market entry or restrict competition, except for those justified on safety, environmental and consumer protection grounds, and prudential oversight of financial institutions;
7. Privatizing their state enterprises while reinforcing the property right;

Privatization in and of itself may do little or nothing to improve economic performance, it may even contribute to its deterioration and may open up new opportunities for corruption. "There is no virtue in converting a state-owned monopoly into a private monopoly, particularly if there is not a set of competition laws in place backed up by a well-resourced regulatory agency" (Globalization for all 2002, p. 74). Further, shedding labour from overstaffed enterprises, through privatization or other means, "improves national productivity only when those workers can find other, more productive employment" (Globalization for all 2002, p. 74). It is clear that the WC's crafters believed deeply that the shorter path to development, more so than international aid, is the opening of local markets to international investment.

Total ODA in the 1990s declined by almost 12% in real terms (German and Randel 2002; Randel and Randel 2002).[13] It becomes clear very quickly that the prosperity promised by the Washington Consensus was merely an illusion; The negative effect of WC on developing assisted countries was, however, real. The Washington Consensus seems to have undermined the traditional economic base of assisted countries and literally erased their manufacturing industries, except for those export oriented (Anderson 2011). Development assistance is also blamed for undermining democratic development processes in developing countries and favour-

[13] Only the former socialist countries in Eastern Europe received increased aid in this period in support of privatisation, market liberalisation and the entry of foreign capital from the West.

ing corruption (Anderson 2011). For the most part, receivers are former colonies of aid donors. What sort of independence can an aid receiver country expect if, after decolonisation, it remains a beggar at the feet of its former colonial masters? asks Anderson (2011). Efficient developing policies may be far from being about laying down a "red carpet" for foreign investors, as suggested by the WC; rather, they are about ensuring all businesses, domestic and foreign alike, optimal investment conditions, in the form of a reasonable set of business rules, sound infrastructure, honest and open government, transparent and fair business regulation, and an effective tax system, (Globalization for all 2002, p. 72).

Faced with WC failure, in 2000 world leaders adopted the so-called Millennium Declaration, committing nations to the path of development (MDGs). This is a series of time targets aimed at reducing extreme poverty by the year 2015, through increased in ODA for health, education, water and sanitation projects and programs, but despite some remarkable progress, this did not happen either, not by the year 2015. ODA seems, however, to work for some developing environments better than for others (Collier 2007), and it is still seen as an important instrument of progress, provided that it is of a temporary duration. It will, however, be deemed effective when developing countries become donors themselves. In the case of the AfDB, for instance, countries like Egypt, Nigeria and South Africa are contributors themselves to African Development Funds, (Kaberuka 2013).

ODA as a proportion of developed countries' GDP, has, indeed, generally fallen over the last few decades. Only Norway, Sweden, Denmark, Netherlands, Luxembourg, Switzerland and Japan now contribute more than $100 per citizen to official development assistance, OECD countries disbursed 0.33% of GDP as aid in 1990. By 2000, this had fallen to 0.22% of GDP, and Japan is the world's major aid donor, followed by the USA, but at only 0.10% of GDP. The USA seems to be the least generous donor of all the developed countries, in term of aid as a percentage of GDP. There has even been strong opposition in the US to ODA to developing countries, mainly because it is believed that it can distort political institutions and foster corruption in these countries (Deaton 2013). It is, however, believed that this cannot be the case for any assistance. Assistance that does not directly meddle with a country's markets, and that is oriented toward human sectors, like medical research, education and so forth, might be highly helpful.

The question as to why in some contexts some approaches to ODA work so well but in others they fail so badly to generate the desired outcome remains unanswered. This may have something to do with the fact that policy coherence over time may barely be easy to achieve, as circumstances constantly change (World Bank 2017b: Governance and Law). It is, however, matter of fact that WC has not explored alternatives for developing countries, other than the opening of their markets to international finance. A more attainable alternative and yet quickly dismissed, would have been the establishment of a fair international exchange system. Rich countries continue manipulating WTO rules for their interests and those of their large multinational corporations. High tariffs, protection rules and support policies are often put in place and have as a direct effect kept developing country from selling their survival products like agricultural products and textiles at derisory prices (Globalization for All 2002, p. 72).

Authors of the Bretton Woods Agreements rightly regarded trade as the other essential basis of their agreement, and not just free trade, but fair trade. They have even thought of an international trade institution, which, unfortunately, has never seen the day. It is only in 2012 that the OECD led a 2-year International Collaborative Initiative on Trade and Employment (ICITE), and "concludes that when supporting policies are in place, growth generated by trade is more inclusive" (IMF_FY_2017_AR). The UNDP, for its part, in its FY 2016 Human Development Report, called for an international agenda that would define rules for trade, goods, services and knowledge that will promote sustainable human development.

Causes of Inefficiencies of Official Development Aid

Many reasons may have caused ODA to appear to be or to be inefficient in the fight against poverty and gain in development. We can mention, for instance:

1. The fact that ODA is usually employed as a Cold War instrument for allegiance purposes, and not for specific development objectives;
2. The fact that international development assistance is often seen as an instrument of dependence, aiming to perpetuate colonization (Sarkin 2008);
3. The use of ODA for trade purposes, in a way in which much of the development assistance is actually tied to purchases from donor countries, as it is highly cancelled by high consultancy fees. Some major donor countries, such as Japan, tie their assistance to the spending of a very large proportion of it, in Japan;
4. The fact that a proportion of ODA is made for humanitarian objectives, such as education, health, sanitation and the like, whose effect on development is felt only in the long term;
5. The promised access of developing countries to the world markets, and facilitating the funding of development projects and trade, did never happen, for most of them;
6. The fact that developing economies are judged not on their real economic performance, but rather on their capacity to generate a set of financial indicators which conform to the standards of the world market (Globalization for all 2002, p. 72). Consequently, policies directed toward achieving full employment have to take second place to policies directed toward achieving balanced and small public budgets (Globalization for all 2002, p. 72);
7. The fact that most developing countries fail to engage in effective development processes aimed at minimizing poverty and promoting growth (World Bank 2017b: Governance and Law); instead, they devote their energy to short-term problem solving.

Conclusion

Recent decades of economic growth have helped lift more than 1 billion people out of poverty (World Bank). While this is a remarkable achievement in and of itself, and one that deserves credit and admiration, it should not obscure the fact that one in five people in developing regions still live on less than $1.25 a day, and still face violence, slow or regressive growth, limited opportunities for advancement, and barriers to personal fulfilment. The international community has responded honourably to the challenge of poverty in the world and not just in words. It took firm engagement to fight poverty and has pledged trillions of dollars for this purpose. The period from 2012 to 2016 alone saw more than a trillion $ spent by the international community on development assistance, and this amount did not include some DAC undeclared assistance. Some major players in international cooperation do not actually report their transactions to the DAC. Official Development Assistance (ODA) is now complimented by other forms of development cooperation, including South-South Cooperation (SSC), Triangular Cooperation (TrC), and peer learning, etc., and this has resulted in the need to coordinate an increased number of partners and modalities of development cooperation and finance (UNDP 2014).

Although official assistance, as a proportion of developed countries' GDP, has generally fallen over the last few decades, huge amounts in the hundreds of billions a year are still involved and a strong correlation between this expenditure and the sought goal of poverty reduction should be expected. The next chapter will try to find out if development assistance really fails expectation, and if this is in fact the case, then it would be essential to find out why and rather than instantaneously blaming development assistance whenever a suggested policy fails to achieve the desired result. Concessional assistance should, however, be free from blame, given the substantial number of poor and vulnerable countries that still need it.

Appendix 7.1: DAC Members and Commitments, $ Billions for Each of the Years from 2012 to 2015, in Billions of Dollars

Year	2015	2014	2013	2012
Australia	3.48934	3.62927	3.75523	3.48934
Austria	1.40439	1.11041	1.19592	1.40439
Belgium	2.05264	2.41905	2.25371	2.05264
Canada	5.67823	3.84801	3.7214	5.67823
Czech Republic	0.2231	0.20154	0.20967	0.2231
Denmark	2.4943	2.48533	2.30925	2.4943
Finland	0.87722	1.36972	1.92699	0.87722
France	12.97823	12.55429	10.69555	12.97823
Germany	21.26428	21.20317	17.3928	21.26428
Greece	0.23869	0.20467	0.23631	0.23869
Iceland	0.03988	0.03498	0.03561	0.03988
Ireland	0.71838	0.71562	0.7327	0.71838
Italy	4.38552	3.66788	3.35465	4.38552
Japan	22.04869	19.18258	20.52143	22.04869
Korea	2.93157	2.55777	2632.89	2.93157
Luxembourg	0.36043	0.35521	0.36833	0.36043
Netherlands	6.62763	6.30402	3.64255	6.62763
New Zealand	0.45191	0.56863	0.39897	0.45191
Norway	4.70295	4.5233	3.85773	4.70295
Poland	0.51735	0.61567	0.42605	0.51735
Portugal	0.38547	0.41681	0.47079	0.38547
Slovak Republic	0.0971	0.07662	0.06894	0.0971
Slovenia	0.05918	0.05242	0.11936	0.05918
Spain	1.73223	1.92875	1.91046	1.73223
Sweden	6.54883	4.50495	3.60794	6.54883
Switzerland	3.07767	4.82018	4.29817	3.07767
United Kingdom	13.37225	12.92885	10.47678	13.37225
United States	34.34183	34.32731	33.71724	34.34183
Total DAC	153.25486	146.607	134.33743	153.25486

Source: OECD (2017), "Detailed aid statistics: ODA Official development assistance: disbursements", *OECD International Development Statistics* (database), https://doi.org/10.1787/data-00069-en, (Accessed on 12 July 2017)

Chapter 8
Empirical Assessment of Official Development Assistance Efficiency

Over the last half century, trillions of official aid funds have been spent in official development aid, ODA and World Bank Group Assistance (WBGA), and some believe the world is nowhere closer to achieving the promised elimination of poverty and development advance (Easterly 2006). In recent years, ODA, including the World Bank Group assistance, has been the topic of many public discussions, often with controversial and contrasting opinions, and after seven decades of ODA, there is still no consensus on whether it works. The chapter argues that if we cannot even agree on whether development aid works at all, how can we address the more important and nuanced questions of how to make it more effective? It, therefore, studies the economic effect of development assistance in the fight against poverty and the scoring of development

This chapter assesses empirically the macro economic success of development assistance and WBG Assistance by comparing yearly assistance to a given developing country to the improvement in its yearly per capita Gross Domestic Product (pcGDP). Section one discusses the Historical development of development aid; section two presents the sample, data, variables and methodology; section three present the results and section four concludes.

Historical Development of ODA

Since the Bretton Woods Agreement, awareness about the damage and deprivation of underdevelopment and extreme poverty has become part of the international community's agenda and a variety of ways to provide economic assistance to poor countries have been experimented with, ranging from loans on nearly commercial terms, to grants and highly concessional conditions. Global ODA has increased considerably. Net official aid reached yet another peak in 2016 of 0.32% of gross national income, driven in part by increased spending on in-donor refugee costs (Development Co-operation's 2016 progress report). ODA expressed as a

A. Naciri, *The Governance Structures of the Bretton Woods Financial Institutions*,
SpringerBriefs in Economics, https://doi.org/10.1007/978-3-319-97906-9_8

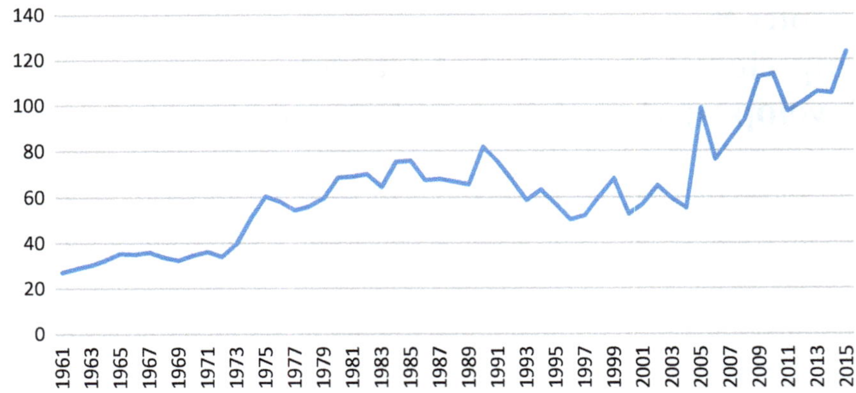

Fig. 8.1 ODF annual average, $ billion (1961–2015). Source: World Bank Data

percentage of the GNI of developing beneficiaries for the year 2015 represented 89.2% of the GNI of a country like Tuvalu and only 0.0214% for a country like Chile. Annual pcGDP growth for developing countries in the sample and for the fiscal year 2015 also oscillated between 7.04% for the Dominican Republic to −28.10 for the Yemen republic. Development assistance is supposed to have three major aims (Severino and Ray 2009; Ocampo 2015):

1. Supporting and complementing efforts of developing countries allowing them to guarantee the provision of universal social basic standards to their citizens, as a means for people to exercise their basic human rights;
2. Promoting the convergence of the developing countries to higher levels of income and wellbeing, correcting extreme international inequalities; and
3. Supporting efforts of developing countries to participate actively in the provision of international public goods.

The number of donor countries has also increased, since the Bretton Woods Agreement, indeed, most industrial countries, OPEC members, and other advanced and middle economies have become bilateral donors, while multilateral institutions such as the World Bank, the regional development banks, the OPEC and European Community development funds, and some UN agencies, have increased their financial contributions to development enhancement. These development-oriented forms of official development aid are generally referred to as official aid flows (ODF) and they are particularly made in the form of concessional flows or official development assistance (ODA), but also made of the World Bank Group assistance (WBGA), such as IBRD loans and IDA assistance, and even of the IMF assistance. Figure 8.1 gives an overview of the extent of the official development flows, including WBGA, for the period 1961–2015. Data are in current $ Million.

Figure 8.1 indicates that ODF to development funding has kept increasing since 1961. From the level of $27.44 billions in 1961, it scored $123,60 billion by FY 2015, an increase of over 440%. The total ODF for the whole period topped $3509.29 billion by the FY 2016, a yearly average of $125.33 billion. This is equivalent to $7000 for each individual on earth, but where does the money go?

Around 60% of aid is actually a long-term contribution to the provision of key services such as education, health, water and sanitation, and an investment in the institutions needed to provide them in the future. There seems to be plenty of evidence of the success of individual aid projects, and its proponents argue that development aid has brought about substantial improvements in people's lives (Sachs 2006; Riddel 2007). Aid has helped to abolish smallpox, to increase the number of children in primary school, and to give families access to clean water and improved sanitation (Barder 2011). It was also argued that when measured by almost every standard other than income, the quality of life has improved substantially in developing countries. Foreign aid has made a significant contribution to these improvements (Kenny 2011).

Others, however, argue that aid is not only ineffective, but it is actually detrimental to development (Moyo 2009) and that trillions of dollars of aid have had little effect (Easterly 2001). Further, "a dependence on aid is akin to 'putting all one's eggs in the same basket" (UNDP 2011). Aid may also expose countries to sharp fluctuations in the volume of aid, but also in terms of donor preferences of the purposes to which aid is used (UNDP 2011). Volatility and pro-cyclicality of aid can have a serious effect: Where aid is volatile or unpredictable, recipient governments are less able to plan expenditures effectively. This can worsen the composition of government spending but not all volatility in aid is necessarily negative; volatility in aid can be associated with aid shortfalls and aid windfalls (UNDP 2011), and the empirical evidence suggests that, on average, aid is pro-cyclical, and can exacerbate rather than mitigate the impacts of business (UNDP 2011).

Official aid effectiveness appears to be weakened by mercantile considerations, geopolitics and security interests of donor countries. US foreign aid, for instance, as the main source of official aid, during its first 40 years, seemed to have been oriented towards containing communism. Indeed, in the 1990s it was tasked with helping "demolish" the Soviet economic and social system (Sogge 2009). Similarly, in the aftermath of the 9/11, only 28% of new aid money was left to honour pledges of increased aid for poverty reduction and MDGs; the bigger part was used for the fight against terrorism (Tomlinson 2008, p. 206). Even in the rare instances where aid was considered a success, in terms of development outcomes, like in the Marshall Plan for Europe in the 1940s, or the aid for South Korea and Taiwan in the 1950s and 1960s, it was granted primarily in the interest of the donor's geopolitical objectives.

If we cannot even agree on whether development aid works at all, how can we address the more important and nuanced questions of how to make it more effective? Our investigation aims, therefore, to study the economic effect of ODF and WBGA, regarding the fight against poverty and the scoring of development.

Sample, Data, Variables and Methodology

In order to study the effect of ODF and WBGA on the fight against poverty and for development advance, the growth of the per capita gross national product (ΔpcGDP) will be used as dependent variable to assess improvement/deterioration in developing countries' economic performance, which might be related to the volume of official aid received. Consequently, the first variable (the dependent variable) to be used in this analysis is the annual percentage growth rate of per capita GDP at market price (ΔpcGDP). Country economic development is commonly measured by the growth of the GDP, defined as the annual percentage growth rate at market prices, based on constant local currency (World Bank). GDP is the sum of gross value added by all resident producers in the economy, plus any product taxes and minus any subsidies not included in the value of the products. It is calculated without making deductions for depreciation of fabricated assets or for depletion and degradation of natural resources. GDP is to be distinguished from GNI, which is a nation's GDP increased by the net income from overseas received by the country. The per capita GDP is the overall GDP divided by the country population. Despite limitations and critics, "per capita income or GDP does capture the main component of well-being" (Bannister and Mourmouras 2018).

Data on ΔpcGDP are retrieved from the World Bank DataBank and aggregates are based on constant 2010 U.S. dollars. The following variables will be used as independent variables to conduct our empirical analysis:

1. ODF representing the inflow of resources to developing countries (OECD, Glossary of Key Terms and Concepts): includes (a) bilateral official development assistance (ODA), (b) grants and concessional and non-concessional development lending by multilateral financial institutions, and (c) Other Official Flows for development purposes (including refinancing Loans) which have too low a Grant Element to qualify as ODA.
2. WBGA, the World Bank group assistance to a given country, whose data are retrieved from the World Bank DataBank. These are the IBRD loans and IDA credits. IBRD lends at market rates; IDA grants are made at concessional rates.
3. G, country grouping, obtained by classifying developing countries of the sample in three categories (the grouping is based on GNI level instead of GDP level, because this is the only classification available):

   - Group #1, composed of "Least Developed Countries", whose GNI per capita in 2013 was under the $1,045 threshold.
   - Group #2, composed of "Lower Middle Income developing countries", whose GNI per capita in 2013, was located within the bracket of $1,046–$4,125; and
   - Group #3, composed of "Upper Middle Income developing countries", whose per capita GNI in 2013, was located within the bracket of $4,126–$12,745.

Data and Sample

The World Bank DataBank is used to gather data on ΔpcGDP, ODF and WBGA. This is a collection of development indicators that are compiled from officially recognized international sources and represents the most current and accurate global development data available. The sample is composed of all eligible borrowing member countries, in the list drawn by the World Bank. Appendix 8.1 gives the list of countries composing the main sample and sub-groupings. It includes 141 developing economies, 52 Least Developed Countries and Territories, 42 Lower Middle Income Countries and Territories, and 47 Upper Middle Income Countries and Territories. In 2012, low- and middle-income economies represented 81.55% of the world population, and 118.18% of its growth. Their GNI, computed by the World Bank Atlas method, represents 30.57% of the world GNI. Table 8.1 describes the main variables used in the study and compares economic performance of low- and middle-income economies to high-income economies and the world.

Beside re-underlining the fact that in 2012, 12.02% of the world population was getting less than 1% of the world's wealth (0.7%), as measured by the GDP, Table 8.1 also indicates that only 31.42% of the world's wealth is shared by 81.55% of the world's population, which lives in low- and middle-income economies, leaving 81.55% of the total wealth to 18.44% of the world population, living in "high-income" economies. It is, however, important to observe that the relative economic progress within low-income and low- and middle-income economies, is higher. For instance, ΔGDP growth in percentage is 4.9% and 6.3% for "low-income" and "low- and middle-income" economies, respectively, while only 1.5% for "high-income" economies. This is also the case for the value added in agriculture in % of GDP, imports of goods and services in % of GDP, and central government cash surplus/deficit in % of GDP, which show higher values for developing economies than for high-income economies. However, low-income and low- and middle-income economies suffer a significant inefficiency at the level of the value added in industry, in % of GDP, value added in services, exports of goods and services, and gross capital formation.

Methodology

The period covered by the study is 1960–2015 for ODF and 1970–2014 for WBGA. A regression analysis is run on data, and Eqs. 8.1 and 8.2 describe the statistical relationship between the growth of the pcGDP and the ODF and WBGA.

$$\Delta GDP_i = \alpha + \beta_1 ODF_i + \varepsilon_i \tag{8.1}$$

$$\Delta GDP_i = \alpha + \beta_1 WBGA_i + \varepsilon_i \tag{8.2}$$

where:

ΔGDP_i is the annual percentage growth rate of GDP at market prices based on constant local currency. Aggregates are based on constant 2010 U.S. dollars. GDP_i is the sum of gross value added by all resident producers in the economy plus any product taxes and minus any subsidies not included in the

Table 8.1 Sample significant characteristics, compared to the world and high-income economies, FY2012

	Population (millions)	Population growth (%)	Surface area (1000 km²)	Pop, living below $1.25 a day (%)	GNI, Atlas ($ billions)	GNI per capita, Atlas ($)	GNI, PPP ($ billions)	GNI per capita, PPP ($)
World	7,043.90	1.10	134.29	–	71,692.40	10,178.00	85,986.80	12,207.00
High income economies	1,299.00	0.30	53.88	–	49,905.70	38,394.00	50,055.10	38,509.00
In % World	18.44	27.27	40.12		69.61	377.23	58.21	315.47
Low and middle income	5,744.10	1.30	80,410	20.60	21,916.10	3,815.00	36,250.50	6,311.00
In % World	81.55	118.18	59,877.88		30.57	37.48	42.16	51.70
Low income economies	846.50	2.30	16,198.00	48.30	499.40	590.00	1,171.10	1,383.00
In % World	12.02	209.09	12,061.96		0.70	5.80	1.36	11.33

Source: Computed based on the little data book WBG

Table 8.2 Models' descriptive statistics

Model	Variable	Mean	Std. deviation
$\Delta GDP_i = \alpha + \beta_1 ODF_i + \beta_2 G_i + \varepsilon_i$ N = 4909 (1961–2014)	ΔGDP_i	4.0403	6.15789
	ODF_i	\$618.66 million	\$980.87 million
	G_i	1.8861	0.75980
$\Delta GDP_i = \alpha + \beta_1 WBGA_i + \beta_2 G_i + \varepsilon_i$ N: 3773 (1970–2014)	ΔGDP_i	3.88%	6.06%
	$WBGA_i$	\$1,350.24 million	\$3,241.9 million
	G_i	1.88	0.752

value of the products. It is calculated without making deductions for depreciation of fabricated assets or for depletion and degradation of natural resources.

ODFi represents the inflow of resources to developing countries.

$WBGA_i$ represents IBRD loans and IDA grants that are public and/or publicly guaranteed debt extended by the World Bank Group.

α, β & ε are regression coefficients and the error term.

It is possible, however, that the effect of development financial assistance is also dependent on developing countries' grouping, following World Bank classification:

- "Least Developed Countries and Territories", (per capita GNI ≤ \$1,045 in 2013) (G = 1),
- "Lower Middle Income Countries and Territories", (per capita GNI between \$1,046–\$4,125 in 2013) (G = 2), and
- **"**Upper Middle Income", (per capita GNI between \$4,126–\$12,745) (**G = 3**).

Equation 8.3 describes the statistical relationship between the growth of the pcGDP and international development assistance and developing countries grouping. Equation 8.4, on the other hand, describes the statistical relationship between the growth of the pcGDP and WBGA and developing countries grouping.

$$\Delta GDP_i = \alpha + \beta_1 ODF_i + \beta_2 G_i + \varepsilon_i \tag{8.3}$$

$$DP_i = \alpha + \beta_1 WBGA_i + \beta_2 G_i + \varepsilon_i \tag{8.4}$$

where: as defined

ODF_i and $WBGA_i$ are as defined before, and
G_i is country grouping: **1** Least Developed Countries, 2 Middle Income, and 3 Upper Middle Income.

Table 8.2 describes the regressions used in the study.

$\Delta pcGDP_i$ is the dependent variable in both regressions one and two, and it represents annual variations of the pcGDP for the period from 1961 to 2014 for regression 1 and from 1970 to 2014, for regression 2, leading to 4,909 and 3,773

Table 8.3 Model summary: $\Delta GDP_i = \alpha + \beta_1 ODF_i + \varepsilon_I$

Model	R	R Square	Adjusted R Square	Std. error of the estimate
1	0.033[a]	0.001	0.001	6.13959

[a]Predictors: (Constant), ODF

Table 8.4 Coefficients[a]: $\Delta GDP_i = \alpha + \beta_1 ODF_i + \varepsilon_i$

		Unstandardized coefficients	Std.	Standardized coefficients		
Model		B	error	Beta	t	Sig.
1	(Constant)	3.920	0.104		37.805	0.000
	ODF	0.000	0.000	0.033	2.307	0.021

[a]Dependent variable: ΔGDP_i

Table 8.5 Model summary: $\Delta GDP_i = \alpha + \beta_1 ODF_i + \beta_2 G_i + \varepsilon_I$

Model	R	R Square	Adjusted R square	Std. error of the estimate
1	0.076[a]	0.006	0.005	6.12784

[a]Predictors: (Constant), G_i, ODF_i

observations, respectively. The means and Standards Deviation of ΔpcGDP, the dependent variable, is \$4.04 and 6.16% for regression one and \$3.88 and 6.06% for regression two. This indicates a significant economic progress in developing countries, but also a large disparity of their economic performance. ODF_i, and G_i are the independent variables for regressions 3, and $WBGA_i$ and G_i, are the independent variables for regressions 4. An annual average of \$618.66 millions, for the period from 1961 to 2014 was handed on average to each developing countries as official development flows, with a standard deviation of \$980.87 million for the period 1970–2014, an annual average of \$1,350.24 million of WBG assistance was on average granted to each recipient, with a standard deviation of \$3,241.90 million. Finally, the independent variable G_i in any regression is meant to detect the effect of the classification of developing countries by their level of economic advance.

Results

As a first step, we consider the result of regressions 1 and 3, trying to discover the relation between ODF and economic development. With an R of 0.33, an R-Square of 0.001 an adjusted R-Square of 0.001(Table 8.3), regression one leads us to conclude that official development flows have a very low impact on the developing countries' progress in their per capita gross domestic product.

The conclusion of the weak effect of development assistance on developing countries' economic advance is confirmed by the low level of the Standardized beta coefficient of the independent variable ODF of 0.033, given in Table 8.4, with its significance at the 5% level ($p = 0.021$).

Table 8.6 Coefficients[a]: $\Delta GDP_i = \alpha + \beta_1 ODF_i + \beta_2 G_i + \varepsilon_I$

Model		Unstandardized coefficients B	Std. error	Standardized coefficients Beta	t	Sig.
1	(Constant)	4.957	0.239		20.738	0.000
	ODFi	0.000	0.000	0.035	2.486	0.013
	G_i	−0.554	0.115	−0.069	−4.807	0.000

[a]Dependent variable: ODF

Table 8.7 Model summary, $\Delta GDP_i = \alpha + \beta_1 WBGA_i + \varepsilon_i$

Model	R	R Square	Adjusted R square	Std. error of the estimate
1	0.025[a]	0.001	0.000	5.735

[a]Predictors: (Constant), WBGA

Table 8.5 gives the regression result of the impact of Official Development Flows (ODF) on developing countries' economic progress, taking into account the classification of developing countries, by the level of their income, etc.

The inclusion of a second independent variable, G, which discriminates the impact of the ODF by the group of countries the recipient belongs to, somewhat increases the explanatory power of the regression. The R is now 0.076, an R-Square of 0.006 and a standardized R-Square of 0.005 (Table 8.6).

The independent G has a negative beta coefficient and seems to represent 55% of the explanatory power of the model, meaning that the impact of ODFs on some groups of developing countries may have been weakened by their level of development. Here again the results are significant (p = 0.000).

As second step, we consider the results of regressions 2 and 4, trying to discover the relationship between WBG assistance and economic development. The R-Square value 0.000, (the "R-Square" Column, regression 2), indicates that IBRD loans and IDA assistance appear to have no significant effect on developing countries' economic progress. The R^2 value (the "R-Square" column) indicates how much of the total variation in the increase in GDP can be explained by the independent variable. The "Sig." indicates the statistical significance of the regression models used. World Bank Group assistance seems to explain 0.000% of developing countries' economic performance, with $p < 0.05$, indicating the overall statistical significance of the regression model and its good fits for the data (Table 8.7).

Table 8.8 gives the beta coefficients, *t*-value and significance of the *t*-value associated for regression 2. The beta analysis may complement our investigation. A beta coefficient is the degree of change in the outcome variable for every 1-unit of change in the predictor variable. The *t*-test assesses whether the beta coefficient is significantly different from zero.

Here again the non-significance of IBRD loans and IDA assistance is clear, with a very low and non-significant beta coefficient (b = 4.479E − 13, p = 0.12). WBGA does not significantly predict economic progress.

Table 8.9 summarizes the results of regression 4 analysis when developing countries are grouped by the level of their economic advance.

Table 8.8 The beta coefficients, $\Delta GDP_i = \alpha + \beta_1 WBGA_i + \varepsilon_I$

Model		Unstandardized coefficients		Standardized coefficients		
		B	Std. error	Beta	t	Sig.
1	(Constant)	4.117	0.102		40.356	0.000
	WBGA	4.479E − 13	0.000	0.025	1.555	0.120

[a]Dependent variable: ΔGDP_i

Table 8.9 Model Summary: $\underline{\Delta}GDP_i = \alpha + \beta_1 WBGA_i + \beta_2 G_i + \varepsilon_I$

Model	R	R Square	Adjusted R square	Std. error of the estimate
1	0.065[a]	0.004	0.004	6.06221

[a]Predictors: (Constant), G_i, WBGA

Table 8.10 Coefficients[a]: $\Delta GDP_i = \alpha + \beta_1 WBGA_i + \beta_2 G_i + \varepsilon_I$

Model		Unstandardized coefficients		Standardized coefficients		
		B	Std. error	Beta	t	Sig.
1	(Constant)	2.764	0.296		9.332	0.000
	WBGA	1.748E − 11	0.000	0.009	0.573	0.567
	G	0.517	0.131	0.064	3.938	0.000

[a]Dependent Variable: WBGA

The R-Square value 0.04, indicates that IBRD loans and IDA development financial assistance appear to account for only 4% of developing countries' economic advance. Such an effect, as underlined in Table 8.10, is only due to the segmentation of developing countries in G1 "**Least** Developed Countries", G2 "Middle Income", and G3 **"**Upper Middle Income". The beta coefficient for WBGA is insignificant, and the one for G is positive and significant ($G = 0.517$, $p = 0.000$). The upgrading of a developing country from one group to the next higher, makes its ΔGDP improve by 51.7%.

Recall from regression 3 that the beta coefficient for G was negative, although insignificant, but here the beta coefficient is positive. It seems that G is more sensitive to World Bank Group Assistance than to official development flows, also including non-concessional development lending by multilateral financial institutions, and Other Official Flows for development purposes (including refinancing Loans), which have too low a Grant Element to qualify as ODA.

The regression results may come as surprise and several elements may explain them:

1. First, the quality of the data can be the cause, given that many developing countries may show a misleading deficit in data collection and presentation;
2. Second, significant part of international official aid is oriented to humanitarian activities;
3. Third, historically, development aid seems to be mainly mercantile and politically oriented (Sogge 2009), and fighting poverty seems to be secondary among foreign aid's main purposes;

4. Fourth, "[…] conflict, disasters and political instability have too often led to uncoordinated, unsustainable, expensive and even dangerous aid projects" (Oxfam 2011).
5. Fifth, the assistance benefit is significantly subdued by the so called the "boomerang" phenomena, where an important portion of the assistance is returned to the "donor" in the form of salaries for highly paid foreign workers and profits for foreign companies, which have the inside running on lucrative aid contracts (Anderson 2011).

Conclusion

Analysis in this chapter could not show the positive impact of development assistance on developing countries in their development endeavour, although common sense would tip the scale in favour of such a possibility. Developing countries' grouping (the independent variable G), appears to have a certain effect, although an insignificant one. This may point to the possibility that aid programs may be poorly monitored. "The outcomes of privately contracted projects are mostly held secret under 'commercial confidentiality' provisions, preventing scrutiny" (Anderson 2011), and therefore are impossible to assess independently. The results may also point to some characteristics of developing countries that may affect their development, besides international assistance. The next chapter will explore such possibilities.

Appendix 8.1: Total and Sub Samples

Upper middle income, (per capita GNI $4126–$12,745). (Sub-sample 1)		Lower middle income countries and territories, (per capita GNI $1046–$4125 in 2013) (Sub-sample 2)		Least developed countries and territories, (per capita GNI ≤ $1045 in 2013) (Sub-sample 3)	
Country	GNI per capita (US$)	Country	GNI per capita (US$)	Country	GNI per capita (US$)
		Georgia	4,120	Djibouti	1,030
Palau	12,180	Guyana	4,090	Senegal	1,000
Panama	11,880	Kosovo	3,960	Tanzania	910
Nauru	11,850	El Salvador	3,940	Chad	880
Venezuela	11,780	Tunisia	3,930	Benin	860
Russia	11,720	Samoa	3,930	Zimbabwe	850
Kazakhstan	11,390	Armenia	3,880	Haiti	820
Malaysia	10,570	Mongolia	3,870	Mali	790
Costa Rica	10,400	Sri Lanka	3,800	South Sudan	790

Upper middle income, (per capita GNI $4126–$12,745). (Sub-sample 1)		Lower middle income countries and territories, (per capita GNI $1046–$4125 in 2013) (Sub-sample 2)		Least developed countries and territories, (per capita GNI ≤ $1045 in 2013) (Sub-sample 3)	
Country	GNI per capita (US$)	Country	GNI per capita (US$)	Country	GNI per capita (US$)
Brazil	9,990	Guatemala	3,590	Comoros	790
Turkey	9,950	Micronesia, Federated States of	3,560	Nepal	730
Mauritius	9,780	Philippines	3,550	Rwanda	700
Mexico	9,710	Indonesia	3,440	Uganda	670
Romania	9,510	Kiribati	3,390	Burkina Faso	660
Suriname	9,360	Egypt	3,340	Afghanistan	630
Gabon	9,200	Cabo Verde	3,280	Sierra Leone	630
Grenada	8,650	Swaziland	3,280	Ethiopia	590
China	7,900	Vanuatu	3,160	Guinea-Bissau	590
Lebanon	7,710	Palestine	3,090	Mozambique	580
Bulgaria	7,480	Morocco	3,030	Togo	654
Turkmenistan	7,380	Bolivia	3,000	Eritrea	530
Saint Lucia	7,350	Nigeria	2,790	Korea, North	500
Montenegro	7,220	Ukraine	2,640	Guinea	192
Colombia	7,140	Congo, Republic of the	2,540	Gambia	470
Maldives	6,950	Bhutan	2,380	Madagascar	420
Dominica	6,800	Timor Leste	2,290	Congo, Democratic Republic of the	410
Belarus	6,470	Honduras	2,280	Niger	390
Botswana	6,460	Papua New Guinea	2,240	Liberia	380
Iran	6,550	Moldova	2,240	Central African Republic	320
Dominican Republic	6,240	Uzbekistan	2,160	Malawi	350
Tuvalu	6,230	Vietnam	1,990	Burundi	260
Peru	6,130	Nicaragua	1,940		
South Africa	6,080	Sudan	1,920		
Ecuador	6,030	Solomon Islands	1,920		
Libya	6,030	Syria	1,850		
Cuba	5,910	São Tomé and Príncipe	1,760		
Iraq	5,820	Laos	1,740		
Thailand	5,720	India	1,590		
Serbia	5,540	Zambia	1,490		
Namibia	5,190	Ghana	1,480		
Macedonia, Republic of	5,140	Pakistan	1,440		

Upper middle income, (per capita GNI $4126–$12,745). (Sub-sample 1)		Lower middle income countries and territories, (per capita GNI $1046–$4125 in 2013) (Sub-sample 2)		Least developed countries and territories, (per capita GNI ≤ $1045 in 2013) (Sub-sample 3)	
Country	GNI per capita (US$)	Country	GNI per capita (US$)	Country	GNI per capita (US$)
Jamaica	4,930	Côte d'Ivoire	1,420		
Algeria	4,850	Mauritania	1,370		
Fiji	4,830	Kenya	1,340		
Marshall Islands	4,770	Cameroon	1,320		
Jordan	4,680	Lesotho	1,280		
Bosnia and Herzegovina	4,670	Tajikistan	1,240		
Belize	4,490	Bangladesh	1,190		
Albania	4,280	Kyrgyzstan	1,170		
Tonga	4,280	Myanmar	1,160		
Paraguay	4,190	Yemen	1,140		
Angola	4,180	Cambodia	1,070		
Number of countries	50	50		30	

Source: World Bank

Chapter 9
Empirical Assessment of the Impact of Public Governance on Development

The previous chapter points to the statistical non-significance of development assistance in developing countries' economic progress. Although the findings may reinforce the believe of the irrelevance of official development aid, it should, however, be kept in mind that such apparent failures may also be the result of elements outside the control of international development assistance institutions, and we must be careful not to quickly underestimate the wise and helpful job undertaken by well-intentioned individuals (officials and non-officials), and the incremental progress that has been made in the fight of poverty. Official development assistance may require more attention to unearth the causes of failure, mainly weakness of public governance.

This chapter explores other possible answers to ODA perceived failure and points to the weakness of public social and economic governance of aid receivers as possible dampening elements to its efficiency. The second section discusses the public economic governance model. The third section discusses the public social governance model. The fourth section presents the sample, the data and the methodology; section five discusses the results; and the last section concludes the chapter.

Public Governance

Governments commonly use a battery of social and economic policies to develop their nations and allows them to prosper, policies that summarized by the term public governance (PG). The notion of PG may find its rational in the neoclassical thinking,[1] as suggested by Adam Smith in his book "The Wealth of Nations", where "basic institutions that protect the liberty of individuals to pursue their own

[1] Neoclassical economics is an approach to economics that relates supply and demand to an individual's rationality and ability to maximize utility or profit. https://www.investopedia.com/terms/n/neoclassical.asp#ixzz54RxHVOnU

A. Naciri, *The Governance Structures of the Bretton Woods Financial Institutions*, SpringerBriefs in Economics, https://doi.org/10.1007/978-3-319-97906-9_9

economic interests, and exploit to the maximum their talent, result in greater prosperity for the larger society". The responsibility of governments is to ensure social and economic freedom for individuals and institutions, allowing them to prosper individually and collectively. Consequently, they will be encouraged to pursue their dreams and free their innovative potential, to secure and protect their human resources, labour and private property. Economic and social freedoms appear usually to be reinforced in developed economies. The purpose of the chapter is to uncover the link between social and economic governance and national economic advances. Public governance can be divided in public economic governance (PEG), and public social governance (PSG), to be discussed in next two sections.

Public Economic Governance (PEG)

Public economic governance is based on the concept of economic freedom and self-ownership. This is the scenario in which individuals have a right to choose and to decide how to use their time and talents to shape their lives and pursue their dreams. Public economic governance has as several foundational principles, such as personal choice, voluntary exchange, open markets, and clearly defined and enforced property rights. Individuals are considered *"to be economically free when they are permitted to choose for themselves and engage in voluntary transactions as long as they do not harm the person or property of others [...]"* (Fraser Institute 2017). Critics, however, have contested the assumption that economic openness necessarily leads to better growth; instead, they pointed out, as examples, that countries with good ratings such as Switzerland and Uruguay had sluggish economic performances, while others like China, with a poorer rating, had very strong economic growth (Sachs 2006). It may make sense, however, that once citizens are permitted to expand and go to the end of their possibilities, domestic energies and local potentialities will work better for national development.

It is expected, at least in theory, that public economic governance (PEG) should foster economic growth, and for multiple reasons (The Heritage Foundation 2017, p. ix): First, "nations with higher degrees of economic freedom prosper", because they tend to capitalize more fully on the knowledge and ability of all individuals in their society; second, the use of the free-market system as a framework for organizing, without coercion, the skills, talents, and effort of individuals helps enhance the production of the goods and services most in demand; and third, for society as a whole, the efficient allocation of resources is supposed to generate dynamic economic growth and promote innovation. It is the responsibility of each government to ensure economic freedom for its citizens, and by doing so, it will hopefully ensure a high level of public economic governance. Attempts were made to measure the degree of public economic governance in the world's nations, with one major attempt made through the Economic Freedom Index (EFI),[2] developed by The

[2]The other index is the *Economic Freedom of the World* (EFW), originally developed by Fraser Institute.

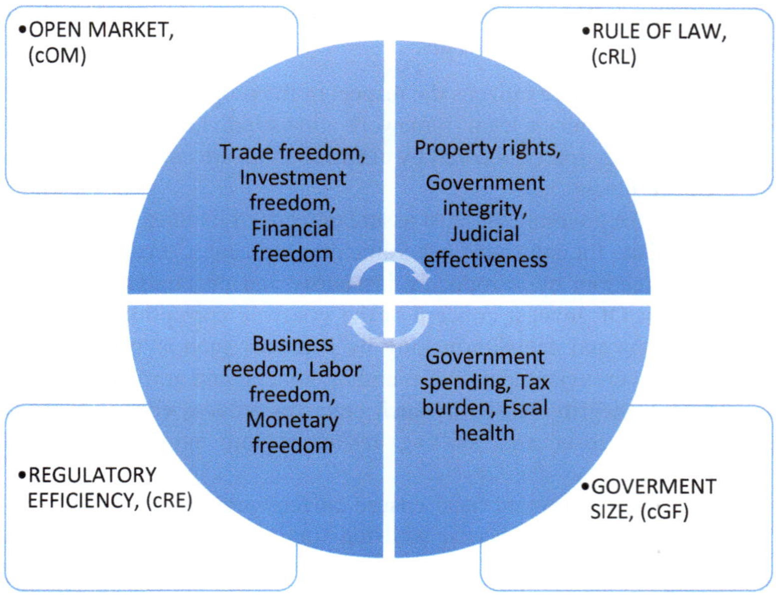

Fig. 9.1 Public economic governance model. Source: The Heritage Foundation

Heritage Foundation and The Wall Street Journal. This index appears to be more helpful, particularly for data work. On the other hand, the Fund for Peace Index will be used as a proxy for public social governance (PSG), also to be discussed. Our objective in this chapter is to find out whether public economic governance and/or public social governance have any impact on economic performance. The economic freedom index will be used as a proxy for public economic governance and the social freedom index will be used as a proxy for public economic governance.

Figure 9.1 summarises the PEG process as deducted from the Economic Freedom Index of the Heritage Foundation.

The PEG model is composed of four categories of economic freedom to be ensured to citizens by their government if economic development is to be sought. Note that a «c» preceding any category abbreviation means category, and the whole is written cRL, cGF, etc.:

1. cRL means the government is ensuring rule of law (Rule of Law),
2. cGS means the government is choosing optimal size for its administration (Government Size),
3. cRE means the government is adopting appropriate and transparent regulations (Regulatory Efficiency), and
4. cOM means the government is refraining from setting unnecessary impediments to free market (Open Market).

The PEG model can also be divided into 12 distinct components of public economic governance. The following is a description of the four categories of public economic governance, broken down into these 12 components.

1. *Rule of law (cRL):* For the government to ensure citizens the rule of law (cRL) it must act on three fronts:

   (a) It must first ensure citizens the respect of the property rights (PR) by making sure a country's legal framework allows individuals to freely accumulate private property, secured by clear laws that are enforced effectively by the government.

   (b) Second, the government must assure citizens of its integrity (GI). This is a prerequisite for any sound economic development. Corruption erodes economic freedom by introducing insecurity and uncertainty into economic relations. Of greatest concern is the systemic corruption of government institutions and decision-making by practices such as bribery, extortion, nepotism, cronyism, patronage, embezzlement, and graft. The lack of government integrity caused by such practices reduces economic vitality by increasing costs and shifting resources into unproductive lobbying activities.

   (c) Third, the government must ensure citizens judicial system effectiveness (JE), which is vital, because well-functioning legal frameworks are essential for protecting the rights of all citizens against unlawful acts by others, including by governments and powerful private parties. Judicial effectiveness requires efficient and fair judicial systems to ensure that laws are fully respected, with appropriate legal actions taken against violations.

2. *Government size category (cGS):* For the government to ensure citizens of the rule of optimal Government size (cGS) it must also act on three fronts:

   (a) The government must curb government spending (GS), capturing the burden imposed by government expenditures on national budget. Such discipline in spending should include not only consumption by the government, but also all transfer payments related to various entitlement programs;

   (b) The government must use fairness in setting its citizens' tax burden (TB). This is a composite measure that reflects marginal tax rates on both personal and corporate income and the overall level of taxation (including direct and indirect taxes imposed by all levels of government) as a percentage of gross domestic product (GDP); and

   (c) The government must always aim for the fiscal health (FH) of the country. Fiscal Health plays an important role in economic freedom; indeed, widening deficits and a growing debt burden, both of which are caused by poor government budget management, lead to the erosion of a country's overall fiscal health. Deteriorating fiscal health, in turn, is associated with macroeconomic instability and economic uncertainty.

3. *Regulatory efficiency category (cRE):* The government must ensure regulatory efficiency (cRE) by establishing and protecting freedom in business and financial affairs. This can be done at three different levels:

   (a) The government should ensure business freedom (BF) by setting conditions and taking measures that render regulatory and infrastructure environments encouraging to the efficient operation of businesses. This concerns an array of factors that affect the ease of starting, operating, and closing a business.

(b) The government should ensure Labour Freedom (LF) by acting on various aspects of the legal and regulatory framework of a country's labour market, including regulations concerning minimum wages, laws inhibiting layoffs, severance requirements, and measurable regulatory restraints on hiring and hours worked; and

(c) Th government should ensure Monetary Freedom (MF), combining measures of price stability with an assessment of price controls. Both inflation and price controls distort market activity. Price stability without government intervention can be the ideal state for the free market.

4. *Open market category (cOM):* The government must ensure open market conditions (cOM) by ensuring that its citizens have three kinds of market freedoms: the government should make sure trade freedom (TF) exits and is protected. This is a composite measure of the extent of tariff and nontariff barriers that affect imports and exports of goods and services.

   (a) The government should also ensure investment Freedom (IF). Ideally, there should be no constraints on the flow of investment capital. In practice, however, most countries have a variety of restrictions on investment. Some have different rules for foreign and domestic investment. Some restrict access to foreign exchange. Some impose restrictions on payments, transfers, and capital transactions. In some countries, certain industries are closed to foreign investment.

   (b) The government should also ensure financial freedom through banking efficiency as well as a measure of independence from government control and interference in the financial sector. State ownership of banks and other financial institutions such as insurers and capital markets reduces competition and generally lowers the level of access to credit.

Once all the 12 components of public economic governance are averaged by first grading each component on a scale of 0–100, they allow the assigning of each country its overall public economic governance score (PEG) score. The $\text{PEG Score i} = \frac{\Sigma \text{Ci}}{12}$, where C_i Represents individual components of public economic governance. The PEG score is computed by averaging these 12 economic freedoms,[3] with equal weight being given to each. Scores on these 12 components of economic freedom, which are calculated from a number of sub-variables, are equally weighted and averaged to produce an overall economic freedom score for each economy.

[3] These are property Rights (PR), Judicial Effectiveness (JE), Government Integrity (GI), Tax Burden (TB), Gov't Spending (GS), Fiscal Health (FH), Business Freedom (BF), Labour Freedom (LF), Monetary Freedom (MF), Trade Freedom (TF), Investment Freedom (IF), and Financial Freedom (FF).

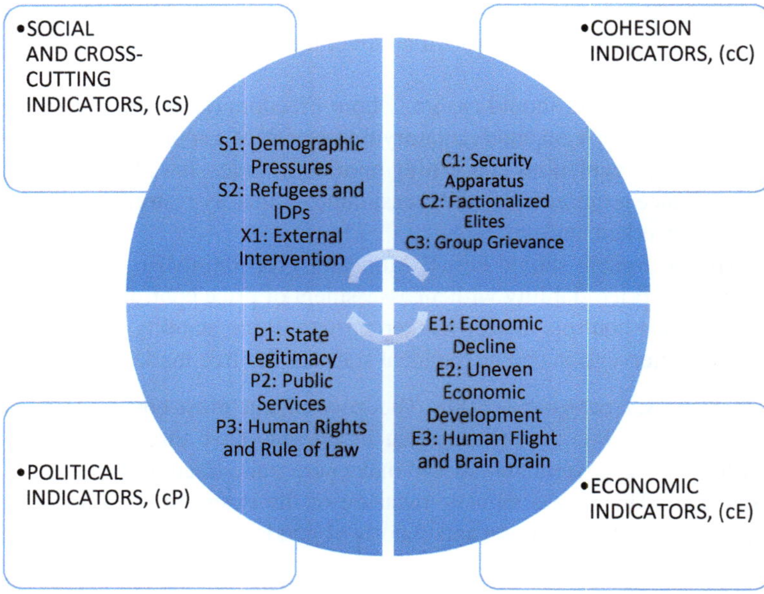

Fig. 9.2 Public Social Governance (Adapted from the Fund for Peace. At: http://fundforpeace.org/fsi/indicators/x1/)

Public Social Governance (PSG)

Public Economic Governance (PEG) usually goes hand in hand with Public Social Governance, (PSG). PSG can be approximated by a model developed and produced by The Fund for Peace (FFP) and named the Fragile States Index (FSI). FSI can represent an acceptable proxy to public social governance. This is an important tool that highlights social and political pressures that any state may experience, given the social governance weaknesses it may show (The Fund for Peace).

Figure 9.2 highlights the model of Public Social Governance, as drawn by The Fund for Peace.

The model of Public Social Governance is based on four categories of indicators, which are the cohesion category, the economic category, the political category, and social category.

1. *Cohesion category* (cC): The Cohesion category is measured through three components:

   (a) The Security Apparatus component (SA) considers the security threats to a state, such as bombings, attacks and serious criminal factors, such as organized crime and homicides, and perceived trust of citizens in domestic security.

   (b) The Fractionalized Elites component (FE) considers the fragmentation of state institutions along ethnic, class, clan, racial or religious lines, as well as brinksmanship and gridlock between ruling elites.

(c) The Group Grievance component (GG) focuses on divisions and schisms between different groups in society—particularly divisions based on social or political characteristics—and their role in access to services or resources, and inclusion in the political process.

2. *Economic category (cE):* The Economic category can also be measured through three components:

(a) The economic Decline component (ED) that considers patterns of progressive economic decline of a society as a whole, is measured by a number of variables: the per capita income, the Gross National Product, the unemployment rates, the inflation, the productivity, the level of debt, the poverty levels, and the business failures.
(b) The uneven Economic Development component (UE) considers inequality within the economy, irrespective of its current performance. For example, the indicator looks at structural inequality that is based on groups (such as racial, ethnic, religious, or other identity groups), or based on education, economic status, and region, such as the urban-rural divide.
(c) The Human Flight and Brain Drain component (HF) considers the economic impact of human displacement and the consequences this may have on a country's development.

3. *Political category (cP):* The Political category is composed of three components:

(a) The State Legitimacy component (SL), which considers the representativeness and openness of government and its relationship with its citizenry.
(b) The Public Services component (PS), which refers to the presence of basic state functions that serve the people. This may include the provision of essential services, such as health, education, water and sanitation, transport infrastructure, electricity power, Internet and connectivity.
(c) The Human Rights and Rule of Law component (HR) considers the relationship between the state and its population insofar as fundamental human rights are protected and freedoms are observed and respected.

4. *Social category (cS):* The Social category (cS) is composed of three components, namely the Demographic Pressures component (DP), the Refugees and Internally Displaced Persons component (RI), the External Intervention component (EI).

(a) The Demographic Pressures component (DP) considers pressures on the state deriving from the population itself or the environment around it. For example, the indicator measures population pressures related to food supply, access to safe water, and other life-sustaining resources, or health effects.
(b) The Refugees and Internally Displaced Persons component (RI) measures the pressure upon states caused by the forced displacement of large com-

munities as a result of social, political, environmental or other causes, measuring displacement within countries, as well as refugee flows into others.

(c) The External Intervention component (EI) considers the influence and impact of external actors in the functioning—particularly security and economic—of a state.

The strength of the FSI is its ability to distil millions of pieces of information into a form that is relevant as well as easily digestible and informative. Daily, the Fund for Peace (FFP) collects thousands of reports and information from around the world, detailing the existing social, economic and political pressures faced by each of the countries analysed.

Results of the previous chapter indicate that the weak impact of official development aid on the economic development performance of developing countries is limited to 7.5% and we ask why in this chapter we ask why and wonder whether the explanation is rooted in the weak economic freedom of countries.

Sample Data and Methodology

Appendix 9.1 lists countries of the sample, composed of countries of the world whose per capita GDP, economic freedom index (EFI), and fragile state index (FSI) are available, for a total of 169 countries. Data come from several important sources:

1. Data on country per capita gross national product (pcGDP) are retrieved from the World Factbook[4] 2016. The pcGDP is commonly used to measure a country's economic advance, and it is defined as the GDP on a purchasing power parity basis divided by population as of 1 July for the same year;
2. Data on the second variable of interest, used in this study, namely a country's public economic governance (PEG) score, are retrieved from the Economic Freedom index (EFI), developed by The Heritage Foundation and The Wall Street Journal; and
3. Data on the third variable used, concerning a country's public social governance (PSG) score, are retrieved from fragile state index (FSI) of the fund for peace[5]

The empirical objective of the study is to find out, using regression analysis, whether public economic governance (PEG) and social economic governance (PSG) have any positive/negative effect on countries' economic performance. Regression analysis is used on data and Eqs. 9.1, 9.2 and 9.3 describe the statistical

[4] The World Factbook provides information on the history, people, government, economy, geography, communications, transportation, military, and transnational issues for 267 world entities.

[5] http://fundforpeace.org/fsi/data/

relationship between the growth of the per capita GDP and the public economic governance (PEG) score and public social governance (PSG) score:

$$pcGDP_i = \alpha + \beta_1 PEG\ score_i + \beta_2 PSG\ score + \varepsilon_I \tag{9.1}$$

where:

$pcGDP_i$ is per capita gross domestic product for a country for the year 2017;
PEG $score_i$ is the public economic governance score allocated to a country by the Heritage Foundation, for the year 2017, using the EFI, as proxy;
PSG $score_i$ is the public social governance score allocated to a country, by Fund for Peace, for the year 2017, using SFI as proxy;
α, β and $+\varepsilon_I$, are regression coefficients and residual, respectively.

Regression 1 will allow the assessment of the overall relation between the per capital gross domestic product behaviour and the public economic governance and the public social governance. To gain more insight into the components of public and social governance, and their individual effect, an additional set of regressions is run on data of governance scores and their respective components:

$$PEGScore_i = \alpha + \beta_1 PR + \beta_2 GI_i + \beta_3 JE_i + \beta_4 GS_i, + \beta_5 TB_i + \beta_6 FH_i + \beta_7 BF + \beta_8 LF_i + \beta_9 MF_i + \beta_{10} TF_i + \beta_{11} IF_i + \beta 12_{12} FF_i + \varepsilon_i \tag{9.2}$$

$$PSGscore_i = \alpha + \beta_1 SA_i + \beta_2 FE_i + \beta_3 GG_i + \beta_4 ED_i, + \beta_5 UE_i + \beta_6 HF_i + \beta_7 SL_i + \beta_8 PS_i + \beta_9 HR_i, + \beta_{10} DP_i + \beta_{11} RI_i + \beta_{12} EI_i + \varepsilon_i \tag{9.3}$$

where:

$PEGScore_i$, and $PSGscore_i$, are governance scores, as defined;
PR, property rights, GI, government integrity and JE judicial effectiveness;
GS, Government spending, TB tax burden, and FH fiscal health;
BF, business freedom, LF Labour Freedom, and MF Monetary Freedom;
TF, trade Freedom, IF, investment Freedom, FF, Financial Freedom;
SA, Security Apparatus, FE, Factionalized Elites, and CG, The Group Grievance.
ED, Economic Decline, UE, Uneven Economic Development, HF, The Human Flight and Brain Drain component
SL, State Legitimacy, PS, Public Services, HR, The Human Rights and Rule of Law.
DP, The Demographic Pressures, RI, The Refugees and Internally Displaced Persons, EI, External Intervention.
α, β and $+\varepsilon_I$, are regression coefficients and residual, respectively.

Table 9.1 Descriptive statistics: $pcGDP_i = \alpha + \beta_1 PEG\ score_i + \beta_2\ PSG\ score_i + \varepsilon_I$

	N	Minimum	Maximum	Mean	Std. deviation
pcGDP	169	$700	$127.700	$19.718.93	$21.446.245
PSG score	169	18.70	113.90	69.3533	23.84466
PEG score	168	5.90	88.60	60.4417	10.83996
Valid N (listwise)	168				

Table 9.2 Model summary: $pcGDP_i = \alpha + \beta_1 PEG\ score_i + \beta_2\ PSG\ score_i + \varepsilon_I$

Model	R	R Square	Adjusted R square	Std. error of the estimate
1	0.704[a]	0.496	0.490	$15.349.163

[a]Predictors: (Constant), PEG score, PSG score

Table 9.3 Coefficients[a]: $pcGDP_i = \alpha + \beta_1 PEG\ score_i + \beta_2\ PSG\ score_i + \varepsilon_I$

		Unstandardized coefficients		Standardized coefficients		
Model		B	Std. error	Beta	t	Sig.
1	(Constant)	−1871.640	10727.720		−0.174	0.862
	PSG score	−369.779	59.411	−0.409	−6.224	0.000
	PEG score	781.285	130.178	0.394	6.002	0.000

[a]Dependent variable: pcGDP

Results

Table 9.1 gives Descriptive Statistics of the variables used in regression model one. One hundred and sixty-nine countries are involved in the regression: 169 for pcGDP and PSG score and 168 for PEG score. A number of countries from the original sample were excluded from the regression because one of the scores was missing.[6] The highest pcGDP of the sample of $127.700 was realised in 2017 by Qatar, and the lowest of $700[7] was scored by Central African Republic. The best PSG score is 18.70, allocated to Finland in the year 2017 and the worst is 113.90, allocated to Sri Lanka. The best PEG score is 88.60 and was registered in 2017 by Singapore, and the worst score is 5.90 and was allocated to North Korea.

Table 9.2: give the model summary and indicates a high level of significance. 70.4% of the variability of the country's cpGDP is explained by either its PEG score or PSG score or by both. The R-Square of 0.496 indicates that 49.60% of the explanatory power of the regression comes from the two independent variables, the PEG score or the PSG score.

Table 9.3 gives explanatory power and significance of each independent variable. The PSG score has, as expected, a negative sign, since the higher the score, the worse

[6]The following were excluded from the original sample: Antigua and Barbuda, Burma, Dominica, Grenada, Hong Kong, Kiribati, Libya, Lithuania, Macau, Myanmar, Saint Lucia, Saint Vincent Grenadines, Somalia, South Sudan, Syria, Taiwan, Tonga, Yemen and Vanuatu.

[7]These countries may have registered higher or lower pcGDP for the year 2017, but are excluded from the sample, because of missing data.

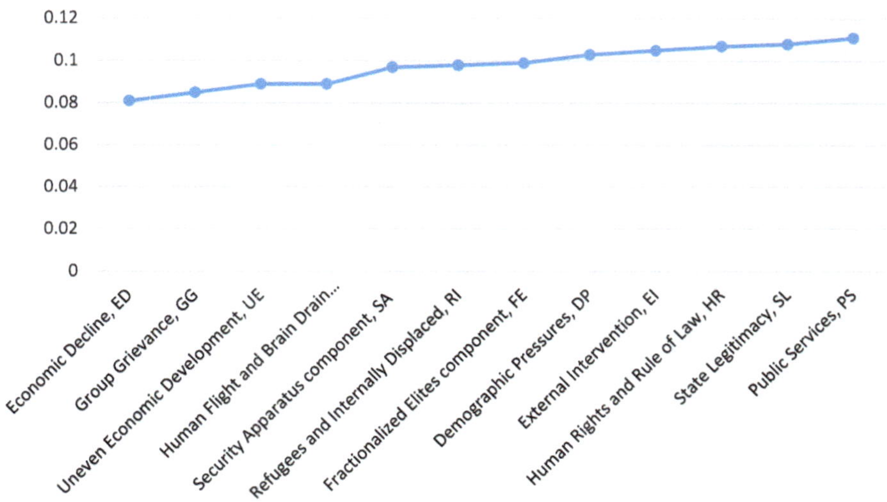

Fig. 9.3 Public social governance components, standardized coefficients

a country's public social governance is. With a standardized beta of −0.409, the PSG score seems to explain 40.9% of the movement in the pcGDP. The PEG score seems to explain 39.4% of the behaviours of country cpGDP. With p = 0.000, both the PSG score, and the PEG score are highly significant in explaining the relationship between governance scores and per capita gross domestic product movement.

Results of the regression seem to point the quality of governance, social and economic, as the main engine of development. The PSG score and PEG score are, however, boxes containing a number of individual components each, and regressions 2 and 3 are meant to explore them more closely. Although components of the PSG score and PEG score explain 100% of the variation of each score, the impact of the individual components may not be similar. Figures 9.3 and 9.4 plot the component of public social governance and the component of public economic governance Standardized Coefficients, classified by ascending order; they are all significant, all having p = 0.000.

Figure 9.3 classifies components of public social governance used in regression 2, by ascending order of impact on the public social governance score. The quality of public services seems to be the more impactful component of the public social governance overall score, followed by state legitimacy, human rights, and external intervention, which for more than 10% of the impact each. Economic Decline, Group Grievance, and Uneven Economic Development, although account for 8% and 9% respectively, are the components of public social governance that have the least impact on the score.

Figure 9.4, on the other hand, also classifies components of public economic governance used in regression 3 by ascending order of impact on the public economic governance score. The Fiscal Health (FH) component seems to show the highest impact on the public economic governance score, with a standardized beta coefficient of 22.7%, followed by Government Spending (GS), 17.9%, Investment

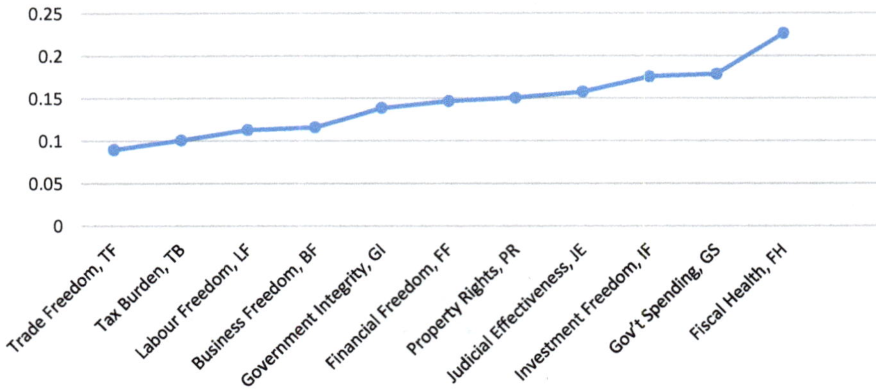

Fig. 9.4 Public economic governance components, standardized beta coefficients

Freedom (IF), Judicial Effectiveness (JE), etc. The component with the lowest impact is Monetary Freedom (MF),with 8%, followed by Trade Freedom (TF) with 9%.

Conclusion

Analysis in this chapter show that, more than international assistance, public governance can have a decisive impact on development progress. Economic governance policies such as Monetary Freedom, Trade Freedom, Investment Freedom, Financial Freedom and other conditionalities that may be imposed on developing countries as part of official development aid may work for some countries only and not for all, when adopted without adaptation to country-specific conditions and can even have disastrous short-term consequences, undermining their own effectiveness. Social governance policies can also have disastrous short-term consequences, on top of being even more difficult to achieve.

Both economic and social freedom policies may work in the long term, although developing countries generally do not have the comfort of waiting on this time scale (Consumer International 2005). For this reason, country-tailored development plans, if developed jointly with each developing country, may prove to be helpful. In other words, the success of economic and social governance may depend on the level of economic advance of the assistance-receiving country and such a possibility is examined in the next chapter.

Appendix 9.1: General Sample

General sample (169 countries)

Country	Country	Country	Country	Country	Country	Country	Country
Afghanistan	Brazil	Cyprus	Guatemala	Kyrgyz Republic	Morocco	Romania	Sweden
Albania	Brunei Darussalam	Czech Republic	Guinea	Laos	Mozambique	Russia	Switzerland
Algeria	Bulgaria	Denmark	Guinea Bissau	Latvia	Namibia	Rwanda	Tajikistan
Angola	Burkina Faso	Djibouti	Guyana	Lebanon	Nepal	Samoa	Tanzania
Argentina	Burundi	Dominican Republic	Haiti	Lesotho	Netherlands	Sao Tome and Principe	Thailand
Armenia	Cambodia	Ecuador	Honduras	Liberia	New Zealand	Saudi Arabia	Timor-Leste
Australia	Cameroon	Egypt	Hungary	Luxembourg	Nicaragua	Senegal	Togo
Austria	Canada	El Salvador	Iceland	Macedonia	Niger	Serbia	Trinidad and Tobago
Azerbaijan	Cape Verde	Equatorial Guinea	India	Madagascar	Nigeria	Seychelles	Tunisia
Bahamas	Central African Republic	Eritrea	Indonesia	Malawi	North Korea	Sierra Leone	Turkey
Bahrain	Chad	Estonia	Iran	Malaysia	Norway	Singapore	Turkmenistan
Bangladesh	Chile	Ethiopia	Iraq	Maldives	Oman	Slovak Republic	Uganda
Barbados	China	Fiji	Ireland	Mali	Pakistan	Slovenia	Ukraine
Belarus	Colombia	Finland	Israel and West Bank	Malta	Panama	Solomon Islands	United Arab Emirates
Belgium	Comoros	France	Italy	Mauritania	Papua New Guinea	South Africa	United Kingdom
Belize	Congo Democratic Republic	Gabon	Jamaica	Mauritius	Paraguay	South Korea	United States
Benin	Congo Republic	Gambia	Japan	Mexico	Peru	Spain	Uruguay

General sample (169 countries)

Country	Country	Country	Country	Country	Country	Country	Country
Bhutan	Costa Rica	Georgia	Jordan	Micronesia	Philippines	Sri Lanka	Uzbekistan
Bolivia	Cote d'Ivoire	Germany	Kazakhstan	Moldova	Poland	Sudan	Venezuela
Bosnia and Herzegovina	Croatia	Ghana	Kenya	Mongolia	Portugal	Suriname	Vietnam
Botswana	Cuba	Greece	Kuwait	Montenegro	Qatar	Swaziland	Zambia
							Zimbabwe

Chapter 10
Empirical Assessment of Developing Countries' Public Governance

Chapter 8 points to the inefficiency of official development aid and Chap. 9 shows that public governance in its social and economic dimensions have an important and significant impact on ODA development success. While extremely important for daily subsistence and humanitarian basic needs, official aid seems to do little to help the world's most underdeveloped nations in their quest for development at least in the short term; public governance, however, in its social and economic dimensions may have an important and significant impact on economic outcomes. Consequently, this chapter wonders whether weak public governance could partially explain the failure of official development aid to attaint objective of poverty eradication and development advance, and indirectly, whether good public governance could partially explain economic success.

The chapter compares governance effects on low-income and high-income countries. Section one gives a summary picture of world development; section two presents the sample and explains the followed methodology; section three discusses the chapter findings; and section four concludes the chapter.

World Development

Economic development expresses a process of change that makes national economies to durably increase their real GDP (Haller 2012). The past two decades have seen enormous progress in economic development around the world that has "helped lift over 1 billion people out of poverty". Many people, however, appear to have been left behind as they are still facing slow growth, privation, and limited opportunities for advancement (World Bank 2017). ODA was mainly intended to push up lower and average economies (G1, G2, and G3) each out of its GNI highest limit. World economies are usually divided in four groups (G1 to G4) according to the World Bank classification and as already presented in Chap. 9. The voluminous literature on aid effectiveness tends, however, to

A. Naciri, *The Governance Structures of the Bretton Woods Financial Institutions*, SpringerBriefs in Economics, https://doi.org/10.1007/978-3-319-97906-9_10

be inconclusive. As of 2017, "aid represents more than 10 percent of GDP for half of all low-income countries and over 30 percent of total revenues for 26 countries" (World Bank 2017, p. 27). It is ultimately concluded that "aid is neither inherently good nor inherently bad for development; what matters is how aid interacts with the prevailing power relations and affects governance" (World Bank 2017, p. 26).

In theory, development assistance will work mostly when supporting transparent and equitable governing arrangements exist and are embedded in a supportive domestic context. It will mostly fail whenever it may undermine the harmonious relationship between the governments and their citizens. It is expected that the higher a state's reliance on revenues from the international assistance, the lower its incentives to build sound public institutions needed to mobilize citizens around its development project. Despite unfavourable domestic conditions, developing countries' governments are expected to make politics work for development, and international development partners should work to orient their actions in that direction by supplying them with the most valuable ingredient of development. The one with the longest-lasting effect: knowledge.[1] Unlike the ravaged Europe of the 1950s, a number of developing economies may simply be lacking administrative and/or organizational systems conducive to development. Development assistance is also expected to be more effective when donor engagement enhances the emergence of more efficient public governance that becomes self-appropriated domestically. Public governance implicates developing states in using of every means at their disposal for the enhancement of their country development and implicates the international community in recognizing that promoting sustained development requires taking seriously the underlying determinants related to governance (World Bank 2017, p. 26). The objective of this chapter is therefore to find out whether low-income economies are more inclined to be affected in their development progress by weaknesses in public governance.

Sample and Methodology

In order to detect the effect of public economic and social governance (PEG & PSG) on development progress as measured by increase of the per capita gross domestic product, the main sample composed of 169 countries as presented in Chap. 8 is, however, divided into four levels of development advance: G1, G2, G3, and G4 and two group combinations, $C_{1.2}$ (GI + G2) and $C_{1.2.3}$ (GI + G2 + G3)

1. Sub-sample 1 (G_1) is composed of low-income economies having a per capita GNI of $1,035 or less
2. Sub-sample 2 (G_2) is composed of lower-middle-income economies with a per capita GNI between $1,035 and $4,085
3. Sub-sample 3 (G_3) composed of upper-middle-income economies with a per capita GNI between $4,085 and $12,616

[1] Even though economic and political freedom may be linked. it will be hazardous for international agencies to engage in the sleepy field of political freedom.

4. Sub-sample 4 (G_4) composed of high-income economies with a GNI per capita higher than $12,616

The sample, sub-samples, and combinations are composed of countries whose per capita GDP, economic freedom index (EFI), and fragile state index (FSI) are available as indicated in Chap. 8. Data come from several main sources: data on countries' per capita gross national product (pcGDP) are retrieved from the World Factbook 2016; data on countries' public economic governance score (PEG score) are retrieved from the Index of Economic Freedom (EFI); and data on countries' public social governance score (PSG score) are retrieved from fragile state index (FSI).

The empirical objective of the study is to find out, using regression analysis, whether public economic governance (PEG) or social economic governance (PSG) or both have any positive/negative effect on countries' economic progress. Regression analysis will, therefore, be performed on data regarding the general sample:

$$\text{pcGDP}_i = \alpha + \beta_1 \text{PSG score} \beta_2 \text{PEG score}_s + G_i + \varepsilon_I \tag{10.1}$$

where:

pcGDPi is per capita gross domestic product for a country for the 2017 for the sample, sub-samples, and combination, respectively.

PEGi score is the public economic governance score allocated to a country. The Heritage Foundation for the year 2017 for the sample, sub-samples, and combination, respectively.

PSGi score is the public social governance score allocated to a country by Fund for Peace for the year 2017 for the sample, sub-samples, and combination, respectively.

G_1 is the group of countries. Country is assigned 1 when it has a per capita GNI of $1.035 or less (low-income economy). Country is assigned 2 when it has a per capita GNI between $1.035 and $4.085 (lower-middle-income), etc.

α, β, and $+\varepsilon_I$ are regression coefficients and residual, respectively for each of the 7 regression models.

Further, in order to assess the impact of public governance on specific country groups, a regression will be performed on the data of each group using the following models:

$$\text{pcGDP}_i = \alpha + \beta_1 \text{PEG scoreG1}_i + \beta_2 \text{PSG scoreG1}_i + \varepsilon_I \tag{10.2}$$

$$\text{pcGDP}_i = \alpha + \beta_1 \text{PEG scoreG2}_i + \beta_2 \text{PSG scoreG2}_i + \varepsilon_I \tag{10.3}$$

$$\text{pcGDP}_i = \alpha + \beta_1 \text{PEG scoreG3}_i + \beta_2 \text{PSG scoreG3}_i + \varepsilon_I \tag{10.4}$$

$$\text{pcGDP}_i = \alpha + \beta_1 \text{PEG scoreG4}_i + \beta_2 \text{PSG scoreG4}_i + \varepsilon_I \tag{10.5}$$

where:

"PEG scoreG1$_i$" and "PSG scoreG1$_i$" represent public economic governance score, and public social governance score, respectively, for low income countries (G1).
"PEG scoreG2$_i$" and "PSG scoreG2$_i$" represent public economic governance score, and public social governance score, respectively, for lower-middle-income (G2).
"PEG scoreG3$_i$" and "PSG scoreG3$_i$" represent public economic governance score, and public social governance score, respectively, for average income economy for (G3).
"PEG scoreG4$_i$" and "PSG scoreG4$_i$" represent public economic governance score, and public social governance score, respectively, for high income economy for (G4).

Results

Table 10.1 gives a model summary of regression 1, independent variables (PSG score, PEG score, and G) explains 76.70% of the behaviour of a country's per capita gross domestic product as indicated by the level of R (column 2, Table 10.1). The model seems to explain 58.10% of the relationship between public governance and pcGDP as underlined by the R-Square (column 2, Table 10.1). The explanatory power of the model seems to have been significantly increased due to the inclusion of the grouping of countries by the level of their development (independent variable G). R has increased from 70.4· to 76.7 and· R Square from 49.6 to 58.9.

Table 10.2 presents standardized beta coefficients for the three independents variables of the regression: public social governance, public economic governance, and the classification by low-income, lower-middle-income, average-income, and high-income countries.

All three independent variables are significant with p = 0.000 (p = 0.011 PSGscore). Variable G, the grouping of countries by the level of their economic advance, seems to explain 44.10% of the significant relation underlined by regression between pcGDP and the three independent variables. Public economic governance, with a standardized beta coefficient of 0.265, would explain 26.5% of this relationship and social governance would explain 18.10%. The negative sign is the right direction because the higher PSGscore is, the worse the public social governance in the country is.

To determine which group is more affected by public governance, either social, economic, or both, we run regressions 2–5, and Table 10.3 gives their summaries.

Table 10.1 Model summary: $pcGDP_i = \alpha + \beta_1 PSGscore + \beta_2 PEGscore_i + G_i + \varepsilon_I$

Model	R	R Square	Adjusted R square	Std. error of the estimate
1	0.767[a]	0.589	0.581	$13,866.042

[a]Predictors: (Constant). PEGscore, PSGscore, G

As of the year 2017 (The Little Green Data Book 2017), low-income economies are countries with a total population of 638.3 millions, land area 13,382 km^2 and GDP of $394.3 billions; lower-middle-income countries are countries with a total population of 2.927.5 billion, land area 1000 km^2 21,753 km^2 and GDP $5.86 billions; the upper-middle-income group is composed of countries with a total population of 2.59 billion; land area 59,525 km^2 and GDP $20.63 billions; the high-income group is formed of countries with a total population of 1.187 billions land area 35,073 km^2 and GDP $47.42 billions.

Figure 10.1 shows the impact of public governance by level of economic development. Lower income countries seem to be affected more drastically by both public social governance and public economic governance, their score of economic governance and a high score social governance. Remember that while public governance sores are classified on a scale 1–100, with 100 being the best. Public social governance scores are classified on a scale of 1–114, with 114 being the worst.

Both governance scores tend to improve by moving on the development saddle. Except for the PEG score for the average-income group. The conclusion is clear: both public social governance and public economic governance seem to impact economic development, and public economic governance does so to a greater degree.

The information in hand allows us to draw a robot portrait of a low-income country, using 10.2, 10.3, from Chap. 8:

Table 10.2 Coefficients[a]: $pcGDP_i = \alpha + \beta_1 PSGscore_i + \beta_2 PEGscore_i + G_i + \varepsilon_I$

Model		Unstandardized coefficients B	Std. error	Standardized coefficients Beta	T	Sig.
1	(Constant)	−24,139.740	10,403.387		−2.320	0.022
	PSGscore	−163.359	63.657	−0.181	−2.566	0.011
	PEGscore	522.489	124.544	0.265	4.195	0.000
	G	9080.474	1485.770	0.441	6.112	0.000

[a]Dependent Variable: VAR00001

Table 10.3 Model summary: Regression 2, 3, 4, 5

Model	R	R Square	Adjusted R square	Std. error of the estimate
2. Low income	0.790[a]	0.624	0.598	$8351.421
3. Lower middle income	0.433[a]	0.188	0.151	$9389.431
4. Upper middle income (Average income)	0.313[a]	0.098	0.059	$10,041.474
5. High income	0.436[a]	0.190	0.145	$20,854.572
Total sample for reference (G included)	0.767[a]	0.589	0.581	$13,866.042

[a]Predictors: (Constant), PEG score, PSG score

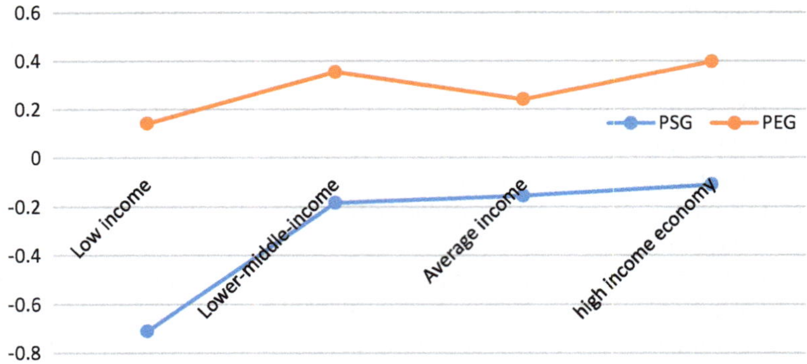

Fig. 10.1 Standardized coefficients for total sample and sub-samples

$$\begin{aligned}\mathrm{PEGScore}_i &= \alpha + \beta_1 \mathrm{PR}_{+}\beta_2 \mathrm{GI}_{i+}\beta_3 \mathrm{JE}_i + \beta_4 \mathrm{GS}_{i,+}\beta_5 \mathrm{TB}_i + \beta_6 \mathrm{FH}_i \\ &\quad + \beta_7 \mathrm{BF} + \beta_8 \mathrm{LF}_{i+}\beta_9 \mathrm{MF}_i + \beta_{10} \mathrm{TF}_i + \beta_{11} \mathrm{IF}_i + \beta 12_{12} \mathrm{FF}_i + \varepsilon_i \\ \mathrm{PSGscore}_i &= \alpha + \beta_1 \mathrm{SA}_{i+}\beta_2 \mathrm{FE}_{i+}\beta_3 \mathrm{GG}_i + \beta_4 \mathrm{ED}_{i,+}\beta_5 \mathrm{UE}_i + \beta_6 \mathrm{HF}_{i+}\beta_7 \mathrm{SL}_i \\ &\quad + \beta_8 \mathrm{PS}_{i+}\beta_9 \mathrm{HR}_i, + \beta_{10} \mathrm{DP}_i + \beta_{11} \mathrm{RI}_i + \beta_{12} \mathrm{EI}_i + \varepsilon_i\end{aligned}$$

where:

PEGScore and PSGscore are governance scores, as defined previously; PR (property rights), GI (government integrity), JE (judicial effectiveness), GS (Government spending), TB (tax burden), FH (fiscal health), BF (business freedom), LF (Labour Freedom), MF (Monetary Freedom), TF (trade Freedom), IF (investment Freedom), FF (Financial Freedom), SA (Security Apparatus), FE (Factionalized Elites), GG (Group Grievance), ED (Economic Decline), UE (Uneven Economic Development), HF (Human Flight and Brain Drain component), SL (State Legitimacy), PS (Public Services), HR (Human Rights and Rule of Law), DP (Demographic Pressures), RI (Refugees and Internally Displaced Persons), EI (External Intervention).

α, β, and $+\varepsilon_I$ are regression coefficients and residual, respectively.

Figure 10.2 is built based on sub-sample of 30 low-income countries and 39 high-income countries. While interpreting Fig. 10.2, it should be remembered again that public social governance scores (PSG scores) are classified on a scale of 1–114, with 1 being the best and 114 being the worst, and public economic governance scores (PEG scores) are measured on a scale of 1–100, with one as the worst score and 100 as the best. Low-income countries diverge from high-income countries at the level of their public social governance and at their ability to capitalise on it for the benefit of their development. Indeed, for most components of PSG, high-income countries are able to make them work more efficiently for development progress.

Figure 10.3, on the other hand, is built on a sub-sample of 25 low-income countries and 53 high-income countries. It can be understood from Fig. 10.3 that for most components of public economic governance, the negative effect on development is high, particularly regarding fiscal health (FH), investment freedom (IF), labour freedom (LF), property rights (PR), and judicial efficiency (JE).

These results may shed some doubt on international development policy for developing countries confronting "one of the greatest myths of our time: that billions of dollars in aid sent from wealthy countries to developing African nations has helped to reduce poverty and increase growth" (Kofi Annan, former UN Secretary-General). In fact, poverty levels continue to escalate and growth rates have steadily declined—and millions continue to suffer.

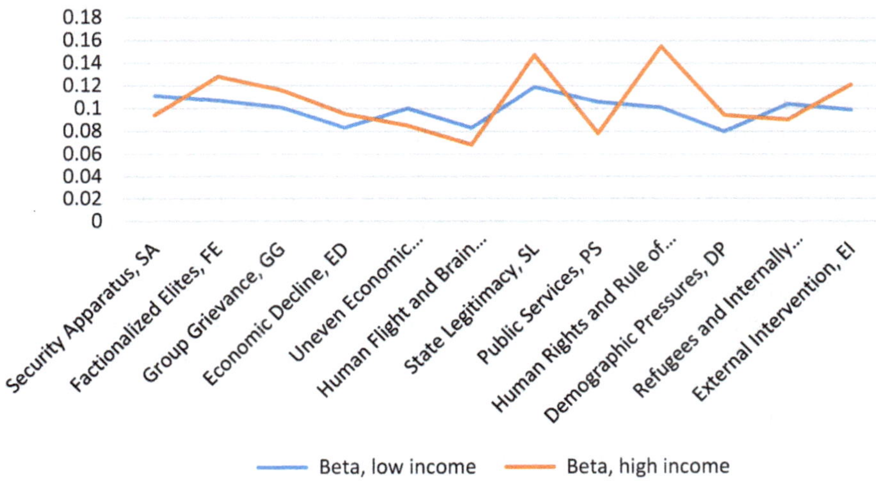

Fig. 10.2 Low-income (in blue) and high-income (in red) countries standardized beta coefficients for PSG components

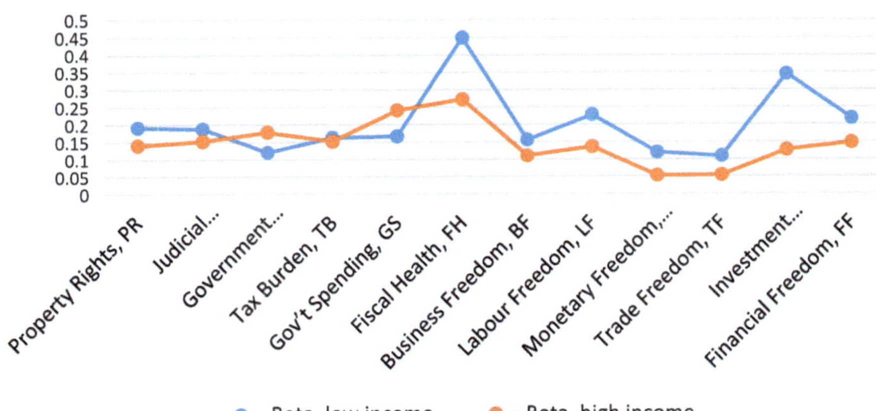

Fig. 10.3 Low-income (in blue) and high-income (in red) countries standardized beta coefficients for PEG components

Countries that have rejected the aid route seem to have significantly prospered, while others that have become aid-dependent may have seen their levels of poverty increase. Their overreliance on aid may have trapped them in the vicious circle of aid dependency, corruption, market distortion, and further poverty, "leaving them with nothing but the 'need' for more aid" (Kofi Annan, former UN Secretary-General).

Figure 10.4 shows the progressive effect of public governance in both its social and its economic dimensions on a country's economic advance.

Recalling again that public social governance scores (PSG scores) are measured on a scale of 1–114, with 1 being the best score and 114 being the worse, and public economic governance scores (PEG scores) are measured on a scale of 1–100, with one being the worst score and 100 being the best. Figure 10.4 shows clearly how public governance is strongly associated with economic development. At the left side of Fig. 10.4, low-income economies (the low-income group with per capita GNI of $1,035 or less) have the worst PSG and PEG scores. While moving to the right in Fig. 10.4, lower-middle-income economies (per capita GNI between $1,035 and $4,085) show a serious improvement at the level of both elements of public governance. Moving even further to the right in Fig. 10.4, upper-middle-income economies (per capita GNI between $4,085 and $12,616) show even more improvement. Finally, it is the high-income economy group (per capita equal to or greater than $12,616) that benefits the most from both public social governance and public economic governance. Such benefits appear to be linear at the level of low-income to upper-middle-income groups and accelerate after in the high-income group. There must be a break-even level of economic advance from where public governance accelerates economic development and under which it decelerates it.

Table 10.4 shows Comparative Public Economic Governance (PEG) for low-income and high-income countries. Overall, low-income economies suffer a 24% deficit in their general economic governance score, or PEG score. Decomposed in individual components, low income compared to high income economies suffer a

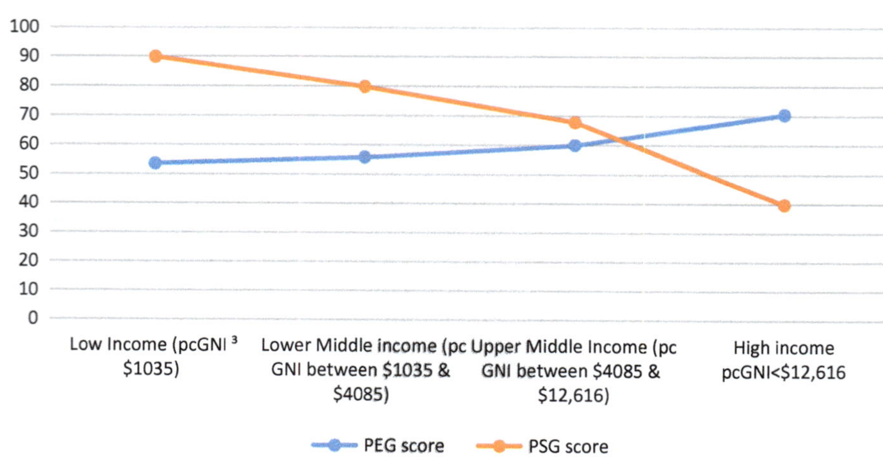

Fig. 10.4 Public governance and economic development (PEG score in blue and PSG score in red)

Table 10.4 Comparative Public Economic Governance (PEG) for low-income and high-income countries (The lower PEG score is the better public economic governance is)

	Mean (high income group), N 52 1–100 scale, 100 the best	Mean (low income group), N25 1–100 scale, 100 the best	Low income PEG score/high income PEG score
PEG score	70.56	53.69	0.76
Property rights, PR	74.66	33.08	0.44
Government integrity, GI	66.68	33.27	0.50
Judicial effectiveness, JE	64.00	30.09	0.47
Government spending, GS	72.02	74.24	1.03
Tax burden, TB	49.04	80.81	1.65
Fiscal health, FH	70.98	66.58	0.94
Business freedom, BF	76.89	49.24	0.64
Labour Freedom, LF	64.36	53.07	0.82
Monetary Freedom, MF	82.39	74.82	0.91
Trade Freedom, TF	85.03	67.35	0.79
Investment Freedom, IF	75.96	48.60	0.64
Financial Freedom, FF	65.96	33.20	0.50

deficit in each component of public economic governance (except for Government spending. and tax burden), notably 56% in public economic governance deficit in property rights, 57% in judicial effectiveness, and 50% in both government integrity and Financial Freedom. Low-income economies seem to register a 65% advantage in tax burden and a 3% in government spending.

Table 10.5 gives Comparative Public Social Governance (PSG) for low-income and high-income countries. PSG scores are, however, set up on a scale of 1–114, with 1 describing the highest level of public social governance and 114, the lowest. Overall social governance of low-income economies is more than twice as bad (225%) as in high-income economies. Such a general deficit of public social governance once broken down into components gives a deeper insight, and all 12 components show a huge deficit in governance: Public Services (PS) component 272% (3.72–1), Demographic Pressures (DP) 194%, Security Apparatus (SA) 139%, Human Flight and Brain Drain component (HF) 149%; All other components seem to have significant impact on low-income countries.

More than public economic governance, public social governance seems have a larger impact on economic development. "It is certainly time for poor countries to assume full control over their economic and political destinies. They should grasp the many means and opportunities available to them for improving the quality of life"

Table 10.5 Comparative Public Social Governance (PSG) for low-income and high-income countries (The higher PSG score is the worse public social governance)

	Mean (high income group), N 39 1–114 scale, 114 the worse	Mean (low income group), N30 1–114 scale, 114 the worse	Low income PSG deficit
PSG score	39.9205	89.9233	2.25
Security Apparatus, SA	2.9077	6.95	2.39
Factionalized Elites, FE	4.1282	7.7233	1.87
Group Grievance, GG.	4.7436	6.6233	1.40
Economic Decline, ED,	3.6769	7.4733	2.03
Uneven Economic Development, UE	3.3692	7.63	2.26
Human Flight and Brain Drain component, HF	2.9	7.2067	2.49
State Legitimacy, SL	3.4821	7.46	2.14
Public Services, PS,	2.2154	8.25	3.72
Human Rights and Rule of Law, HR	3.3205	7.1067	2.14
Demographic Pressures, DP	2.9051	8.5333	2.94
Refugees and Internally Displaced Persons, RI	3.3641	7.2267	2.15
External intervention, EI	2.9077	7.7400	2.66

Table 10.6 Model summary[a]

Model	R	R Square	Adjusted R square	Std. error of the estimate
1	0.770[a]	0.593	0.562	7.17715

[a]PEG score $=\alpha + \beta_1 SA_{i+}\beta_2 FE_{i+}\beta_3 GG_i + \beta_4 ED_{i,+}\beta_5 UE_i + \beta_6 HF_{i+}\beta_7 SL_i + \beta_8 PS_{i+}\beta_9 HR_{i,}+\beta_{10} DP_i + \beta_{11} RI_i + \beta_{12} EI_i + \varepsilon_i$

(Kofi Annan, former UN Secretary-General). It is time for them to opt for public governance as means of economic development. The task is, indeed, Colossal, but this should not discharge developed countries from their responsibilities, as there is still some possibility for them to act on social governance. However, there will never be sense for developed countries in using development assistance to support poor countries, while undermining their own efforts through control of decision-making, trade restrictions, unfair subsidies, political pressure, and alike. All developed country policies towards the world's poorest countries should be consistent with a commitment to sustainable development and poverty reduction (U.K. White Paper 2000).[2]

As expected, the two dimensions of public governance seem to be highly related. Table 10.6 gives the summary of the model linking public economic governance scores to the 12 components of public social governance whose variables were defined previously in this chapter.

[2]U.K. White Paper on International Development (2000). Eliminating World Poverty Making Globalisation Work for the Poor. At: http://webarchive.nationalarchives.gov.uk/+/http:/www.dfid.gov.uk/Documents/publications/whitepaper2000.pdf

The 12 components of public social governance (PSG) appear to explain 77.00% of the variation of the public economic governance (PEG). The six first components of PSG listed in Table 10.7 appear to be inversely related to public economic governance, meaning any increase in the component is translated in an amelioration of public economic governance. Conversely, the six other components listed at the end of Table 10.7 seem to be directly related to public economic governance, where any increase would indicate a deterioration in public economic governance. The four components of social governance in Table 10.7 show an acceptable level of significance.

Conclusion

This chapter has shown how important public governance for economic development can be. Its impact seems to be progressive in the sense that low-income economies tend to register negative scores of governance while higher income economies register more favourable scores. Developing countries, if they are to maximise the benefits of international assistance, are required to have effective systems of government and to take serious actions against corruption and for justice (U.K. White Paper 2000). Unfortunately, this chapter shows how developing countries are failing dramatically to put all their potential in the service of their development. Many reasons may explain this disastrous situation, notably the legacy of colonialism, unfair international exchange terms, the imminence of rich countries in poor country affairs, etc. (U.K. White Paper 2000). All these conditions make it hard to pursue their development on more equal terms. The most impactful failure seems, however,

Table 10.7 Standardized coefficients beta of PSG components

Model	Standardized coefficients beta
Public Services, PS,	−0.425[a]
Economic Decline, ED,	−0.423[a]
State Legitimacy, SL	−0.19
External Intervention, EI	−0.151
Human Rights and Rule of Law, HR	−0.097[a]
Security Apparatus, SA	−0.077
Fractionalized Elites, FE	0.027
Uneven Economic Development, UE	0.028
Group Grievance, GG.	0.037
Demographic Pressures, DP	0.097
Refugees and Internally Displaced Persons, RI	0.178[a]
Human Flight and Brain Drain component, HF	0.239

[a]Significant at 5% level

to result from developing countries' inability/unwillingness to take their economic destinies into their own hands, as seen in the weakness of their public governance systems. However, it is not clear how this might be accomplished (Frieden 2016).

Appendix 10.1: General Sample

General sample (169 countries)							
Country	Country	Country	Country	Country	Country	Country	Country
Afghanistan	Brazil	Cyprus	Guatemala	Kyrgyz Republic	Morocco	Romania	Sweden
Albania	Brunei Darussalam	Czech Republic	Guinea	Laos	Mozambique	Russia	Switzerland
Algeria	Bulgaria	Denmark	Guinea Bissau	Latvia	Namibia	Rwanda	Tajikistan
Angola	Burkina Faso	Djibouti	Guyana	Lebanon	Nepal	Samoa	Tanzania
Argentina	Burundi	Dominican Republic	Haiti	Lesotho	Netherlands	Sao Tome and Principe	Thailand
Armenia	Cambodia	Ecuador	Honduras	Liberia	New Zealand	Saudi Arabia	Timor-Leste
Australia	Cameroon	Egypt	Hungary	Luxembourg	Nicaragua	Senegal	Togo
Austria	Canada	El Salvador	Iceland	Macedonia	Niger	Serbia	Trinidad and Tobago
Azerbaijan	Cape Verde	Equatorial Guinea	India	Madagascar	Nigeria	Seychelles	Tunisia
Bahamas	Central African Republic	Eritrea	Indonesia	Malawi	North Korea	Sierra Leone	Turkey
Bahrain	Chad	Estonia	Iran	Malaysia	Norway	Singapore	Turkmenistan
Bangladesh	Chile	Ethiopia	Iraq	Maldives	Oman	Slovak Republic	Uganda
Barbados	China	Fiji	Ireland	Mali	Pakistan	Slovenia	Ukraine
Belarus	Colombia	Finland	Israel and West Bank	Malta	Panama	Solomon Islands	United Arab Emirates
Belgium	Comoros	France	Italy	Mauritania	Papua New Guinea	South Africa	United Kingdom
Belize	Congo Democratic Republic	Gabon	Jamaica	Mauritius	Paraguay	South Korea	United States
Benin	Congo Republic	Gambia	Japan	Mexico	Peru	Spain	Uruguay
Bhutan	Costa Rica	Georgia	Jordan	Micronesia	Philippines	Sri Lanka	Uzbekistan
Bolivia	Cote d'Ivoire	Germany	Kazakhstan	Moldova	Poland	Sudan	Venezuela

General sample (169 countries)							
Country	Country	Country	Country	Country	Country	Country	Country
Bosnia and Herzegovina	Croatia	Ghana	Kenya	Mongolia	Portugal	Suriname	Vietnam
Botswana	Cuba	Greece	Kuwait	Montenegro	Qatar	Swaziland	Zambia
							Zimbabwe

Appendix 10.2: Sub-samples

Low income	Country 2017	Country 2017	Country 2017
Country 2017	Armenia	Albania	Australia
Afghanistan	Azerbaijan	Algeria	Austria
Bahrain	Bangladesh	Angola	Bahrain
Benin	Bhutan	Argentina	Belgium
Burkina Faso	Bolivia	Bahamas	Canada
Burundi	Cambodia	Barbados	Cyprus
Central African Republic	Cameroon	Belarus	Czech Republic
Chad	Cape Verde	Belize	Estonia
Comoros	Congo Republic	Bosnia and Herzegovina	Finland
Congo Democratic Republic	Cote d'Ivoire	Botswana	France
Denmark	Djibouti	Brazil	Germany
Eritrea	Egypt	Brunei Darussalam	Greece
Ethiopia	El Salvador	Bulgaria	Hungary
Gambia	Equatorial Guinea	Chile	Iceland
Guinea	Georgia	China	Ireland
Guinea Bissau	Germany	Colombia	Israel and West Bank
Haiti	Ghana	Costa Rica	Italy
Japan	Guatemala	Croatia	Kuwait
Liberia	Guyana	Cuba	Latvia
Madagascar	Honduras	Dominican Republic	Luxembourg
Malawi	India	Ecuador	Malta
Mali	Indonesia	Fiji	Netherlands
Mozambique	Kenya	Gabon	New Zealand
Nepal	Kyrgyz Republic	Iran	Norway
Niger	Laos	Jamaica	Oman
North Korea	Lesotho	Jordan	Poland
Rwanda	Mauritania	Kazakhstan	Portugal
Senegal	Micronesia	Lebanon	Qatar
Sierra Leone	Moldova	Macedonia	Saudi Arabia
Tanzania	Mongolia	Malaysia	Singapore
Togo	Morocco	Maldives	Slovak Republic
Uganda	Nicaragua	Mauritius	Slovenia

Low income	Country 2017	Country 2017	Country 2017
Zambia	Nigeria	Mexico	South Korea
Zimbabwe	Pakistan	Montenegro	Spain
	Papua New Guinea	Namibia	Swaziland
	Philippines	Panama	Switzerland
	Samoa	Paraguay	United Arab Emirates
	Sao Tome and Principe	Peru	United Kingdom
	Sri Lanka	Romania	United States
	Sudan	Russia	
	Sweden	Serbia	
	Tajikistan	Seychelles	
	Timor-Leste	Solomon Islands	
	Tunisia	Suriname	
	Ukraine	Thailand	
	Uzbekistan	Trinidad and Tobago	
	Vietnam	Turkey	
		Turkmenistan	
		Uruguay	
		Venezuela	

Chapter 11
Concluding Remarks: A Lightened Cooperation and Assistance!

In the closing days of the Second World War, the world's political leaders made a commitment to global security and development. Their legacy materialized substantially in a set of international institutions of economic cooperation and conflict resolution, indirectly leading to the formalisation of the concept of official development assistance (ODA). Although such assistance seems only occasionally to have reached its promised objectives of poverty elimination and development enhancement, its designers, crafters and multiple contributors deserve much respect, recognition and admiration. Despite geopolitical considerations, a large part of their action can only be motivated by their high believe in human common destiny and solidarity. Development is a difficult process, always subject to multiple impediments. Some of these impediments may appear obvious, while many others are unsuspected, and unless all human efforts are joined for the same objective, the fight against global poverty risks fought in vain. The main instrument for this purpose is, by far, the official development assistance, which is significantly delivered through the BWFIs, which despite their efforts could not escape much criticism, to which they responded through timid governance reforms.

This book has tried to study BWFIs, looking especially at the efficiency of their development assistance action and the way it may have been affected by weaknesses in their governance structure. It also explores alternative explanations for official development aid's seeming failure, particularly possible weaknesses in public governance of assistance recipients.

This concluding chapter summarizes the findings of the book: in section one, it gives an overview of BWFIs; in section two, it exposes the Quotas system; in section three, it discusses BWFI's governance reform; in section four, it discusses the IMF governance and shareholding review; in section five, it presents the World Bank governance and shareholding review; in section six, it proceeds to an overall *Discussion of Bretton Woods Financial Institution governance;* in section seven, it concludes.

A. Naciri, *The Governance Structures of the Bretton Woods Financial Institutions*, SpringerBriefs in Economics, https://doi.org/10.1007/978-3-319-97906-9_11

Bretton Woods Financial Institutions Overview

The world financial architecture is built around BWFIs where membership is gradual and expertly granted. First, a country must join the IMF and only then can it apply for IBRD membership and later register for membership in IDA, IFC and MIGA. At Regional Development Banks, membership is more closely related to the member directly interest in the concerned region, (Africa, Asia, Europe, etc.). The clear picture of the world taken at Bretton Woods in 1944 has been only insignificantly retouched in the following decades (Villafranca 2014). The global economy has, however, undergone tremendous upheavals, underscoring the need for the redefinition of the international balance of power. BWFIs' original modus operandis has been submitted to timid reforms only in 2010, and only recently in 2016 was it ratified by the major shareholders of the Institutions. For critics, this reform, intended to give stronger representation to emerging economies, only perpetuated the control of rich countries over them.

Similarities between BWFIs are very important, but each institution has a distinct structure, receives its funding from different sources, and assists often different categories of members. For critics, the governance structure and mandate of BWFIs, established at the Bretton Woods Conference of 1944, are becoming out-dated and their action seems to fade. Criticisms expressed toward BWFIs are based on a number of worries:

1. BWFIs' governance structures and decision-making are firmly controlled by a few rich countries which represent the largest contributors/donors without much consideration for poor/developing countries interest (Bretton Woods Project 2005a, b);
2. There exists also a serious apprehension regarding BWFIs' role in shaping the development discourse through their research, training and publishing activities; and
3. It is feared that BWFIs views and prescriptions may undermine or even eliminate alternative perspectives on development, as they are regarded as experts in the field of financial regulation and economic development (Bretton Woods Project 2005a, b).

Given the original structure of BWFIs, founding shareholders found themselves, quite naturally, in charge of the decision-making of the whole multilateral development funding system. Consequently, ownership and voting power at BWFIs become literally a function of the amount of capital provided by each member country, which is typically based on the country's economic weight. Under such a model, the United States found itself quite naturally the dominant shareholder in most international institutions in which they have participations in the capital, in WBG, AsDB, AfDB, IaDB, and EBRD. The US is followed by Japan, Germany, France and the United Kingdom. In aggregate, the US accounts for 17% of shareholdings across these institutions, or twice as much as Japan, the next largest shareholder. Further, the US remains, directly or indirectly, the largest shareholder of the broader RDB's system, which includes many institutions in which they are not member, such as AIIB and the 40-year-old IsDB. Across the broader multilateral financial system, the US accounts for 12% of shareholdings, twice as much as China, currently the next largest shareholder (Morris 2017). It is, however, suggested that this shareholding approach of dominant shareholder(s) may have served the RDBs well by "engendering greater efficiency" in decision making, compared to a "one country, one vote" model of governance. Many others do not see it that way.

The original shareholding system of BWFIs carries some limitations, one of which has to do with its inability to accommodate countries' desire to increase institutions' capital or shareholding without the agreement of leading shareholders. The other limitation resides in its failure to recognize other sources of financing besides capital subscription that countries may provide to BWFIs. Emerging countries have directly encountered both limitations, and they are neither able to significantly increase their shareholding in the rich countries-led institutions nor can they participate in large increases in institutions' capital bases. These barriers force some emerging countries to look for alternative solutions. China, for instance, has established large trust funds, each exceeding $1 billion, at the IaDB and AfDB, and more modest funds at the World Bank and AsDB. The fundamental question regarding BWFIs that comes to mind is whether and how their current governance system will accommodate the demand for growth coming from the developing and emerging world (Morris 2017). The IMF and the WBG have tried to respond to this pressure for growth and democracy by launching governance reforms, and for more than two decades there have been efforts to reform the IMF and the WBG by changing their voting structure, which is fundamentally based on the so called quota system. It would seem that there will be growth in the RDBs system, even with US resistance to reform (Morris 2017).

Quotas System (QS)

The quotas system (QS) is a formula by which each country member of the BWFIs is assigned a proportion of an institution's shares, based broadly on its relative position in the world economy. The quotas system is actually central to the Bretton Woods Institutions' establishment (Silver 2010). The QS was presented in Chap. 3 as the weighted average of several elements with different assigned weights, including the GDP, with an assigned weight of 50%; the openness of the economy, having a weight of 30%; the economic variability, with a weight of 15%; and the international reserves, with a weight of 5%. For quota assessment purposes, the GDP is measured through a blend of GDP, based on market exchange rates, with a weight of 60% and on purchasing power parity (PPP[1]) exchange rates with a 40% weight.

---

[1] PPP is calculated with the following formula: [$\$ = P_1/P_2$]. Where: \$ is exchange rate of currency 1 to currency 2; P_1 the cost of good g in currency 1; and P_2 represents the cost of good g in currency 2.

Table 11.1 IMF list of general quota reviews since its establishment

Quota review no	Resolution adopted	Overall quota increase (%)	Quota review no	Resolution adopted	Overall quota increase (%)	Quota review no	Resolution adopted	Overall quota increase (%)
1	No increase proposed	–	6	February 1970	35.4	11	January 1998	45.0
2	No increase proposed	–	7	March 1976	33.6	12	No increase proposed	–
3	February and April 1959	60.7	8	December 1978	50.9	13	No increase proposed	–
4	No increase proposed	–	9	March 1983	47.5	14	December 2010	100.0
5	March 1965	30.7	10	June 1990	50.0			

Source: IMF (2017a)

The formula also includes a "compression factor" that reduces the dispersion in calculated quota shares across member countries (IMF quotas, 2017). Quotas are denominated in IMF's unit of SDRs,[2] and they determine countries' financial and organizational relationship with the IMF, mainly its subscription to the capital of the IMF,[3] its voting power at the IMF decision making instances, and its funding from the IMF. The more recent reforms fixed the number of basic votes at 5.502% of total votes. The 14th general quota review increased each of the IMF's 189 members to a combined SDR477 billion (about US$652 billion) (from about SDR238,5 billion about US$326 billion). The current share of basic votes in total votes represents close to a tripling of their share prior to the implementation of the reforms (IMF_FY_2016_AR).

The IMF conducts general quota reviews at regular intervals, usually every 5 years. Eventual changes to quotas must, however, be submitted to the approval of 85% majority of the total voting power, and a member's quota cannot be changed without its consent. Until 2017, it has been 14 general quota reviews (IMF quotas, 2017) of which nine have been increases. Table 11.1 gives the list of the general quota reviews undertaken by the IMF since its establishment.

The third general review of 1959 has brought an increase of quotas of 60.7%, followed by 30.7% in the fifth general review of 1965; 35.4% in the sixth general of

[2] The largest member of the IMF is the United States, with a current quota (as of March 2017) of SDR82.99 billion (about US$113 billion), and the smallest member is Tuvalu, with a quota of SDR2.5 million (about US$3.4 million).

[3] Up to 25% must be paid in SDRs or widely accepted currencies (such as the US dollar, the euro, the Japanese yen, or the British pound sterling), while the rest is paid in the member's own currency.

1970; 33.6% in the seventh general review of 1976; 50.9% in the eighth general review of 1978; 47.5% in the ninth general review of 1983; 50% in the tenth general review of 1990; 45.0% in eleventh general review of 1998; 45% of 1998; and lately, in the fourteenth general review of 2010, 100%. General quota reviews allow the IMF to assess the adequacy of quotas, not only in terms of members' balance of payments financing needs, but also in terms of its own ability to help meet those needs (IMF 2017a). A general quota review also allows for increases in members' quotas to reflect changes in their relative positions in the world economy. Ad hoc increases outside general reviews do not occur often, but the increases in quotas for 54 member countries approved under the 2008 Reform are a recent example.

WBG member countries are allocated votes at the time of membership and subsequently for additional subscriptions to capital, and like at the International Monetary Fund, the World Bank Articles of Agreement (Article V, section 3) state that each member of the Bank receives 250 basic membership shares, plus one additional vote for each share of stock detained. The distribution of votes at the World Bank was also set up to reflect each member country's comparative economic strength. It is actually based on a combination of several elements, such as reserves, international trade volumes and national income. The allocation of voting shares at the World Bank is accompanied by paid-in capital requirements. Thus, there is a direct link between the scale of financial backing provided to the Bank and the degree of decision-making power granted to the bank member country. Recent capital increases at the Bank, have seen the number of other shares held increased, while the number of basic membership shares kept constant. This has resulted in a situation where basic votes are losing weight, which has relatively weakened the voice of small countries, mostly borrowing developing countries, and has made their participation in decision-making remain insignificant. Consequently, the majority of developing countries have the negative feeling of being voluntarily retained as under-represented, compared to their shares of the world GDP, when measured in purchasing power parity (PPP). This imbalance in decision-making has placed BWFIs in the first stage of responsibility in the apparently failing official assistance, to eradicate poverty and score development. Institutions have reacted with a battery of reform of their governance, apparently without success in appeasing the contestation.

Bretton Woods Financial Institutions' Governance Reform

Although the world economy has changed quite significantly since the signing of the Bretton Woods Agreement, in the sense that while some emergent economies have grown tremendously, most developed economies have grown less sizably, BWFIs' governance seems to have failed to follow the pace of change. However, there seem to be structural limits to any attempt change in the original governance rules at Bretton Woods institutions, and these limits constantly weaken any gain that may be gained from any change. Those structural limits are embodied in two barrier rules within BWFIs: The first barrier is materialised in the fact that any amendment on reform of Executive Boards must be submitted for adoption to a double requirement of a very high percentage of member institutions coupled with a high percentage of total voting power. The second barrier is embodied in the rule that requires, for any quota increases adoption (under the 14th General Review of Quotas), the consent of the Executive Board as well as the consent of members having no less than 70% of voting shares.

The recent IMF quota review, ratified with a 5-year delay, and the World Bank "voice reform" to increase developing countries' representation in their governance structures, seem to have brought small changes to the institution decision-making structure and were also met with little enthusiasm (Bretton Woods Project 2016).

IMF Governance and Shareholding Review

The quota at the IMF largely monitors members' relations with the institution; it determines, for instance, their voting power at IMF decision-making bodies, where each country member's votes are composed of basic votes, plus one additional vote for each SDR100,000 of quotas. The quotas also determine the amount of financing a member can obtain from the IMF (its access limit). For example, under Stand-By and Extended Arrangements,[4] a member can borrow up to 145% of its quota annually and 435% cumulatively, and its access may even be higher, in exceptional circumstances (IMF 2017a). The 2008 reforms have fixed the number of basic votes at 5.502% of total votes. Currently, however, the proportion of basic votes in total votes represents close to a tripling of their share prior to the implementation of the more recent reforms, and representing the first increase in basic votes since the Fund's establishment (IMF 2017a).

In 2010, the Board of Governors of the IMF completed its 14th General Review of Quotas, which involved a package of "far-reaching reforms" of the IMF's quotas and governance, becoming effective only in 2016, following the US Congress approval. Since then, the basic votes of each member are supposed to be the number of votes that results from the equal distribution among all members of 5.502% of the aggregate sum of the total voting power of all of the members.[5] The recent reform, once it officially became effective in 2016, has had four main implications;

1. Doubling quotas, increasing them from approximately SDR238,5 billion to approximately SDR477 billion (around $653 billion, at current exchange rates)[6];

[4] The Stand-By and Extended Arrangements (SBA) are designed to help countries address short-term balance of payments problems. The length of an SBA is typically 12–24 months, and repayment is due within 3¼–5 years of disbursement.

[5] Under the amended Article XII, Section 5(a).

[6] As of January 2018, SDR1 = US$1,428120.

Table 11.2 IMF voting shares current and prior to latest reform

Countries	Old voting shares (%)	New voting shares (%)	Percentage point change	Countries	Old voting shares (%)	New voting shares (%)	Percentage point change
Saudi Arabia	2.80	2.01	−0.789	Austria	0.87	0.81	−0.058
Belgium	1.86	1.30	−0.555	Norway	0.78	0.77	−0.002
Germany	5.80	5.31	−0.495	Malaysia	0.73	0.75	0.017
Canada	2.55	2.21	−0.34	Australia	1.31	1.33	0.02
Venezuela	1.08	0.77	−0.317	Thailand	0.60	0.67	0.066
Netherlands	2.08	1.76	−0.315	Indonesia	0.85	0.95	0.097
France	4.29	4.02	−0.262	Iran	0.62	0.74	0.113
U.K.	4.29	4.02	−0.262	Poland	0.70	0.84	0.142
U.S.	16.73	16.48	−0.248	Russia	2.39	2.59	0.201
Switzerland	1.40	1.17	−0.227	Singapore	0.59	0.80	0.213
Argentina	0.87	0.66	−0.208	India	2.34	2.63	0.292
Nigeria	0.72	0.52	−0.208	Spain	1.62	1.92	0.295
Kuwait	0.58	0.41	−0.164	Mexico	1.47	1.80	0.329
Italy	3.15	3.02	−0.138	Turkey	0.61	0.95	0.346
South Africa	0.77	0.63	−0.136	Korea	1.36	1.73	0.367
Japan	6.23	6.14	−0.087	Brazil	1.71	2.22	0.504
Sweden	0.98	0.91	−0.072	China	3.81	6.07	2.265
Denmark	0.78	0.71	−0.068				
Advanced economies	57.90	55.30	−2.6	Emerging Markets	42.10	44.70	2.6

Source: International Monetary Fund

2. Shifting more than 6% of quota shares from over-represented rich countries to dynamic emerging and under-represented member countries;
3. Realigning significantly some quota shares, meaning that China, for instance, became the third largest member country in the IMF, and Brazil, China, India, and Russia, are now among the ten largest shareholders in the IMF, and
4. Preserving the quota and voting share of the poorest member countries. These are countries defined as those eligible for the low-income Poverty Reduction and Growth Trust, PRGT and whose per capita income fell below $1,135 in 2008, the threshold set by the International Development Association.

As of March 2017, 179 of the 189 members of the IMF had already made their quota payments, accounting for over 99% of the total quota increases, and total quotas stood at SDR475 billion (about US$650 billion). This reform also entitles an Executive Director elected by at least 19 members to appoint two Alternate Executive Directors to further enhance the capacity of the two Executive Directors' offices representing African constituencies (IMF 2017a). The proposed changes in voting shares have recently been made effective, and Table 11.2 underlines the extent of such shareholding changes.

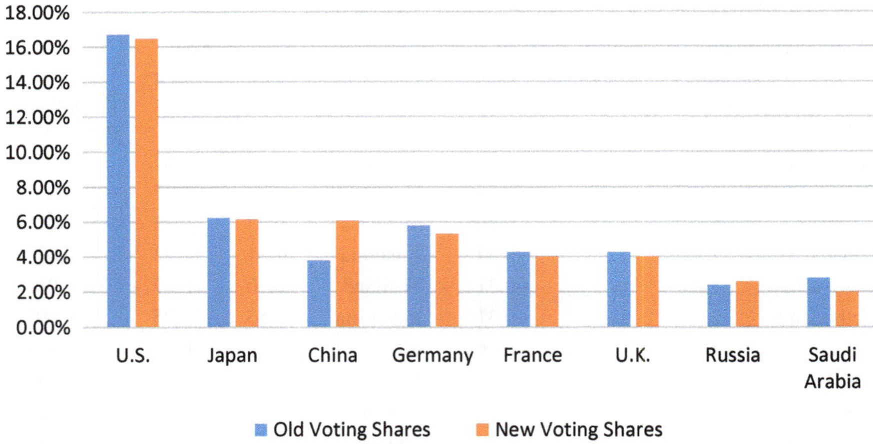

Fig. 11.1 IMF voting shares current and prior to 2010–2016 reform

A number of interesting observations can be drawn from the figures presented in Table 11.2:

1. OECD countries still retain an overwhelming majority of the voting share within the IMF even after recent reforms: 63.09%, compared to 63.55%, before;
2. The voting shares of the United States and Japan did not change during the most recent re-shuttling of votes and remain at 16.73, and 6.23%, respectively. As can be seen from the figures, this dwarfs all other member countries' voting shares, both before and after the latest changes;
3. Except for Brazil, Russia, India, and China, the rest of the developing countries actually see their voting share decrease by 3% points;
4. The emerging economies of Brazil, Russia, India, China, and South Africa (BRICS) have seen their voting shares improved, although mostly to modest degrees, except for China, which has gained more than two-thirds of the total transfer to emerging markets (3.46%), and seen its share increase by 2.35–6.16%, the largest increase; and
5. Poor countries included in the rest of the world have suffered the biggest drop in their voting shares, a −3.01% decrease from their level before the reform of 26.21%.

Figure 11.1 shows that European countries and Saudi Arabia appear to have conceded to lower votes in favour of China and to a lesser extent in favour of Russia.

Despite the readjustment in voting shares brought by the recent reform, dissatisfaction is still prevalent and voices are still asking for fairness. This is especially true given the current voting system continuing to retain the United States' veto over most important decisions, including changes to the IMF's charter, which always require an 85% majority. This kind of veto has allowed the U.S. to block the most recent changes in voting shares, which were approved by almost everyone else in

Table 11.3 Allocation of votes at the World Bank Group by organization, as FY 2017

Organization	Vote
International Bank for Reconstruction and Development (IBRD)	Each member receives one vote for each share of the Bank's capital stock held by him, plus basic votes calculated so that the sum of all basic votes is equal to 5.55% of the sum of basic votes and share votes for all members
International Finance Corporation (IFC)	Each member receives one vote for each share of IFC's capital stock held by him, plus basic votes calculated so that the sum of all basic votes is equal to 5.55% of the sum of basic votes and share votes for all members
International Development Association (IDA)	Each member receives subscription votes and membership votes according to the rules established in each IDA replenishment resolution
Multilateral Investment Guarantee Agency (MIGA)	Each member receives one vote for each share of MIGA's capital stock held by him, plus parity votes, calculated so that the aggregate number of votes of category 1 and category 2 members is the same. Members choose which category they want to join at the time of membership. Category 1 members were originally defined as developed countries and category 2 members as developing countries

Source: WBG Voting Powers at: http://www.worldbank.org/en/about/leadership/votingpowers. Accessed September 4, 2017

2010, but were held up by the U.S. Congress for 5 years (until December 2016). As the world economy continues to change, fears are still expressed that the same dynamic that has delayed the past reforms will likely to delay or prevent further reforms in the future.

World Bank Governance and Shareholding Review

The World Bank has a similar governance structure to the IMF, with the board of governors overseeing the board of executive directors, composed of the Bank's president and 25 members. Votes at the WBB are allocated differently in each constituency, as specified in Table 11.3, as of the FY 2017.

Apart from some minor discrepancies among constituencies (Table 11.3), conditions for the allocation of voting rights are comparable across the WBG. As a rule, each member country receives two kinds of voting rights: first, a member country receives a basic voting number of shares, so that the sum of all the basic votes is equal to 5.55% of the total sum of votes, and second, a member country also receives one vote for each share it holds in the capital of the institution.

Figure 11.2 graphically summarizes representation at the executive board level of the World Bank. 40.57% of the votes, or 938,080 votes, appoint their representatives on the Executive Board of the IMF and 59.43% of the votes, or 1,422,241 votes, elect their representatives.

Figure 11.2 shows that the six largest shareholders of the WBG are, in order of importance, the United States, retaining 16,32% votes; Japan, retaining 7.04%;

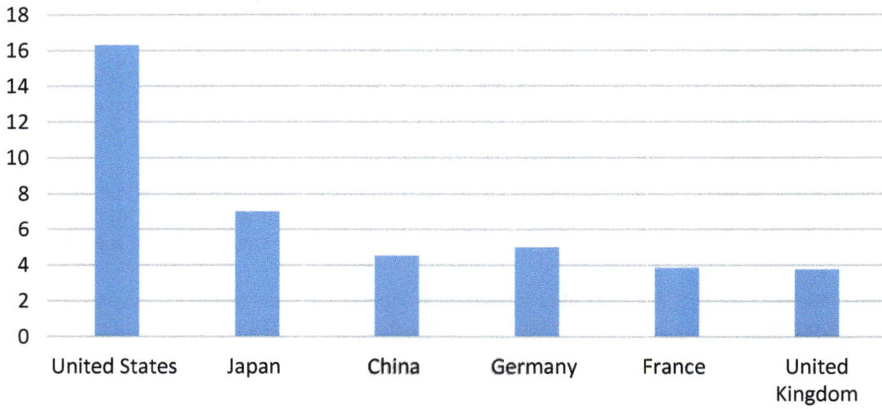

Fig. 11.2 International Bank for Reconstruction and Development, voting power of the seven more important executive directors, % of total

Germany, retaining 5%; China, retaining 4; 55%, France, retaining 3.86%; the United Kingdom, retaining 3.8%; additional to Saudi Arabia, retaining 2.78%. Each of these major shareholders appoints its own executive director, in addition to its governor. The remaining 18 Executive Directors represent countries from the rest of the world, and Sub-Saharan Africa has the right to representation of three directors.

Since the year 2008, the World Bank has launched a "voice reform" process, to increase developing countries' representation, thus recognising that the distribution of shareholding is important for the legitimacy of the institution. Initial reforms in 2010 increased developing countries' shares to 47.19% from 44.06% in 2009, with periodic shareholding reviews scheduled every 5 years based on agreed principles and a dynamic formula for calculating voting shares (World Bank). The September 2015 shareholding review acknowledged the growing share of developing and emerging economies, scoring 49.19% of global GDP, between 2012 and 2014, when measured by a blend of market rates and purchasing power parity. In line with this, the Bank expects the voting share of developing countries to increase to 52.76% when all the capital subscriptions (World Bank).

The voting shares review considered the economic weight of members, their contributions to the Bank's development mission and assessed "progress towards equitable voting power". Among the proposed measures to increase representation and board effectiveness are the reduction of the size of underlying committees and realigning them with the board of directors, and the building capacities of Executive Directors and their potential elections. Election of ED would, however, require changes to the Bank's Articles of Agreement, but the situation keeps gaining in urgency, given that developing countries currently represent over 80% of the world's population and are the main financial contributors to the Bank, through loan repayments. Not to mention that development membership of the Bank represents the environment where almost all of the Bank's activities are taking place.

Many remain skeptical about the recent reform's effect. At the Bretton Woods project, for instance, stakeholders have concluded that the reforms inadequate and believe that it stakeholders have concluded that the reform is inadequate and "stunts the Bank's legitimacy, limits its capacity to serve the interests of developing countries, and violates democratic principles". In its briefing analysis of the recent BWFIs' governance reform, the Bretton Woods project is still convinced that "World Bank will continue to be overwhelmingly dominated by rich countries", and underscores that **in** the end**,** high-income countries are set to hold onto over 60% of voting power, middle-income countries are only allocated around one-third of the votes, and low-income countries can aspire to just 6%, averaged across the different constituencies of the World Bank. Such imbalance in voting is also encountered in different arms of the WBG (Bretton Woods project 2010).

Currently the 78 IBRD country borrowers will retain only 34.1% of the votes, compared to more than one quarter of votes held by the 27 countries of the European Union. At IDA, high-income countries will still also retain over 61% of the votes, while middle-income countries will retain under 28%, and low-income only 11% of the total votes. At the IFC, **which** considers investing in poorest countries its priority**,** high-income countries will still retain 66.24% of total votes, middle-income countries 30.59% and low-income countries only 3.09% (Bretton Woods project 2010).

Equal voting shares for developed and developing countries are commonly demanded, and should be based on a formula that reflects the democratic principles that have been at the heart of the BWFIs' development mandate. An end is also required to the practice of some rich countries having permanent seats on the BWFIs' boards, where they are particularly over-represented. These demands, if exhausted, it is believed it can place BWFIs on a stronger footing to support development.

Discussion of Bretton Woods Financial Institution Governance

The felt unfair allocation of voting power at the Bretton Woods Institutions, at the expense of weaker economies, might have been the result of particular historical circumstances and has, however, been wrongly perpetuated, rather than corrected. The imbalance in voting remained unchanged for such a long time, to the point where even countries that have joined the institutions in more recent years have received far less favourable treatment, compared to predecessors (Griffith-Jones 2002). Recent reforms have, however, a number of positive effects, such as the advocating for the strengthening of the representation of dynamic emerging economies through ad hoc quota increases for some member countries; the shifting of more than 6% of quota shares to dynamic emerging market and developing countries (EMDCs); the making of China as the third largest member country in the IMF; and the allowing of Brazil, China, India, and Russia to be among the ten largest shareholders in the IMF. However, to some observers, the reform does not go far enough and does not fundamentally change the situation for the following reasons:

1. Since 1944 other economies besides the US[7] have grown to have larger shares in BWFIs' voting, yet they only get a minor voting change (Griffith-Jones 2002).
2. Boards at BWFIs continue to usually operate on a consensus basis, with few decisions formally going to the vote. The composition of the Board and the number of the EDs does, as expected, affect the type of issue to be brought to the Board and the decisions to be made, and thus, indirectly, the consensus does reflect the voting power of member countries, i.e. the U.S. (Griffith-Jones 2002).
3. Outside of Europe, the major international decision-maker is still the US Treasury Department. This means that Treasury is the main power for policy decisions affecting low- and middle-income borrowing countries.
4. At the World Bank, the borrowing countries still retain only a minority of the votes of 38%, and consequently, they can only nominate a minority number of the executive directors. Given the structure of the vote, which holds back poor countries, the president of BWFIs risks never coming from a borrowing country. Further, by some informal arrangement, the managing director of the IMF is always from Europe and the president of the World Bank always from the United States. The chosen European, however, must still be acceptable to the US Treasury department. There have been major efforts to put someone from the developing world in charge of WBFIs, given their primary mission is to encourage economic development, but they have so far failed (Griffith-Jones 2002). The dynamic is, however, reportedly quite different at the regional development banks, where some RDBs, like the IaDB and the AfDB, have voting rules that provide for the President of bank to come from a borrowing country.
5. In both the IMF and the World Bank, small economies must still be grouped into just a few constituencies and be represented at the Board by just few Executive Directors, and this seriously compromises the strength of their voice at institutions. Developing country Executive Directors that represent large number of constituencies, such as the two representing the Sub-Saharan Africa region, may have an unreasonable workload just trying to follow the huge number and variety of projects run by the institutions (Griffith-Jones 2002).
6. In a strategy of the "lesser evil", developing countries more than emergent will have no other choice than to accept whatever is offered to them as Bretton Woods governance reform.

Increase in retained reserves, out of substantial net income from loans made to developing countries coupled with the virtual absence of defaults since establishment, may mean that institutions' risks have always been low, even close to zero (Kapur 1999). "As a result, the financial case for strong developed country domi-

[7] Currently, the United States' power in the IMF and the WBG is vastly greater than the charter-determined right to veto decisions that require an 85% majority.

nance on the World Bank Board has weakened considerably" (Griffith-Jones 2002). This fact is not considered in quota allocation.

Quota shares and board voting of countries constitute a very important political issue, and one that is probably irreconcilable without a prior agreement on the future role of the BWFIs. There is, however, an absence of a meaningful consensus on what the role of the WBWFIs should be (Bernes 2013), and a large divergence of opinion on the subject continues to exist among countries. Once the specification of the purposes and mandates of the BWFIs are ensured, their appropriate governance should also become clear, and ODA governance might also be possibly improved. The issue has two sides: the institution and the client sides. On the institutional side, the commonly suggested governance reform revolves around the following:

1. Institutions' purposes and mandates should lead to institutions governance, instead of historical considerations and/or capital rights.
2. Greater involvement of institution governors and executive directors in providing strategic direction and accountability
3. Surveillance functions in institutions should be separated from lending functions, thus ensuring appropriate oversight and accountability of management
4. The size of institutions' capital base and the relevance of their boards should be determined by institutions' operations (Bernes 2013).
5. An "open and transparent process" should be set for the selection of the senior leadership of institutions (Bernes 2013).

Recent governance reform of Bretton Woods' institutions has opened the door for changes yet to come that favour a significant increase in the weight of developing country's voice, should the main shareholders agree to do so. This ideally implies increasing the number of votes and just as importantly, increasing the support to developing country Executive Directors to help them carry out their jobs more effectively (Bretton Woods project 2010). Additionally, a number of suggestions have also been made regarding the mechanisms through which changes to Bretton Woods governance could happen.

1. For instance, it was suggested to follow a path, similar to the one once adopted by the Inter-American Development Bank, and where donor countries were invited to sell part of their shares to borrower countries. The cost to borrower countries should not be very high, given that paid-in capital is representing only a small fraction of the total capital.
2. Another suggested alternative concerns a replenishment of capital, where borrower countries would purchase all (or a large part) of the amount involved. This would have the double benefit of increasing the power of borrower countries in the institutions' governance, and, at the same time, increasing institutions' resources for lending. This option should not necessarily imply a high—or even any—cost for developing countries. Indeed, it has been argued that eventual capital increases could be envisaged without any paid-in capital (Mistry 1995). It seems that there should be no reason the usual AAA ratings of institutions would be affected (Griffith-Jones 2002). This can be a formula

where a United Nation or another international institution would guaranty the capital shares of developing countries can even be envisaged.

3. Another idea is to establish, within the Board of institutions, auditing committees made up only of borrowing country members that have separate meetings from those of institutions' Boards. The only purpose of this additional mechanism would be the protection of the rights of minority borrower shareholders.
4. In all institutions, an open and competitive processes for the selection of top management is suggested, and should be established and hiring conditions for the positions should be clarified, with competence to be put above all other considerations, or citizenship.
5. Another crucial suggestion concerns the availability of good statistical data showing whether policy and programs are effectively working, and which work better than others. Good statistics can be critical for evidence-based policy-making, and can also be crucial in mobilising political will around development initiatives. Achieving development priorities certainly takes financial resources, but just as much, it requires data, evidence, and knowledge on how to best use those resources for development gains (World Bank_FY_2017_AR). Indeed, when institutions cannot tell with accuracy whether their development actions are effective, they will have a harder time increasing public support for those actions.
6. One might also think of a system of governance wherein institutions' financing is separate from their grant operations. Institutions' funding can, for instance, be assured by an independent global funding mechanism, under the auspices of the United Nations, for example, or the like, to which donor countries would entrust their contributions, for which international financial institutions would compete, based on the quality alone of their development projects.
7. Regarding RDBs specifically, they are invited to enter into more collaboration with client countries in policy guidance and capacity-building activities at the country level. They should share their experience and good practices and intensify guidance and toolkits in key areas, including illicit financial flows (The World Bank Group Annual Report 2015).

Observed weaknesses in BWFIs' governance may explain the weak efficiency of ODA they were set to administer. Such result, however, can only be partially attributed to them. Debates on institutions and official aid governance have focused almost exclusively on the quota share and Board representation of country members. Governance of ODA may, however, suffer from other important setbacks that stand to be considered. As important as the improving of BWFIs governance may be, it should not be allowed to obscure the unavoidable need to better manage the client side of ODA.

No real development improvement can be expected from official development aid unless a clear commitment to it is made by developing countries themselves. Indeed, the empirical investigation of Chaps. 8–10 has clearly shown the failure of the current Bretton Woods official aid system. Chapter 8 points to the overall failure of official development assistance in enhancing development, while recognizing that development

Table 11.4 Low-income economies versus high-income economies, deficit in public governance

	Low income PEG score/high income PEG score		Low income PSG score/high income PSG score
Overall PEG score	0.76	Overall PSG score	2.25
Property rights, PR	0.44	Security Apparatus, SA	2.39
Government integrity, GI	0.50	Factionalized Elites, FE	1.87
Judicial effectiveness, JE	0.47	Group Grievance, GG	1.40
Government spending, GS	1.03	Economic Decline, ED	2.03
Tax burden, TB	1.65	Uneven Economic Development, UE	2.26
Fiscal health, FH	0.94	Human Flight and Brain Drain component, HF	2.49
Business freedom, BF	0.64	State Legitimacy, SL	2.14
Labour Freedom, LF	0.82	Public Services, PS	3.72
Monetary Freedom, MF	0.91	Human Rights and Rule of Law, HR	2.14
Trade Freedom, TF	0.79	Demographic Pressures, DP	2.94
Investment Freedom, IF	0.64	Refugees and Internally Displaced Persons, RI	2.15
Financial Freedom, FF	0.50	External intervention, EI	2.66

assistance may have longer-term development objectives, such as educational objectives, sanitation objectives, and the like. Although inefficiency in development assistance is often attributed to donor weak governance, it is shown in Chap. 9 that such failure can be better explained by recipient public governance. Further, Chap. 10 finds that weakness in public governance of aid receivers can cancel a country's efforts for development. A number of negative features may explain such situations, and Table 11.4 highlights them by comparing low-income economies and high-income at the level of their public economic and social governance (Low income PEG score divided by high income PEG score) and (Low income PSG score divided by high income PSG score). While considering the numbers in table 11.4, it should be remembered again that while public governance sores are classified on a scale 1–100, with 100 being the best. Public social governance scores are classified on a scale of 1–114, with 114 being the worst. Therefore according to table 11.4, low income economies accuse deficit, compared to high income, virtually in all components of economic governance, except for government spending and tax burden components. Similarly they also a deficit components of social governance. Improving governance, however, is far from being an easy task, but the aim here, rather than to change everything within governmental systems, is to improve consciousness about the impact of public governance on development assistance efficiency. It also concerns the start of the process of change, which is expected to be progressive, and whose benefits will be cumulative. Any serious dealing with one of listed components of public governance can have a significant positive effect, though some components may have more indirect implications. Take, for instance, dealing with corruption, which can be defined as the illegitimate use of public power to benefit a private interest (Morris 1991). Corruption is widespread and commonly linked to poor quality of public services, and it can only diminish government efficiency and contribute to the weakening of its legitimacy in the eyes of its citizens, who usually respond to corruption with a disrespect for state institutions and a disregard for its laws (The World Bank Group Annual Report 2011). Corruption negatively affects state legitimacy in many ways: first by weakening its judicial system's effectiveness through neglect of the rule of law and second by the jeopardizing all freedom, business, labour, trade, investment, and property. It also kills tax fairness. Corruption, therefore, represents a real threat to the participation of citizens in "selecting and sanctioning the leaders who wield power in government, including by entering themselves as contenders for leadership" (The World Bank Group Annual Report 2015). Research on corruption has generally concluded that it has pernicious consequences for both efficiency and fairness (Olken and Pande 2012).

One main element that can diminish the devastating effect of corruption on public governance is transparency. Governments of developing countries stand to commit themselves to ensuring citizens access to information about their activities and decisions in an open, comprehensive and timely manner. All state departments and agencies should be required to conform to well-defined transparency rules. Citizen engagement and public transparency are interconnected and usually lead to good public governance. Citizen adhesion and transparency in the political process "can shape incentives and behavioural norms in the public sector" (The World Bank Group Annual Report 2015) with profound consequences for economic development. Success in these two areas can yield beneficial results for developing countries' governments who want to build effective public sector institutions that can secure the appropriate conditions needed for development.

Because of weaknesses in their public governance, most underdeveloped countries show features that make them unable to make appropriate use of their financial resources for development, including assistance. The qualities of public governance should be taken into account when analysing or leveraging development factors. Hence, the process of development official aid stands to be revised, in order to focus on assessing and gauging capabilities of each assistance receiver country's actual public governance system, in the interest of inducing development (Villafranca 2014).

If institutions' objective is poverty reduction and development enhancement, their policy should better reflect and serve the interests of the majority of the world's population, especially in low- and middle-income countries (Weisbrot and Johnston 2016), and the appropriate action of BWFIs should be to link non-concessional assistance to public governance progress. The findings of this book show the importance of the public governance deficit suffered more seriosly by developing countries as well as how development funding decisions may stand to be subjected to improved performance in the area of public social and economic governance.

The IMF and the World Bank have already introduced what is called the Standards and Codes Initiative, referring to institutional environment, essentially the rules of the game for economic and financial policy. They developed Standards and Codes in several areas, in accordance with evolving best practices. The IMF and the World Bank classify international standards under three broad groups: (1) Policy transparency, (2) Financial sector regulation and supervision, and (3) Institutional and market infrastructure. According to the IMF and the World Bank, countries with well-regulated and transparent institutions tend to enjoy better economic health and greater financial stability; however, they warn that compliance with international standards is only one element of the crisis (IMF 2017b). The United States, having the upper hand on Bretton Woods' institutions decision making, seems to have constantly minimized the impact of conditionality, discouraging any linking of development assistance decisions to conformity to conditionality respect by the recipient (Svensson 2003). Poor macroeconomic performance and non-compliance with conditions only leads to lower loan disbursements (Kilby 2009).

Globalization has weakened the power of national governments in economics and politics without a corresponding increase in effective international co-operation or supra-national government, which could regulate this market-driven process. Consequently, reforming the governance of the international development financial architecture cannot be achieved without an international system of governance for transnational corporations, focussing not only on the rights, but also on obligations (Nayyar 2001). An international mechanism for co-operation and transnational monitoring, which facilitates co-ordinated action and co-operative behaviour is needed. It is essential to create institutional mechanisms that give poor countries and their people a voice in the making of their destiny (Nayyar 2001).

Conclusion

Bretton Woods Financial Institutions and official development assistance have been Key instruments in development funding, and their role is greatly appreciated and so is the contribution they can make to development and the fight against poverty. Empirical findings of the book tend to show inefficiencies in the process of development funding, at different levels. "Were they to survey the world today, the architects of official development aid would be dismayed to see how many of the world's people are still in poverty, but would be pleased to see what progress has been made, and even shocked to see how inequality has widened" (Globalization for all 2002, p. iii). But their dismay would have been even greater knowing that advances in technology of information are creating unprecedented global opportunities for the fight against poverty. Using the right policies, many millions more people can escape the trap of privation.

In cases of success, just as in cases of failure of ODA, donors as well as receivers, bear responsibility. Consequently, reform of the governance of BWFIs, and public governance of assistance receiver countries, is strongly felt, not only as way of overcoming democratic deficits and weak legitimacy, but also as a means of strengthening the effectiveness of development assistance and reviving the Bretton Woods Spirit. However, no matter the chosen approach to reform, it must place a stronger focus on knowledge. BWFIs are recognizing the need to align their assistance to nationally owned education and training strategies. "Speeding the spread of education and skills will make the single greatest difference to the way the world's poorest countries can harness globalisation to eradicate poverty" (Globalization for all 2002).

Bibliography

Anderson, T. (2011), « Aid: is it worth it? ». At : http://actnowpng.org/sites/default/files/Aid%20-%20 is%20it%20worth%20it.pdf
AfDB (2004), « Bank Group policy on poverty ». At : https://www.afdb.org/fileadmin/uploads/afdb/ Documents/Policy-Documents/10000028-EN-BANK-GROUP-POLICY-ON-POVERTY-RE
AfDB (2016), African Development Banks, 2016 Annual report. At: https://www.afdb.org/en/ documents/document/afdb-annual-report-2016-95954/
AIIB « Governance » (n.d.). At : https://www.aiib.org/en/about-aiib/governance/members-of-bank /index.html
AIIB (2016), Asian Infrastructure Investment Bank 2016 Annual Report. At: https://www.aiib.org/ en/news-events/news/2016/annual-report/index.html
AsDB (2016a), "2016 Financial Report". At: https://www.AsDB.org/sites/default/files/institutional-document/237881/AsDB-financial-report-2016.pdf
AsDB (2016b) "2016 Annual Report". At: https://www.adb.org/documents/adb-annual-report-2016
Bank watch network, (n.d.) Citizens' guides to international financial institutions. At: https://bankwatch.org/get-involved/citizens-guides
Bannister, G. and A. Mourmouras (2018), « Welfare Versus GDP: What Makes People Better Off ». IMF Blog. At : https://blogs.imf.org/2018/03/07/welfare-versus-gdp-what-makes-people-better-off/. Accessed March 12, 2018
Barder, O. (2011), « Aid Effectiveness: Being Clear about Objectives » (11 August). At : http:// www.cgap.org/blog/aid-effectiveness-being-clear-about-objectives. Accessed June 29, 2016.
Bernes, T. A. (2003), "Strengthening international Financial inStitutionS to Promote eFFective international cooPeration" CIGI PaPers no. 13. https://www.cigionline.org/sites/default/files/ cigi_paper_13.pdf
Birdsall, N. (2000), 'The World Bank of the Future: Victim, Villain, Global Credit Union?', Policy Outlook, Carnegie Endowment.
Bretton Woods Project (2003), "Open statement on steps to democratize the World Bank and IMF". At: http://www.brettonwoodsproject.org/2003/04/art-16202/. Accessed September, 2016.
Bretton Woods Project (2005a), « What are the Bretton Woods Institutions? ». At : http://www. brettonwoodsproject.org/2005/08/art-320747/
Bretton Woods Project (2005b), « What are the main concerns and criticism about the World Bank and IMF? ». At : http://www.brettonwoodsproject.org/2005/08/art-320869/

A. Naciri, *The Governance Structures of the Bretton Woods Financial Institutions*, SpringerBriefs in Economics, https://doi.org/10.1007/978-3-319-97906-9

Bretton woods Project (2010), « Analysis of World Bank voting reforms, Governance remains illegitimate and outdated ». At : http://www.brettonwoodsproject.org/2010/04/art-566281/. Accessed August 3, 2016.

Bretton woods Project (2016), « IMF & World Bank decision-making and governance ». At : http://www.brettonwoodsproject.org/2016/03/imf-world-bank-decision-making-and-governance-existing-structures-and-reform-processes/. Accessed March 7, 2018.

CABEI (2016), "Central American Bank for Economic Integration, 2016 Annual Report". At: https://www.bcie.org/en/

CAF (2016), "*Corporación Andina de Fomento, 2016 Annual Report". At: http://www.caf.net/upload/accionista/CAF-2016_english.pdf.*

Canada's Action Plan on Open Government 2012–2014, at : http://open.canada.ca/en/canadas-action-plan-open-government.

Carrasco E.R., W. Carrington and H. Lee (2009), "Governance and accountability: the regional development banks". At: http://www.bu.edu/law/journals-archive/international/volume27n1/documents/carrasco.pdf.

CBD (n.d.) "Agreement of the Caribbean Development Bank ». At : http://www.caribank.org/uploads/2012/03/agreement.pdf.

CBD (2016), "Caribbean Development Bank, 2016 annual report. At: http://www.caribank.org/publications/featured-publications/2016-annual-report.

CEB (2016), "*Council of Europe Development Bank, CEB*, 2016 annual report". At: https://coebank.org/media/documents/Annual_Report_2016.pdf.

Chervalier, B., (2015), «Concessional financing windows or the need to reform the magic triangle ». WP 129 Development policies. Ferdi, Paris. At : http://www.ferdi.fr/sites/www.ferdi.fr/files/publication/fichiers/p129_-_reforming_the_magic_triangle_-_b_chervalier.pdf. Accessed March 7, 2018.

CIA (n.d.), "World Factbook", At: https://www.cia.gov/library/publications/the-world-factbook/

Cissokho, M. (2009), Dieu n'est pas un paysan. Présence africaine, Paris, 2009, p. 295

Collier, P., (2007), « The Bottom Billion: Why the Poorest Countries are Failing and What Can Be Done About It ». New York, Oxford University Press.

Consumer International (2005), Globalization for all – reviving the spirit of Bretton Woods. At: http://www.consumersinternational.org/media/319899/globalization%20for%20all%20%E2%80%93%20reviving%20the%20spirit%20of%20bretton%20woods.pdf

Collins dictionary. (n.d.) At: https://www.collinsdictionary.com/dictionary/english/colonialism.

Darrow, M. (2003), « *Between Light* and. *Shadow*, The *World Bank*, The. *International Monetary Fund* and. *International Human Rights Law*. Oxford: Hart Publishing. p. 376.

Deaton, A, (2013), « The great escape*: health, wealth and the origins of inequality*", Princeton University Press.

Diallo, M. et J. Vogel (1996), " L'Afrique qui résussit. Paris, Syros.

Dictionart.com. (n.d.) At : http://www.dictionary.com/browse/atlantic-charter. https://doi.org/10.1787/dcr-2017-en

Driscoll D.D. (1996), « The IMF and the World Bank How Do They Differ? ». At : https://www.imf.org/external/pubs/ft/exrp/differ/differ.htm.

Easterly, B., (2001), "The Elusive Quest for Growth". MIT Press.

Easterly, W., (2006) The White Man's Burden: Why the West's Efforts to Aid the Rest Have Done So Much Ill and So Little Good. Penguin Press..

EIB (2016), "European Investment Bank, 2016 annual report". At: http://www.eib.org/infocentre/publications/all/financial-report-2016.htm

Encyclopedia. (n.d.) At: https://www.encyclopedia.com/history/modern-europe/ancient-history-middle-ages-and-feudalism/colonialism.

Fraser Institute (2017), "Economic Freedom of the World 2017 annual report". At : https://www.fraserinstitute.org/sites/default/files/economic-freedom-of-the-world-2017.pdf.

Friedman B. M. (2002), « The New York Review of Books. Globalization Stiglitz's Case. At : http://www.nybooks.com/articles/2002/08/15/globalization-stiglitzs-case/. Accessed January 12, 2018.

Frieden, J. (2016). The governance of international finance. Harvard University. *Annual Review of Political Science.*

Fuhrer, JC (1996), “Monetary policy shifts and long-term interest rates”, The Quarterly Journal of Economics 111 (4), 1183–1209.

Fund for Peace. (n.d.) At: http://www.fundforpeace.org/fsi/indicators/x1/

German, T and Randel, J. (2002), The Reality of Aid: Never Richer, Never Meaner. Available online at http://www.devinit.org/ktrends.pdf

Global Exchange (2018), “Why the World Bank Must Be Reformed and How We Can Do It”. http://www.globalexchange.org/resources/wbimf/reform). Accessed February, 20, 2018.

Griffith-Jones, S. (2002), » Governance of the World Bank ». At : https://www.ids.ac.uk/files/GovernanceWorldBank.pdf. Accessed June 5, 2017.

The Guardian (2012), «Developing countries deserve a greater say in World Bank governance ». At : https://www.theguardian.com/business/economics-blog/2012/apr/04/developing-countries-world-bank-governance. Accessed November 2017.

Haller, A. P, (2012), « Concepts of Economic Growth and Development. Challenges of Crisis and of Knowledge ». Economy Transdisciplinarity Cognition. Vol. 15, Issue 1/2012, pp. 66–71. At : www.ugb.ro/etc

Held, D. (2006), “Reframing Global Governance: Apocalypse Soon or Reform!” New Political Economy Vol. 11, No. 2, pp. 157–176..

Heritage Foundation, (2017), “2017 index of economic freedom”. At: https://www.heritage.org/international-economies/report/2017-index-economic-freedom-trade-and-prosperity-risk.

Hind, M. (2002), « Role of Regional Development Banks in Rebuilding the International Financial Architecture ». At : http://www.cgdev.org/sites/default/files/9780881323535-FinDev5.pdf .

Howard-Hassmann, Rhoda E. and Anthony P. Lombardo (2011) ‘Reparations to Africa’, Pennsylvania Studies in Human Rights, University of Pennsylvania Press.

IDA, (2017), “Towards 2030: Investing in Growth, Resilience and Opportunity ». At : http://documents.worldbank.org/curated/en/471761467993490105/IDA18-IDA18. Accessed March 4, 2018.

IaDB (2016), “Inter-American development bank, 2016 annual report”. At: https://publications.iadb.org/handle/11319/8218.

IBON Foundation, Inc,, 2002. Manila. At: http://ibon.org/about/

IBON, 2009. At: http://ibon.org/

IBRD and IDA (2016), “IBRD and IDA 2016 Financial statement”. At: https://openknowledge.worldbank.org/bitstream/handle/10986/24985/210852v2.pdf?sequence=4&isAllowed=y.

ICSID (n.d.) Convention. At: https://icsid.worldbank.org/en/Pages/icsiddocs/ICSID-Convention.aspx.

IDA and IBRD (2016), “IBRD and IDA 2016 Financial statement”. At: https://openknowledge.worldbank.org/bitstream/handle/10986/24985/210852v2.pdf?sequence=4&isAllowed=y

IFC (2016), “ International finance corporation, 2016 Annual Report”. At: http://www.ifc.org/wps/wcm/connect/corp_ext_content/ifc_external_corporate_site/annual+report+2016/2016+online+report/printed+version/printed+version.

IMF (2002), “Globalization for All”. At: http://www.imf.org/external/pubs/ft/fandd/2002/03/hausler.htm

IMF (2016a), IMF Financial Operations 2016”. At: http://www.imf.org/external/pubs/ft/finop/2016/. Accessed October 9, 2016.

IMF (2016b), « By-Laws Rules and Regulations of the International Monetary Fund Sixty-Third Issue ». At : https://www.imf.org/external/pubs/ft/bl/blcon.htm. Accessed 12 of December 2017.

IMF (2016c) « Historic Quota and Governance Reforms Become Effective ». Press Release No. 16/25, January 27, 2016: www.imf.org/

IMF (2017a), “International monetary fund 2017 Annual Reports. At: https://www.imf.org/external/pubs/ft/ar/2017/eng/index.htm

IMF (2017b), « Making Trade an Engine of Growth for All: The Case for Trade and for Policies to Facilitate Adjustment ». At : https://www.imf.org/en/Publications/Policy-Papers/Issues/2017/04/08/making-trade-an-engine-of-growth-for-all. Accessed March 11, 2018.

Lagarde, C. (2017a), «2017 Annual Report. At : http://www.imf.org/external/pubs/ft/ar/2017/eng/pdfs/IMF-AR17-English.pdf. Accessed March 11, 2018.

IMF (2017c), « Members' Quotas and Voting Power, and IMF Board of Governors », July 23, 2017. At : https://www.imf.org/external/np/sec/memdir/members.aspx. Accessed 23 of July, 2017.

IMF (2017d), IMF Extended Credit Facility (ECF). At : https://www.imf.org/en/About/Factsheets/Sheets/2016/08/02/21/04/Extended-Credit-Facility

IMF (2017e), « IMF Rapid Credit Facility (RCF) ». At : https://www.imf.org/en/About/Factsheets/Sheets/2016/08/02/21/08/Rapid-Credit-Facility

IMF (2017f), How does the IMF support low-income countries? At : http://www.imf.org/en/About/Factsheets/IMF-Support-for-Low-Income-Countries

IMF Regulations. (n.d.) At: https://www.imf.org/external/pubs/ft/bl/blcon.htm

IMF (2017g), « Governance Structure ». At : https://www.imf.org/external/about/govstruct.htm. Accessed, 12 of September 2017.

IMF (2017h), « Annual Meetings of the Boards of Governors of the World Bank Group (WBG) and the International Monetary Fund (IMF) ». At : http://www.imf.org/external/am/2017/. Accessed March 5, 2018.

IMF's Articles of Agreement (n.d.), at https://www.imf.org/external/pubs/ft/aa/. Accessed February 7, 2018.

IMF (2018a), "IMF Members' Quotas and Voting Power ». At : https://www.imf.org/external/np/sec/memdir/members.aspx. Accessed 2 of March, 2018.

IMF (2018b), « IMF at glance, February 21, 2018. At : http://www.imf.org/en/About/Factsheets/IMF-at-a-Glance. Accessed March 13, 2018.

Islamic Development Bank (n.d.), isdb. At: http://www.isdb.org/irj/go/km/docs/documents/IDBDevelopments/Internet/French/IDB/CM/Publications/AnnualReports/41st/annrepen1436.pdf.

Kaberuka, D. (2013), "We need to rethink how we provide aid to Africa, Aid, Poverty matters" blog, At : https://www.theguardian.com/global-development/poverty-matters/2013/sep/25/aid-africa-development-donald-kaberuka

Kanbur, R. (2006), "The economics of international aid", in Kolm, Serge-Christophe; Ythier, Jean Mercier, Handbook of the economics of giving, altruism and reciprocity: foundations, volume 1, Amsterdam London: Elsevier, ISBN 9780444506979.

Kapur D. (1999), « Processes of Change in International Organisations ». Prepared for UN Wider research project 'The New Role and Functions for the UN and the Bretton Woods Institutions'.

Katasonov V. (2014), "Reform of the Bretton Woods Institutions: The IMF Might Not Live to See Its Anniversary". Global research. At: http://www.globalresearch.ca/reform-of-the-bretton-woods-institutions-the-imf-might-not-live-to-see-its-anniversary/5378544.

Kenny, C., (2011), 'Getting Better', Basic Books.

Kilby, C. (2009). The Political Economy of Conditionality: An Empirical Analysis of World Bank Loan Disbursements. Journal of Development Economics, 89(1): 51–61.

Kofi, A. (2017),"Human Rights Day (Kofi Annan,10 décembre 2017).

Lagarde (2017b), « Message from the Managing Director, IMF, 2017 Annual Report. At : http://www.imf.org/external/pubs/ft/ar/2017/eng/pdfs/IMF-AR17-English.pdf. Accessed March 11, 2018.

Mallampally P. and K. P. Sauvant (1999), "Foreign Direct Investment in Developing Countries". At: http://www.imf.org/external/pubs/ft/fandd/1999/03/mallampa.htm

Masood, A (2000), «**Making Globalization Work for the Poor ».** Policy Development and Review Department, IMF. At : https://www.imf.org/en/News/Articles/2015/09/28/04/54/vc121200. Accessed, January 22, 2016.

MIGA (2016), "Multilateral Investment Guarantee Agency 2016 Management Discussion and Analysis. At: https://www.miga.org/resources/reports/annual-reports.
Mistry, P. S. (1995), "The New Regionalism: Impediment or Spur to Future Multilateralism?" https://link.springer.com/chapter/10.1007/978-1-349-27268-6_5.
Morris, S., (2017), "What the AIIB Can Do for the Multilateral System". Center for Global development. At : https://www.cgdev.org/publication/what-aiib-can-do-multilateral-system.
Morris, S.D. (1991), « Corruption and Politics in Contemporary Mexico ». University of Alabama Press, Tuscaloosa.
Moyo, D., (2009), "Dead Aid, Why Aid Is Not Working and How There Is a Better Way for Africa ». Frrar, Straus and Giroux, NY. At: http://dambisamoyo.com/publications-articles-videos/books/dead-aid/
Nayyar, D. (2001), « Reform the UN and the Bretton Woods Institutions », United Nations University, At : https://www.wider.unu.edu/publication/reform-un-and-bretton-woods-institutions. Accessed July 21, 2016.
Nelson, R. M. (2015), "Multilateral Development Banks: Overview and Issues for Congress". At: https://fas.org/sgp/crs/row/R41170.pdf. Accessed August 7, 2017.
NYE, J.S. Jr (2003), «The democracy deficit in the global economy: Enhancing the legitimacy and accountability of global institutions.
Ocampo, JC. (2015), "A Post-2015 Monitoring and Accountability Framework", CDP Background Paper No. 27 ST/ESA/2015/CDP/27 AT: https://www.un.org/development/desa/dpad/wp-content/uploads/sites/45/publication/CDP-bp-2015-27.pdf.
Oxfam (2011) 'Whose Aid is it Anyway?' 10 February, online at: https://www.oxfam.org/en/research/whose-aid-it-anyway
Oxfam (2015), « Foreign Aid And Its Importance In Relieving Poverty ». At : https://www.oxfam.org.au/wp-content/uploads/2015/09/Oxfam-Foreign-Aid-GeoDate-Vol-28-No-3-July-2015.pdf. Accessed March 3, 2018.
OECD (2017), « *Development Co-operation Report 2017: Data for Development* », OECD Publishing, Paris.
OECD (2009), Better managing aid. At : https://www.oecd.org/dac/peer-reviews/35051857.pdf
OECD (n.d.-a), DAC1 Official and Private Flows (*op. cit.*). The calculation is Net Private Grants / ODA.
OECD (n.d.-b), « Glossary of Key Terms and Concepts. From the Development Co-operation Report: Efforts and Policies of Members of the Development Assistance Committee ».
OECD/UNDP (2016), « Making Development Co-operation More Effective : 2016 Progress Report », OECD Publishing, Paris. At : https://doi.org/10.1787/9789264266261-en
OECD/WTO (2017), « Aid for Trade at a Glance (2017), Promoting Trade, Inclusiveness and Connectivity for Sustainable Development ». WTO, Geneva/OECD Publishing, Paris. https://doi.org/10.1787/aid:glance-2017-en
OECD (n.d.-c) "Global Relations". At: http://www.oecd.org/global-relations/
Olken, B.A. and R. Pande (2012), "Corruption in Developing Countries Annual Review of Economics Vol. 4:479–509 (Volume publication date September 2012) First published online as a Review in Advance on April 25, 2012 https://doi.org/10.1146/annurev-economics-080511-110917
OECD (2008), « Guidance for multilateral agencies reporting to the DAC ». At : https://www.oecd.org/dac/stats/45896056.pdf
Ottenhof, J. (2011), « Regional Development Banks », in GDP Brief, At : https://www.cgdev.org/sites/default/files/1425484_file_IFI_Briefs_RDB_FINAL_r1_0.pdf
Pilger J. (1991), "War By Other Means". At : https://www.pinterest.ca/pin/380976449713899959/
Randel, T. G. and J. Randel (2002), "Never richer, never poorer," In The Reality of Aid 2002: Focus on Conditionality and Ownership, by Reality of Aid Network, 145–157, Manila: IBON Foundation, Inc.
Riddel, R. (2007), Does Foreign Aid Work? Oxford University Press.

Rossi, M. (1999), "Financial Fragility and Economic Performance in Developing Economies: Do Capital Controls, Prudential Regulation and Supervision Matter?" International Monetary Fund Working Paper.

Sachs, J. (2006), « The End of Poverty, Economic Possibilities for Our Time", Penguin Books. https://www.amazon.com/End-Poverty-Economic-Possibilities-Time/dp/0143036580#reader_0143036580

Sarkin, Jeremy (2008) 'Colonial Genocide and Reparations Claims in the 21st Century: The Socio-Legal Context of Claims under International Law by the Herero against Germany for Genocide in Namibia, 1904–1908', Praeger, Westport

Severino, J.M. and O. Ray, (2009), "The End of ODA: Death and Rebirth of a Global Public Policy" At: https://www.cgdev.org/files/1421419_file_End_of_ODA_FINAL.pdf

Silver, M. (2010), IMF Application of Purchasing Power Parity Estimates. IMF WP/10/253

Smith, A. (1776), An Inquiry into the Nature and Causes of the Wealth of Nations (1776)

Sogge (2002), Give and Take: What's the Matter with Foreign Aid? Zed Books

Sogge, D. (2009) 'Inequality: Can the foreign aid industry help roll it back?', Transnational Institute, March. at: http://www.tni.org/article/inequality-can-foreign-aid-industry-help-roll-it-back

Joseph E. Stiglitz J.E. (2002) *Globalization and Its Discontents. At :* https://doi.org/10.1046/j.0391-5026.2003.00107

Stiglitz, J. E. (2017), Globalization and Its Discontents Revisited: Anti-Globalization in the Era of Trump Paperback – November 28. https://www.amazon.com/Globalization-Its-Discontents-Revisited-Anti-Globalization/dp/0393355160/ref=asap_bc?ie=UTF8

Svensson, J. (2003). Why Conditional Aid Does Not Work and What Can Be Done About It? Journal of Development Economics, 70(2): 381–402.

Tian, N., A. Fleurant, P.D. Wezeman and S. T. Wezeman (2017), « TRENDS IN WORLD MILITARY EXPENDITURE, 2016 ». IPRI Fact Shee. At : https://www.sipri.org/sites/default/files/Trends-world-military-expenditure-2016.pdf. *Retrieved 2 March 2018.*

Tomlinson, B. (2008), "World aid trends: Donors distorting the reality of aid in 2008." In The Reality of Aid (2008), Aid Effectiveness, Democratic Ownership and Human Rights , by Reality of Aid Network, 200–223. Manila: IBON Foundation, Inc., 2008.

The World Bank Group Annual Report (2011), Annual Report-201. https://www.openknowledge.worldbank.org/handle/10986/2378.

The World Bank Group Annual Report (2015), Annual Report-2015 http://www.worldbank.org/en/about/annualreport-2015.

U.K. White Paper (2000), "Eliminating World Poverty: A Challenge for the 21st Century". At : http://webarchive.nationalarchives.gov.uk/20050404190659/http:/www.dfid.gov.uk/Pubs/files/whitepaper1997.pdf. Accessed on October 10, 2017.

UK White Paper (2000), «Making Globalisation Work for the Poor ». White Paper. At : http://www.bris.ac.uk/poverty/downloads/keyofficialdocuments/Making%20globalisation%20work.pdf. Accessed November 10, 2017.

UN (n.d.) "International Development Strategy for the Second United Nations Development Decade ». General Assembly Resolution 2626 (XXV). At: http://www.un-documents.net/a25r2626.htm

UN (1948), « Universal Declaration of Human Rights », Adopted and proclaimed by General Assembly resolution 217 A (III) of 10 December 1948. At : http://www.ohchr.org/Documents/Publications/Compilation1.1en.pdf. Accessed. February 28, 2018.

UNDP (2011), "Official Development Assistance". At :http://www.undp.org/content/dam/undp/library/Poverty%20Reduction/Inclusive%20development/Towards%20Human%20Resilience/Towards_SustainingMDGProgress_Ch5.pdf

UNDP (2014), « Global-Project on Capacity Development for Aid Effectiveness » At : http://effectivecooperation.org/wp-content/uploads/2016/08/2014-UNDP-Global-Project-on-Capacity-Development-for-Aid-Effectiveness-9.pdf

UNDP (2016), "The 2016 Human Development Report". At: http://hdr.undp.org/sites/default/files/2016_human_development_report.pdf

Vestergaard J. (2013), « Protecting Power: How Western States Retain The Dominant Voice in The World Bank's Governance ». World Development Volume 46, June, Pages 153–164

Villafranca A. (2014), Reforming the global economic governance: Public Goods and Balance of Power. ISPI Working Paper, no 54. At :

Vivien, F. D. (2009), Pour une économie patrimoniale des ressources naturelles et de l'environnement. De Boeck Supérieur.

Waqf Fund, (2015). "Realizing the social role of islamic finance". At: http://www.mifc.com/index.php?ch=28&pg=72&ac=130&bb=uploadpdf

World Bank (n.d.-a) « data/databases ». At : http://databank.worldbank.org/data/databases.aspx?qterm=IBRD%20loans%20and%20IDA%20credits%20(DOD,%20current&pagenumber=1

World Bank (n.d.-b), « PovcalNet ». At : http://iresearch.worldbank.org/PovcalNet/povOnDemand.aspx.

World Bank (n.d.-c), « IDA 18 ».At : http://ida.worldbank.org/financing/replenishments/ida18-overview. Accessed March, 10, 2018.

World Bank (n.d.-d), « What is IDA ? ». At : http://ida.worldbank.org/about/what-ida. Accessed March,10, 2018.

World Bank (n.d.-e) « Metadata » . At : http://databank.worldbank.org/data/Views/Metadata/MetadataWidget.aspx?Name=GDP

World Bank (2015a), "Global Financial Development Report 2015/2016: Long-Term Finance. World Bank. Washington, DC. https://openknowledge.worldbank.org/handle/10986/22543 License: CC BY 3.0 IGO."

World Bank (2015b), "The Little Data Book on Financial Development 2015/2016". Washington, DC. World Bank. At: https://openknowledge.worldbank.org/handle/10986/22553 License: CC BY 3.0 IGO."

World Bank (2016a), Multilateral Development Banks, Issue Brief. At : https://datahelpdesk.worldbank.org/knowledgebase/articles/378832-the-world-bank-atlas-method-detailed-methodolog

World Bank (2016b), Multilateral Development Banks. At: http://www.un.org/esa/ffd/wp-content/uploads/2016/01/Multilateral-Development-BanksWBGIATF-Issue-Brief.pdf

World Bank (n.d.-f), "Open knowledge". At: https://openknowledge.worldbank.org/bitstream/handle/10986/5968/9780195204827_ch07.pdf?sequence=8

World Bank (n.d.-g) « Leadership ». At : http://www.worldbank.org/en/about/leadership. Accessed October 10, 2017.

World Bank (2017a), « Fact Sheet on World Bank Trust Funds ». At : http://siteresources.worldbank.org/CFPEXT/Resources/TFfactsheetapril2017.pdf. Accessed March 9, 2018.

World Bank (n.d.-h) « The World Bank Atlas method - detailed methodology ». At : https://datahelpdesk.worldbank.org/knowledgebase/articles/378832-the-world-bank-atlas-method-detailed-methodology

World Bank (2017b), « World Development Report 2017, Governance and the Law». http://www.worldbank.org/en/publication/wdr2017. Accessed 10 January, 2018

World Bank (2017c), "Allocation of Votes by Organization » At: World Bank http://www.worldbank.org/en/about/leadership/votingpowers

World Bank's little data book. At: https://data.worldbank.org/products/data-books/little-data-book. Accessed July 9, 2017

World Banks (2016), IBRD 2016-Annual Report, Management's discussion and analysis ».

World Bank Data base. At : http://databank.worldbank.org/data/databases.aspx?qterm=IBRD%20loans%20and%20IDA%20credits%20(DOD,%20current&pagenumber=1

Weisbrot, M. and J. Johnston (2016), Voting Share Reform at the IMF: Will it Make a Difference? *cepr.net/images/stories/reports/IMF-voting-shares-2016-04.pdf*

Websites

http://www.adb.org/
http://www.afdb.org/
http://www.brettonwoodsproject.org/2009/02/art-563643/. 16 February 2009 | Inside the institutions
http://www.cgdev.org/sites/default/files/1425484_file_IFI_Briefs_RDB_FINAL_r1_0.pdf
http://www.ebrd.com/
http://www.IADB.org/
http://www.imf.org/
http://www.isdb.org/irj/go/km/docs/documents/IADBDevelopments/Internet/English/IADB/CM/Publications/IADBGroupBrief2013.pdf.
http://www.ispionline.it/sites/default/files/pubblicazioni/wp_54_2014bis.pdf.
http://www.un.org/esa/ffd/ffd-follow-up/inter-agency-task-force.html
https://www.aiib.org/en/news-events/news/2016/annual-report/.content/download/AnnualReport2016.pdf.

MIX
Papier aus verantwortungsvollen Quellen
Paper from responsible sources
FSC® C105338
FSC
www.fsc.org

If you have any concerns about our products,
you can contact us on
ProductSafety@springernature.com

In case Publisher is established outside the EU,
the EU authorized representative is:
Springer Nature Customer Service Center GmbH
Europaplatz 3, 69115 Heidelberg, Germany

Printed by Libri Plureos GmbH
in Hamburg, Germany